THE COMPLETE GUIDE TO
DIGITAL
IMAGING

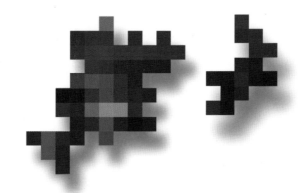

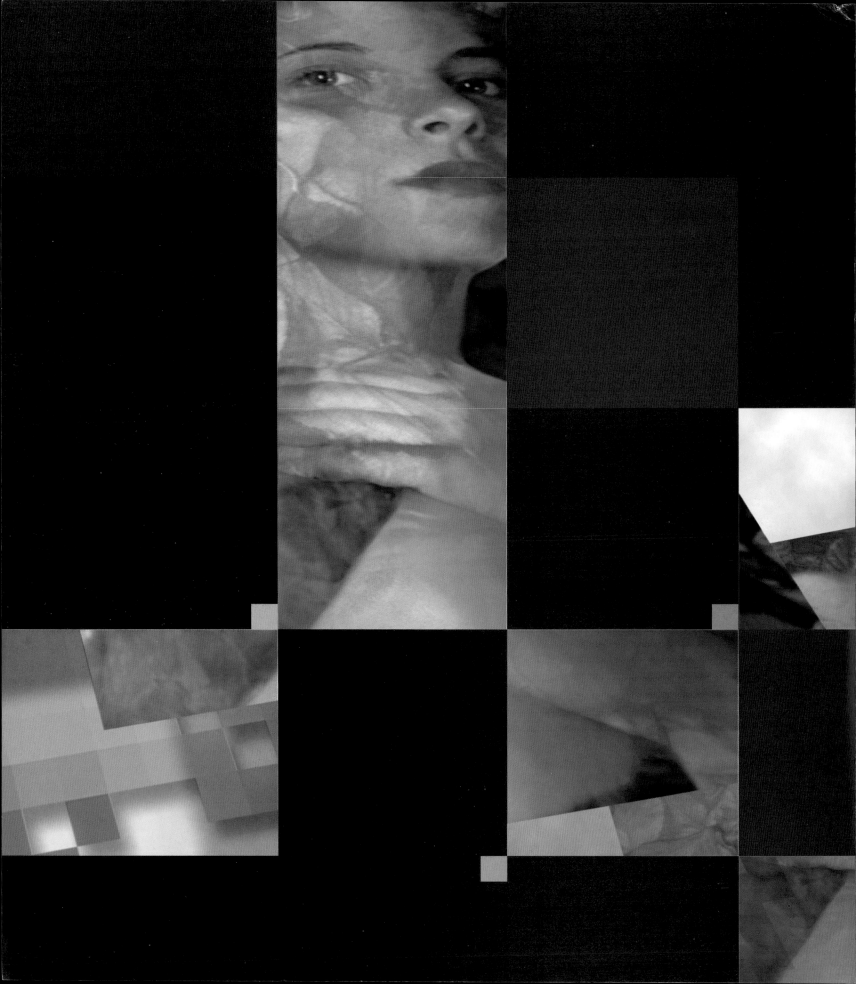

THE COMPLETE GUIDE TO
DIGITAL
IMAGING

JOËL LACEY

Watson-Guptill
Publications
New York

First published in the United States in 2001 by
Watson-Guptill Publications, a division of VNU Business Media, Inc.
770 Broadway, New York, NY 10003
www.watsonguptill.com

This book was conceived,
designed, and produced by
THE ILEX PRESS LIMITED
Cambridge
England

Art Director Alastair Campbell
Designer Axis Design Editions Ltd
Design Manager Tony Seddon
Project Editor Lachlan McLaine
Contributors Peter Cope and Philip Andrews

Library of Congress Cataloging-in-Publication Data

Lacey, Joël.
    The complete guide to digital imaging / Joël Lacey.
        p. cm.
    ISBN 0-8230-0779-0
    1. Image processing—Digital techniques. I. Title.

    TA1637 .L313 2001
    621.36'7—dc21

                                                2001046514

ISBN 0-8230-0779-0

Printed and bound in China

The Photoshop tools and procedures described in this book are
based on Photoshop version 6. Earlier versions of Photoshop may
not operate in the same way.

contents

introduction

Opposite *Not thinking things through makes for slower output and lower quality.*

Below *The sensible digital imager takes a measured, structured approach.*

There is a great deal of confusion about the complex subject of digital imaging (DI). As with many things, its complexity depends on how much you know and how much you want to know. In a fundamental sense, digital imaging is extremely simple. Every digital image you see represents no more than combinations of two digits—0 and 1.

Unfortunately, knowing the composition of an image is not the same as being able to use it as you would wish. That is only a little more complex. In this book I have tried to separate the various concepts that go under the umbrella term "digital imaging." In isolating these concepts, simplicity starts to return. It is not quite as simple as the difference between 0 and 1, but it is certainly not rocket science, despite the fact that the first digital image to be transmitted ever was from the moon during the 1969 Apollo 11 mission.

Before we begin to examine individual aspects of digital imaging, however, I will explain the structure of this book. We are going to start with the output, or end product. Then we will consider ways of manipulating images to get that end product. And finally we will learn how to get the appropriate type of image into the digital domain: that is, how you go about getting the images onto your computer in the first place.

The important thing is to know what you want to achieve; only by knowing where you are going will you know where to begin. Before you can understand how you need to manipulate an image, before you even decide how you're going to input it, you need to know in what form you are going to output it.

There are plenty of ways to immerse yourself in jargon and abbreviations and join the Tower of Babel that is all things computer-related. I have tried, as far as possible, not to get too wrapped up in jargon. Knowing what an abbreviation stands for is not the same as knowing what it does, and is significantly less useful. Inevitably, though, there are the many "standards" that digital artists have to navigate their way through. Each of these has its own lexicon. Where appropriate, I will explain them in the text, but where no purpose is served other than to say what they stand for, I will define them in the glossary.

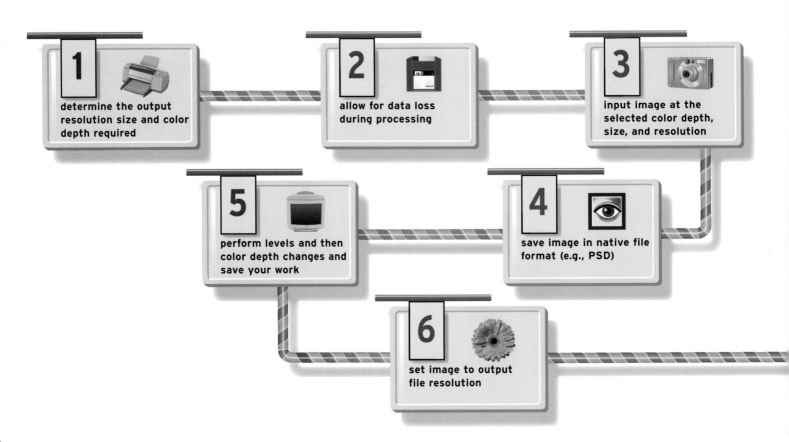

1 determine the output resolution size and color depth required

2 allow for data loss during processing

3 input image at the selected color depth, size, and resolution

5 perform levels and then color depth changes and save your work

4 save image in native file format (e.g., PSD)

6 set image to output file resolution

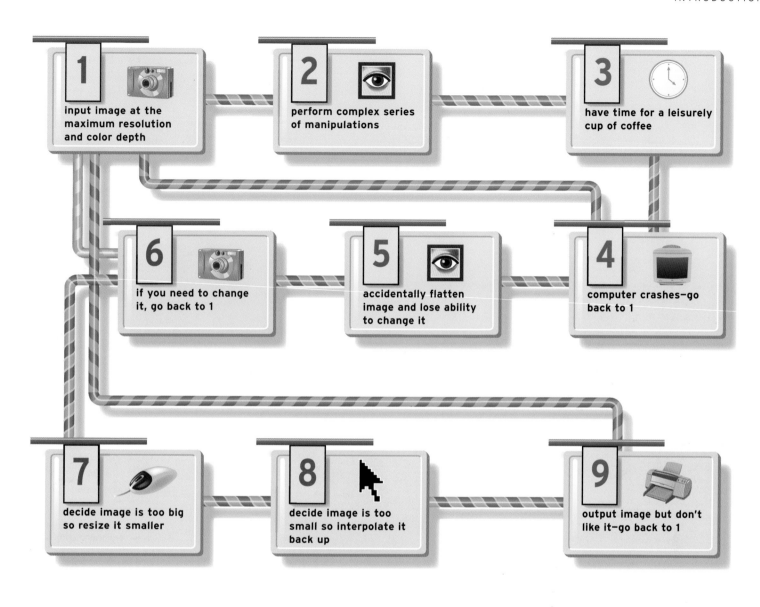

1 input image at the maximum resolution and color depth

2 perform complex series of manipulations

3 have time for a leisurely cup of coffee

6 if you need to change it, go back to 1

5 accidentally flatten image and lose ability to change it

4 computer crashes—go back to 1

7 decide image is too big so resize it smaller

8 decide image is too small so interpolate it back up

9 output image but don't like it—go back to 1

7 make creative changes on this smaller file

8 if saving to Web, perform image compression

9 save, then output in appropriate method

what is digital imaging?

Twenty years ago, there was little cause for confusion between analog and digital in the creative world. Photography was analog (film and paper), graphics were black and white and produced by photomechanical transfer, and video was analog (levels of voltage sent twenty-five times a second to a screen). How digital imaging came into existence was really a function of the changes in the field of printing, predominantly in the world of prepress. Images had previously been converted to digital form in order to take advantage of new technology in the production of plates used by printing presses. The process of "digital imaging" then started to creep backward along the production chain to the design office as part of the desktop publishing

Below PCs and Macs can now be used for sophisticated nonlinear video editing.

revolution, which has affected all areas of the industry. At first typesetters no longer played a part in the process, because the text was all digital, and then photographs and artwork (graphics) also started to move into the digital domain.

What is this digital domain? In essence, it is a place where all images speak or are expressed in the same language, or at least are defined in the same terms, the 0s and 1s of the binary code. "Digital imaging" is just a coverall term; it may be a common language, but there

Above You can use digital imaging software to create various animation sequences, from simple to complex.

Below With digital imaging you can create in seconds effects that would take hours using traditional photographic methods. Left to right, original image, pinch, radial blur, and stretch.

are many different dialects. In the words of one observer of the computing industry, whose comment is delivered with a tinge of irony: "The great thing about standards is that you have so many to choose from."

The most obvious incarnation of digital imaging is the conversion of photographs to digital format. This may be carried out at the moment of taking the image (with a digital camera), recording it using a scanner (see *chapters 5 and 6*), or making a screen-grab (capturing a still image from analog video or television picture).

Below *Software enables you to create contact sheets and so manage your picture filing.*

Right *Programs like ArcSoft's PhotoMontage allow special effects to be created digitally.*

Fortunately, for those with large investments in traditional camera equipment, conventional films can be converted into digital format either at the time of processing or later.

There is another benefit for images encoded digitally; once they are in the computer they can be shared instantly and without compromising on quality. Digital images can be emailed with the confidence that any copy will be as good as the original.

But this is not the principal reason many get involved with digital imaging. Though it is not as expedient, you could easily post a picture or video tape. No, the real reason for getting into digital is that once any image—whether it is still or moving, 2D or 3D, large or small—has been moved into the digital domain, it has been converted into a series of digits. The series can be large and complex with billions of bits of information. And what is the primary purpose of computers? Is it not to crunch numbers at our behest?

Every method of altering a photograph, picture, graphic, or sound, can be expressed as an equation. You can alter the picture as a whole, or an individual tiny component of it, as well as all of the points in between. If you place a few pictures together in sequence, you create a short piece of animation. If you place millions of images together, you create a movie.

It is at this point that the numbers involved start to reach mind-boggling size (which is why we made sure that computers were involved in the first place). But it is instructive to know a little about what is going on in the gray, beige, or increasingly, multicolored box when the screen appears to be doing nothing, and you have already made yourself another cup of coffee. Why are computers so slow when dealing with digital imaging?

Without going into too much detail at this point, let us look at a single still digital image. Let us say it is a 7 x 5-inch image, which is at the appropriate resolution for printing in, for example, a book. It has been captured on the latest digital equipment, and each pixel (or component cell of that image) contains information on the color and brightness of the bit of the world it is representing. Because it was taken on a top-of-the-line piece of equipment, it has a very subtle control of colors. In fact, each picture cell can represent any one of a combination of 65,536 shades of red, 65,536 shades of blue, and 65,536 shades of green. Given that each shade of red can

Below *How you see an image and how your computer sees an image.*

```
1010101011010110101 0
1011100101110101101 1
1010101010101101010 1
1010101011010101001 0
0101101000101010101 0
0101011010101010101 0
1010101001010110101 0
1010101010101101010 1
0101010101011010101 1
0101010101010101010 1
0101011010010111010 1
0101101010101111010 1
1010101011010101101 0
0101011010101010101 0
1010101001010110101 0
1010101010101101010 1
0101010101011010101 1
```

be used in combination with any combination of green and blue, there are two hundred and eighty-one trillion (281,000,000,000,000) possible combinations for this one pixel. This smallest component part of our digital image is already quite a large number. But this little pixel is not alone; within our simple 7 × 5-inch picture there are already 2,100 × 1,500 pixels.

working backward

So, before cursing your computer, bear in mind that at any one moment it might be trying to do more than three million calculations on numbers of the order of two hundred and eighty-one trillion in size. In light of this, it is frankly surprising that computers manage to handle the workload at all. Luckily, digital artists never have to deal with this level of detail. You do not need to know how it works, but it is sometimes useful to know why it does not work instantly.

You do not always need to work at the highest resolution, but you do need to work at the appropriate one. This is why "working backward" makes sense. The output is often the only part of the imaging chain that is not negotiable. Clearly, if someone asks you for a high-

quality printed poster for a shop window, he or she will not thank you for turning in a low-resolution screen image blown up to poster size. But the real reason for working backward is that it will save you time and improve the quality of your results. If you have four hours to do a job and spend three and three-quarter hours looking at an egg timer or spinning watch, the chances are that you have committed the major sin of digital imaging: overengineering.

Many digital artists fail to obtain the best possible image, despite their efforts, because they choose an input method that gives them too much resolution, too large a file size. They are therefore effectively wasting time at every step of the manipulation process. That means less time thinking, and more time asking your boss (or even worse if you are self-employed, your loan manager) for a better computer, more memory, more storage space, and a more powerful image processing package—and more time to resent the emphatic "no" that you get in response.

The other benefit of thinking backward is that the question "Why am I doing this?" becomes a positive, creative question rather than a self-pitying one.

Above *More thought, less time. Just "trying things" is a good way to learn but a bad way to work.*

Below *How many different shades you decide to mix, along with the bit depth you select in order to achieve the desired color, affects not only the result but also how long it takes to manipulate. Bit depth is explained fully on page 18.*

24 BIT COLOR

8 BIT COLOR

8 BIT GRAYSCALE

1 BIT BITMAP

1 need to know

Before we launch into the intricacies of digital image processing, it is vital to know the basics of what digital images are, how they work, and how they can be manipulated. This chapter introduces fundamentals that appear throughout this book, such as pixels, color depth, and interpolation. With a grasp of each of these basics, the image creator can make a series of enhancements and improvements to digital images—as will be outlined in the chapters that follow.

visual glossary

A picture may not quite be worth a thousand words, but it makes explanation significantly easier. This chapter offers you a whistle-stop tour of the most important aspects of digital imaging.

The smallest constituent of any digital image is the pixel. A single pixel will show up on a screen if it is much magnified, but it is unlikely to show up in print. Pixels are not the same as information; pixels are just tiny little showcases for information. If you have an office full of filing cabinets, that is not the same as having an office full of information, it just means you have an awful lot of room to put it in. Similarly, the pixel is merely a specified place in the computer's memory where there is a number. That number is the definition of the color and brightness of a part of an image.

pixels per inch

Though the number of pixels in an image defines the amount of information in that image, it is the number of pixels *per inch* (ppi) (otherwise known as dots per inch or dpi) that defines the physical size of an image. Typically, computer monitor screens offer a resolution of 72dpi (determined by the physical size of the phosphor dots on the screen), while a printed image would need to feature at least 300dpi to appear of photographic quality. Hence an image of 1,800 × 1,200 pixels would yield a 6 × 4-inch image when printed at 300dpi, but would be significantly larger when displayed on screen.

Now while many monitors allow much higher resolution than this (some 22-inch monitors allow up to 2,048 × 1,536 pixels to be displayed), any text would have been reduced to an unreadable size if you selected that on-screen resolution.

A pixel has a single color, thus the fewer pixels an image has, the more jagged any graduation of tone is going to be (see also color depth, *pages 18 to 19*).

Right *The more pixels, the smoother the definition of an image—especially where it contains text.*

100 X 100 PIXELS

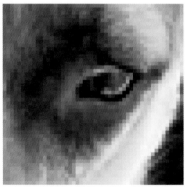

50 X 50 PIXELS

Right *Different numbers of pixels affect the quality of an image if you use the images all at the same physical size.*

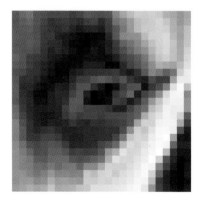

25 X 25 PIXELS

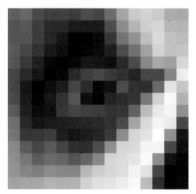

15 X 15 PIXELS

combinations

Most image manipulation applications are pixel-based; that is, all edits and transformations are performed on individual or groups of pixels. As such, the resolution of the image (in terms of the number of pixels it contains) is irrelevant (although images can be resized by altering the number of pixels it contains either up—increasing image size—or down).

If you try to combine a 300ppi scan with a portion of a 72ppi screengrab, you will need to give the images a common resolution before proceeding. Your screengrab may well be four inches wide on screen, but if you try and combine it with a 300ppi four-inch-wide image, your screengrab will shrink to less than one inch wide when its resolution is adjusted correspondingly and the image combination will not succeed as envisaged. If you absolutely must use images of two different resolutions together, you may have to choose between reducing the size of the final image to accommodate the lowest resolution part of your image

combination (this will entail reinputting the screen resolution element of your combination at a higher resolution), or (and only as a final measure) using interpolation. Interpolation is a technique that allows you to make the transition from one resolution to another by creating equally scaled images through the introduction of intermediate pixels. (Interpolation is covered in detail on pages 20 to 21.)

Interpolation can be both a boon and a drawback in image manipulation. It can be used constructively to resize a good image. It is important to note that interpolation inserts new pixels but does not add to the information (or definition) of the image. Some "large" image files are created by scanners (and even some digital cameras) by virtue of interpolating a smaller file. There is rarely any justification in this.

Below *The definition, sharpness, and smoothness of tone increases as the number of different pixels contained within an image increases.*

1 PIXEL

2 X 2 PIXELS

3 X 4 PIXELS

5 X 7 PIXELS

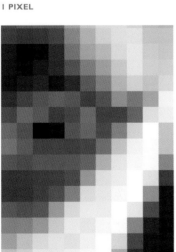

10 X 15 PIXELS

25 X 35 PIXELS

50 X 70 PIXELS

100 X 145 PIXELS

colors in the computer

As far as light is concerned (as opposed to pigments), the three primary colors are red, green, and blue (RGB). These three colors can, between them, represent every known color shade. It is probably best to regard the number of shades as infinite, but the essential thing to know is that if you shine a red light, a green light, and a blue light so that they overlap, they will give white light.

The amount of light—brightness—does not affect the actual color. The formal definition of brightness is the relative lightness or darkness of the color, usually measured as a percentage from 0% (black) to 100% (white). Hence, a color can have the same shade but, depending on the brightness, be a deep maroon or a pale pink.

If you add blue and green together you get cyan; add red and blue together and you get magenta; and if you add red and green together you get yellow. Cyan, magenta, and yellow are known as the secondary colors. If you add cyan light to red light, you get white light; the same goes for adding magenta to green, and yellow to blue.

By using filtration, you can employ these complements to creative effect at the moment of capture. For example, a dense pure yellow filter placed in front of a lens allows only yellow light through, and blocks all blue light (its complementary color). This is a useful device for darkening skies without losing cloud detail (which is white, and thus contains yellow light).

The key to how these colors affect digital imaging is, as usual, the output mode. If you are engaged in Web work, you will have only a limited palette of colors (see color depth, *pages 18 to 19*) with which to work. With print work, it becomes even more important to think very carefully about the colors in an image. Cyan, magenta, and yellow are the colors used for printing. In theory, just as red, green, and blue light should combine to make white light, so cyan, magenta, and yellow inks should combine to make black. In practice, however, this is not strictly the case, and so a fourth ink, black, is added to the mixture to make for the CMYK ink system. The letter "K" is used to represent black in this acronym so as to differentiate it from blue.

limitations

In the real world, where printers' inks and computer monitor phosphors are not 100% pure, it is impossible to reproduce every theoretical color defined by mixing pure red, green, and blue colors. In fact the ability of an output device to represent color varies from device to device. The colors that a particular device can represent are called its "color space" and can be depicted graphically (see below). Depending on the device, the color space is somewhat smaller than the theoretical maximum number of colors possible. The methods used to maintain the color of an image from capture to manipulation to printing is known as color management. This is covered in more detail in chapter 3.

Right *Different methods of output have different limitations in terms of which colors they can show.*

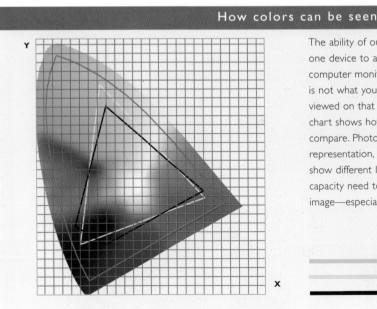

How colors can be seen

The ability of output devices to represent color varies from one device to another. When you examine something on a computer monitor, you need to be aware that what you see is not what you are going to get, unless an image is to be viewed on that exact same monitor. The CIE chromaticity chart shows how the limitations of three typical output media compare. Photographic films have the widest color representation, while CMYK printing and an RGB monitor show different limitations. These variations in color display capacity need to be taken into account in the creation of an image—especially if it is destined for print processes.

FILM

MONITOR

PRINTING PRESS

4-BIT, PRODUCING 16 COLORS

8-BIT, PRODUCING 256 COLORS

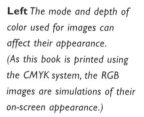

Left *The mode and depth of color used for images can affect their appearance. (As this book is printed using the CMYK system, the RGB images are simulations of their on-screen appearance.)*

24-BIT RGB (8 BITS FOR EACH CHANNEL = 16.7 MILLION COLORS)

32-BIT CMYK (8 BITS FOR EACH CHANNEL)

color depth

Whether you are looking at input devices such as scanners, software such as image manipulation programs, or are even examining images on your monitor, the color depth, bit depth or how many hundred, million, or even trillion colors you want, confounds many digital-imaging novices. When faced with this mathematical challenge, it is helpful to start with the simplest color combination, namely no color or black-and-white type.

The key to digital imaging is that it uses a binary counting system (binary uses only two digits, 0 and 1). Information is stored in bits, and each bit has two possible states: 0 or 1. So how does this system translate to defining and assessing color depth?

An image with 1-bit color can by definition only have two states, black or white. But what we usually call a black-and-white image is more correctly known as a monochrome, or single-color, image. That does not mean it only has two states, rather that it lacks the three primary colors. A truly black-and-white (1-bit color) image lacks any tonal variation. What we need are intermediates between those two extremes, in other words, shades of gray. A 2-bit image has four states: expressed in bits, these are 00, 01, 10, and 11 (00 is black, 11 is white, and 01 and 10 are shades of gray). At this 2-bit level, the image will obviously lack smooth tonal detail.

For smooth monochrome images we need something more. A 3-bit image has eight states expressed as 000, 001, 010, 011, 100, 101, 110, and 111. We now have black as 000, white as 111, and six intermediate shades of gray. Add a fourth bit and we multiply the shades by two. This gives 0000 as black, 1111 as white, and fourteen shades of gray. With eight bits of data, we increase our total to 256 combinations with 00000000 as black, 11111111 as white, and 254 intermediate shades of gray.

1-BIT BLACK AND WHITE

2-BIT GRAYSCALE

3-BIT GRAYSCALE

4-BIT GRAYSCALE

8-BIT GRAYSCALE

continuous tone

At this complexity, the image has become what is known as a continuous tone. While practically no image is truly "continuous"—even traditional photographs are made up of tiny colored dots—the term is used in this book to refer to images that appear to be so when viewed at normal size with the unassisted human eye. But how do we progress from this smooth gray image to a colored one?

Digitally, color can be split into three primary colors: red, green, and blue. If each pixel is defined by three lots of data (one each for red, green, and blue) then for each primary color, 00000000 means no color (black), and 11111111 means 100% color (or 100% each of red, green, and blue respectively).

Any combination of these three 8-bit numbers will refer to any one of 256 x 256 x 256 possible combinations of red, green, and blue. This level of color is known as 8-bits per channel or 24-bit color. With 24-bit color, up to 16.7 million different shades can be described.

8-BIT BLUE CHANNEL

8-BIT COLOR

8-BIT RED CHANNEL

Left *You can see how adding extra levels between black and white eventually leads to a continuous-tone gray image up to a total of 256 levels. Add these smooth channels of 256 levels of each primary color together and you have a continuous tone color image, showing 16.7 million colors.*

24-BIT 16.7 MILLION COLORS

8-BIT GREEN CHANNEL

interpolation

You may have noticed that there are often two figures quoted for a scanner's resolution. Flatbed scanners (normally used to digitize flat artwork or photographic prints) may have, for example, from 1,200ppi resolution up to 9,600ppi resolution. Given that the 1,200ppi is the maximum optical resolution (i.e., the number of pixels per inch the scanner can actually scan), how can they achieve this stunning 9,600ppi resolution?

The brief answer is that 8,400 of the 9,600 pixels per inch are "made up," or to give it its technical name, interpolated. Interpolation is the technique of adding pixels to an image where none exist. The process is carried out by software that examines an image pixel by pixel and, based on one of a number of different algorithms (preset processes), converts a preset number of pixels into a much larger number of pixels. This technique can make an image look smoother, but remember that it does not add detail, it only boosts the number of pixels.

Interpolation is to be completely avoided except when you are scanning in black and white (1-bit color). By scanning in grayscale (256 shades of gray) at its maximum optical resolution, the scanner is able to recognize the edges of the black-and-white artwork. It can make sensible judgments about the shapes it is scanning in, and so give much more accurate results. Given that text is in effect black-and-white artwork,

interpolation is actually very useful if a scan is then to be used by text recognition software. In all other cases, trying to increase, or even reduce, the size of an image by interpolation is not a worthwhile option.

When you are changing the size of an image in order to make a screengrab (see pages 132 to 133) for example, interpolation will soften the image and destroy its realism as a screengrab. That may well be what you are attempting to do, but interpolation does not really achieve anything other than blurring the boundaries of an image.

wysiwyg

An abbreviation for What You See Is What You Get, WYSIWYG should really be given the more appropriate title of ARABSTRAPS (A Rough Approximation Bearing Some Tenuous Relation After Prolonged Searching). WYSIWYG is used for digital camera LCD (liquid crystal display) viewfinders, on-screen scanning previews, and applications of special effects in some manipulation software programs. Often the images look nothing like the final image, and the windows in some software programs are so small that it is difficult to examine the image.

In short, the acronym WYSIWYG is used to enhance a product's marketability. In many cases, the best way to assess how your image will look is simply to do the necessary work, and study the results for yourself. As with driving, taking shortcuts on the advice of someone else rarely leads to the shortest, least painful route.

Below *To show the limitations of interpolation, here are ten images, originally of 512 x 512 pixels, each reduced to its captioned size, then resampled back up to 512 x 512 pixels.*

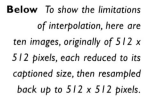

| 1 X 1 PIXEL | 2 X 2 PIXELS | 4 X 4 PIXELS | 8 X 8 PIXELS | 16 X 16 PIXELS |

| 32 X 32 PIXELS | 64 X 64 PIXELS | 128 X 128 PIXELS | 256 X 256 PIXELS | ORIGINAL, 512 X 512 PIXELS |

Below *Without interpolation,
some scanners will produce
jagged edges on curved detail.*

Below *With interpolation
smoother edges on curved
detail can be obtained.*

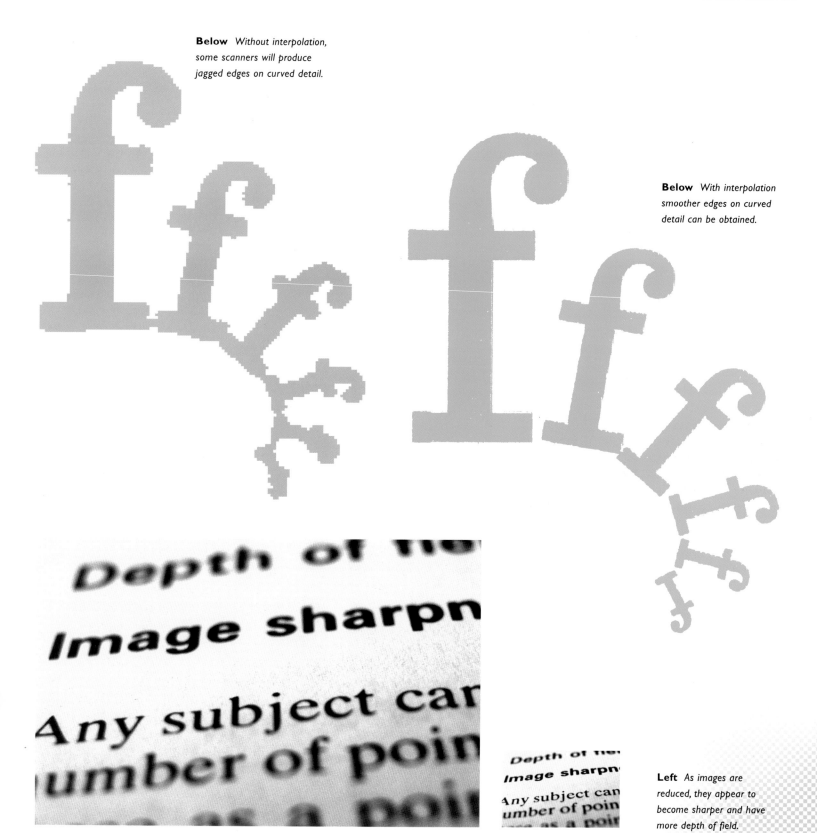

Left *As images are
reduced, they appear to
become sharper and have
more depth of field.*

sharpness and artifacts

Many digital cameras and scanners have "sharpening" algorithms built in to their operation. These make a punchier image out of the one that has been captured. You can sharpen an image by increasing the general contrast. You can also give the perception of greater sharpness if you identify the edges of subjects and simply increase the contrast on them.

Both these options have two things in common: they are overused, and they should never be done after an image has been compressed. When an image is compressed using the common JPEG system, information is discarded, producing a potentially "blocky" image when the image is decompressed. When a sharpening filter is applied to such an image these artifacts tend to be emphasized more than genuine image elements (we look more closely at this "lossy" compression method and

"lossless" alternatives later). If possible, switch off the sharpening facility on input devices. Treat sharpening as the last option for an image, or at least save a version without sharpening, so you can adjust it later.

color management

Although color management is the most complex aspect of digital imaging, it is an essentially simple concept at its core. Some elements of the digital imaging chain cannot cope with all the colors, and even those that can will not necessarily show the colors in the same way. When you have an image on screen, you need to know what it will look like at output (whether to a Web site or to print). In Adobe Photoshop, the difference between what can be represented by RGB and CMYK (see pages 16 to 17) can be shown as a gamut warning on screen. Everything that cannot be represented by printed inks is shown in a block of the user's specified color (often an eye-catching green or red). For Web work, depending on which color

ORIGINAL

COMPRESSED AND SHARPENED ONCE

COMPRESSED AND SHARPENED TWICE

COMPRESSED AND SHARPENED THREE TIMES

palette you are working to, you may find that the subtle shades of your perfectly designed artwork look more like a child's first attempt at painting by numbers. This is an appropriate analogy as the colors available to you in both Web and printed work are defined within a set of numbers, which is referred to as the color space.

Knowing which color space you are working toward (at the output stage) allows you to avoid any nasty shocks at the end of the process. Nowadays, every element of the digital imaging chain has a profile (as defined by the International Color Commission). By setting up all the elements in your imaging chain properly, and assigning the correct ICC profiles to your image for the output, input, and viewing elements of the process, you should have a good idea of how your image looks at every stage. This is the essence of color management.

If you ignore the concept of color spaces there is a chance that the color fidelity of your image will be compromised (required colors will not be "available") and the amount of detail that can be represented (with more limited color ranges) may decrease. But perhaps most importantly, you could equally be deluding yourself about how good an image can look. It might look perfect on your monitor, but if you haven't picked the correct final color space, the screen image may bear no relation to the final result.

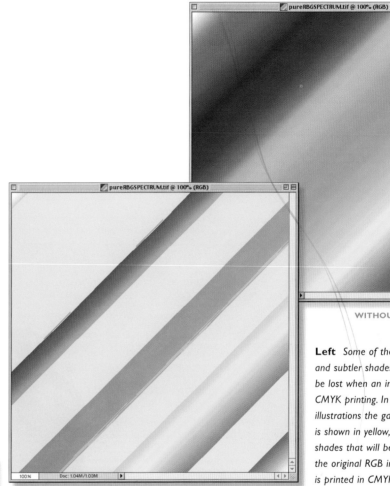

WITHOUT GAMUT WARNING

WITH GAMUT WARNING

Left *Some of the brighter and subtler shades of color will be lost when an image goes to CMYK printing. In these illustrations the gamut warning is shown in yellow, revealing the shades that will be lost from the original RGB image when it is printed in CMYK.*

WITHOUT GAMUT WARNING

WITH GAMUT WARNING

Left *As can be seen here, it is often shadow detail that will be lost in the journey from screen to printed image.*

2 output

 There are many purposes for digital imaging, one of which is archiving for the future. For all other aspects of DI, the ultimate aim of your manipulations and input, the be-all and end-all of digital imaging, is output. Everything else you do is useless unless you get this aspect of the job right. Over the next pages, we'll look at all the common forms of output and how best to optimize your images for the particular form or forms of output you want to use. Only when you know what you want to output and how you want to output it can you start to work out the best way to manipulate it and import it in to your computer.

what is output?

You can define output in two ways: it can be the point of no return (the final product) or a way-marker (a proof output). In this chapter, we will look at how to achieve the perfect output, but first we need to establish exactly what "perfect output" really means. Perfect in a proofing sense relates to how closely what you are looking at matches what the final image will look like. In terms of a finished product, it means being exactly what is required. For each of the output methods used in digital imaging, there is a slightly different set of factors that goes into making them perfect images.

To achieve the outputs as described and discussed here, image editing software is generally required. Most results can be achieved with any such editor but in some cases a specific application is required.

As discussed in the Introduction, the key to successful digital imaging is to deal only with as much data as you need. Output resolution, image size, and color depth are key factors in the final look and size of an image. By assessing your final requirements, you can establish what you will need to work with at the input stage, and how to view your images during the processing of the image to get a good idea of the final look. This idea of

previewing, or "soft proofing," is fundamental to controlling how accurately your final image will resemble the desired effect. It is particularly useful to soft proof in this way when preparing images for the Web. Subtle gradations of tone will end up as great blocks of color when transferred from true color RGB to a limited palette of 256, 216, or even 16 colors.

color differences

You also need to be aware of the difference between the representation of colors achieved on an RGB computer monitor and that achieved using the conventional four-color printing process. Being aware of, and able to compensate for, such differences is critical for the accurate adjustment of tonal values. Whether you are dealing with single images or movies you can use Adobe Photoshop software (see pages 168 to 169) to examine the color of a single frame. This will enable you to assess how the image will look, either in a restricted palette or when printed.

In order to do the latter (see pages 56 to 57) you need to know the profile of the press with which you are dealing. While it is possible to redo screen-based images, or change the color profile of an image destined for an inkjet output, asking a publisher to reprint a publication is simply not going to be possible. The important rule of output is to get it right the first time.

Right *The left part of this image is at Web color level, the rest of it is at 16.7 million colors.*

Opposite *Image quality—and file size—is primarily affected by the variables of resolution and color depth.*

72PPI 32 COLORS

72PPI 256 COLORS

72PPI MILLIONS OF COLORS

150PPI 32 COLORS

150PPI 256 COLORS

150PPI MILLIONS OF COLORS

300PPI 32 COLORS

300PPI 256 COLORS

300PPI MILLIONS OF COLORS

27

desktop output 1

One of the fastest-moving technologies within digital imaging has been in printers designed for your desktop. Whether inkjet, laser, dye-sublimation, thermal autochrome, or other technology, they provide you with very high-quality results. Although the technology has improved, confusion exists as to image resolution.

With printers that give resolutions of up to 1,440 or even 2,400 dots per inch, surely that means huge input resolutions? Not necessarily. The key lies in the ability of the printer to smooth things out (see *dithering,* opposite) and also the human eye's ability to resolve detail. For inkjet output, 150 pixel per inch (ppi) files will give an acceptable output. Acceptable, however, may not be good enough for some people, and 200ppi as a baseline

number may then be regarded as giving acceptable printed reproductions for inkjet printers. A larger file resolution may give enhanced quality, especially in deeply colored and complex patterned images, but it might not. Some people prefer to use 300ppi as a baseline for their printing. This allows them to keep the same setting for whatever printing they are doing (see *pages 34 to 35*).

If, however, you are only going to output to an inkjet printer, then this is unnecessary and wastes time, memory, and storage. The difference between a 200ppi image and a 300ppi image in terms of file sizes is greater than you might think. A 6 × 4-inch 200ppi image in CMYK for printing is a 3.67Mb (Megabyte) file. An equivalent 300ppi image will be 8.25Mb, more than twice the size. As well as being wasteful, using an unnecessarily high resolution may also be ineffective. The larger the image, the further away you will view it from.

Below *The main picture shows what inkjet printing can achieve. The close-ups show in light, dark, and mixed areas what results different levels of print resolution and dithering will give.*

360DPI

720DPI

720DPI, DITHERED

Dithering

When a section of an image has graduated tones, rather than a solid block of the same color, it is called a "continuous-tone" image. With CRT (cathode ray tube) monitors and LCD (liquid crystal display) screens, as in real life, tiny blocks of different levels of light of different colors make up what appears to be a smooth-toned image. With printing, it becomes a little harder to achieve this appearance, and if you were to print just the pixels in an image, you would need a huge resolution for the pixels not to be visible. Printers overcome this hurdle by using a technique known as "dithering."

Rather than laying down a single dot for each pixel, dithering lays down a number of them around the area of the pixel to achieve a smooth-toned image. For example, when printing a 200ppi image on a 1,200 × 1,200-dpi (dots per inch) printer, the printer can lay down thirty-six dots of ink for each pixel. It could arrange them in a square block, but as the human eye is good at detecting regular patterns, the printer lays them in a random pattern or varies the size of the droplets of ink. The result is that images are anti-aliased, or smoothed, to reduce the jagged effect of the blocks that form images on computer screens.

MONO ORIGINAL

MONO DITHER

FULL-COLOR ORIGINAL

FULL-COLOR DITHER

360DPI

720DPI

720DPI, DITHERED

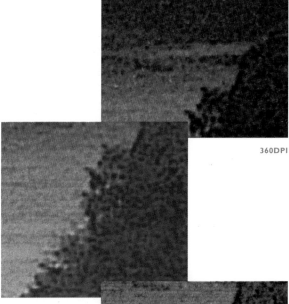

360DPI

720DPI

720DPI, DITHERED

desktop output 2

Color management is a crucial aspect of image quality. Most printers have their own color modification software, although this may be a limited feature on lower-priced models. For the most part, the medium onto which you output, and the inks you use, have as much impact on the final image as your color software settings. By changing the paper type or the resolution level on an inkjet printer, you affect how ink is laid down, as well as how much is laid down. This will change how the image looks. The ideal, if you must use more than one type of ink or paper, is to get to know how a particular combination works. Set up a color management chart for that combination (perhaps just a screen image and a reference print to see how those two are related) and judge your subsequent printing on that combination.

One of the hardest things to set up properly is "four-color black." This is where you have a black-and-white image in RGB mode on your computer, and you want to achieve a neutral, i.e., noncolored, black. In case you are wondering, there are two reasons why you might want to have a "color" black-and-white image. First, using a four-color black means more dots on the page, which means smoother, denser blacks and grays and thus more natural-looking images. Second, if you manage to set up four-color black correctly, then your printer will be perfectly set up for normal color printing. Think of it this way: for a four-color black to be neutral, all three of the cyan, magenta, and yellow inks must be in perfect balance; this is a lot more noticeable on an ostensibly neutral image than it is on a colorful shot of a landscape or a portrait.

One additional benefit of having black-and-white images in a color rather than a grayscale color space, is that it becomes very simple to produce subtle duotones or tritones.

Below *You can adjust the saturation settings from subtle to very saturated with most inkjet printers.*

DUOTONE

TRITONE

ADJUSTING LEVELS

Duotone *The right-hand side of this color image has been converted to a duotone featuring only black and green as colors. The mode was changed to Monochrome (to remove color) and then Duotone selected.*

Tritone *By adding a third, specific, color (an electric blue) to the duotone, an iridescent, metallic effect is achieved.*

Adjusting levels *Using the Levels command in Photoshop the original "flat" image was converted to one that exhibits a more realistic contrast range and color saturation.*

Thermal dye sublimation

There was a time when thermal dye-sublimation printers ruled every design office. To some extent, this still holds true, but the rule is nowhere near as absolute these days. In order to form an image, these printers melt different colored wax onto the printing paper. The colors, as with most printing, are cyan, magenta, yellow, and black, although some specialist photo printers eschew the black.

The more advanced printers are starting to use variable-sized dots to increase the continuous-tone look of an image, but their ability to form fine images is being overtaken by inkjet printers. The key advantage of advanced printers is their speed.

In terms of resolution, advanced printers have significantly lower resolution capacity than inkjet printers of equivalent price. Generally dye-sublimation printers will include, as part of the software that comes with the machine, a PostScript RIP (raster image processor) that enables such printers to interpret and print page layouts accurately.

BLOWUP

MAIN IMAGE

output to photographic film / paper

One of the secondary benefits gained from the introduction of the Advanced Photo System film format in 1996 was the wholesale change to photo processing machinery. In order to take advantage of what this format offered, many printing machines were converted to digital both for input and for output.

The advantage of outputting images to photographic paper is a relatively simple one. It gives the images a stronger resemblance to photographs. There is also the benefit that real photographs do not smudge, which means that they will have good archival performance. In fact, they have an average life expectancy of sixty years before any loss of color becomes apparent. Physically, photographic papers have an impressive structural integrity as compared with many inkjet papers.

The resolution of digital photo output may seem a little on the low side at 133 lines per inch (for scanning beam devices) or 150ppi for LED (light emitting diode) array printers. The final result, however, has an "analog" smoothness that can rarely be matched by any other printing device. As with output to slide film (see opposite), the dyes within the paper smooth pixellation away, and you can use image resolutions of 200 to 300ppi with very little noticeable difference to the naked eye.

Color management is, without the necessary ICC device profile, a case of "try it out and see what happens." There is, however, a naturalism about the results, irrespective almost of any color management, that makes photo printing output one of the easier methods of output from a digital image in terms of its color.

Finally, if you want to achieve the best black-and-white images, the digital photo printer is the perfect choice since it can make images with real impact when used with special black-and-white paper. This process is worth doing—it gives very classy-looking results.

Below *Although specialist photographic paper is a more expensive option, the output quality is far superior to normal plain paper.*

PRINTED ON PHOTOGRAPHIC PAPER

PRINTED ON PLAIN PAPER

ORIGINAL IMAGE

+10 SATURATION

+20 SATURATION

+30 SATURATION

+40 SATURATION

Output to slide

It may seem ironic that having originated an image digitally, and having adjusted it digitally, you would then want to output it to film. Slide does, however, have a number of advantages. First, it needs only the human eye to view it (about as cross-platform compatible as you can get). Second, it has more visual impact than a print because transmitted light images, as opposed to reflected light prints, have better color and contrast characteristics. The third advantage is that slides are a secure means of data storage. For example, original Kodachrome slides dating from 1935 are still in existence, and they can still be scanned. There are, however, few digital storage media readers from ten years ago, let alone any surviving images. Film also has a built-in dithering capability in the form of dye grains. These are disposed, in a random fashion, in the emulsion layer, and unless you use too low a resolution to output to slide, there will be no sign that an image has been brought into the digital arena at all. Given that some people are still wary of digital imaging, outputting to slide, especially for a single photo image, represents a way of delivering digital images in an acceptable form to many clients.

To avoid evident pixellation, image files should have a resolution of about 2,800 to 3,000ppi for a 35mm slide. Higher resolution does slightly improve definition beyond this point, but it is very much a question of diminishing returns above 3,500ppi.

output to press

With the advent of the Internet, outputting to the printing press is no longer the ultimate goal in many cases, but with the wealth of new books and magazines being launched every year, learning the art of outputting to a CMYK press is still a necessity for the digital imager.

Before considering how to set up for output to press, it is worth looking at how presses work. Magazines and books are printed in sections, which are normally made up of thirty-two, sixteen, or occasionally, eight pages. Covers are printed four pages at a time (outside front, outside back, inside front, and inside back). The reason for this is that it is quicker to print on wide rolls of paper than narrow ones, so printing thirty-two pages all at once is quicker than printing single pages at a time.

magazine printing

A typical 100-page saddle-stitch magazine, that is, one held together by a staple in the middle, will be printed as three thirty-two-page sections (pages 3 to 98) and one four-page section for the cover (pages 1, 2, 99, and 100). When these huge sheets of thirty-two pages (sixteen on each side) are pulled off the press, they are cut from the roll in a section, folded in on themselves three times, and then trimmed down to their correct size. It is important to be aware of the sections because pages with heavy color on them may cause "color carry"—overinking of other less colorful pages—since the blanket press (the

drum that carries out the actual printing) picks up ink from the printing plates for each color. You should be aware of this, especially when involved in magazine work where the page output is extraordinarily fast.

Printing inks are not applied from a single printing plate, but in four different applications from four plates (one each for CMYK). The image has previously been broken down into halftones, which are composed of dots of different sizes. When paper runs through the presses, the different colored dots are laid down near each other in a shape known as a rosette. This rosette is the basis for every detail that appears on a press-printed image.

dot gain

Different papers and inks create various ink spreading characteristics known as "dot gain;" the more absorbent the paper or the lower the surface tension of the solvent in the ink, the greater the dot gain. Too much dot gain makes your image look dark and soft since not enough of the paper's whiteness shows through the rosette. Too little dot gain makes the image look high in contrast because the dots are obvious to the eye. If the four colors are out of register and not positioned correctly in relation to one another, the colors themselves will look wrong and the image resembles an anaglyph (red/green stereo imagery). An example of this is where a nominally black line has different colors on either side of it. It is often best, especially when using white type out of a black background, to use a heavier weight (i.e., bold) type so any registration errors do not make the text illegible.

Right *In press printing, four dots of color are laid down one on top of another to blend colors and tones, producing a so-called "rosette" shape. When the colors are out of register, quality suffers.*

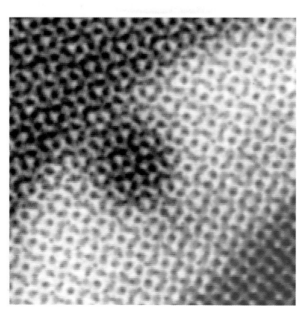

THE CMYK ROSETTE

REGISTRATION PROBLEMS

NO SHARPENING

Left and below *These three pictures show the effects of sharpening and resharpening an image with an unsharp mask. The mask has been applied with a setting of two pixels radius (the radius describes the number of pixels beyond the edges we wish to emphasize that will be affected by the sharpening).*

UNSHARP MASK APPLIED WITH 2 PIXELS RADIUS SETTING

SHARPENED TWICE

preparing a digital image for press output

When you are preparing an image for output to press, the first thing you need to do, other than making sure that you have enough resolution (see the Q factor, below), is to ensure that you have the right color mode. If you are working with a continuous tone image, i.e., a photograph or any image where there are subtle gradations of tone, you should work on your image in 24-bit color (see pages 14 to 15). Once you have made final adjustments you should convert it to CMYK mode for output.

Provided that your color settings are arranged correctly (see pages 38 to 39), you should be able to get a good idea of what your images will look like in color and contrast terms when they are eventually printed out. One of the benefits of working in Photoshop is that it has Gamut Warning and Proof Colors settings. These features allow you respectively to see which colors cannot be reproduced in your chosen output medium, and to see how colors will be reproduced. If you are working with black-and-white images and want to output to grayscale, you will need to be aware that purely grayscale images will look less rich than an image in four-color black; however, there is no risk of color fringing or other registration problems.

the q factor

While there is often a problem when scanning press-printed images into a digital form (where moiré, or distorted, patterns can occur), there is also a similar problem when converting pixels into rosettes, particularly where images containing patterns are concerned. Unlike inkjet printing, press printing does not have a dithering process. If you try to output an image with the same pixel per inch resolution as the line per inch screen (the measure of press printing), you may get disappointing results. To prevent this from

Below *Here we have the processes involved in selecting a gamut color warning, and how that warning is shown.*

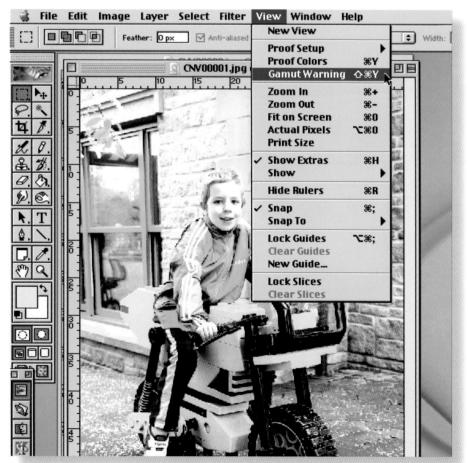

TURNING GAMUT WARNING ON

GAMUT WARNING APPLIED (SHOWN IN PURPLE)

happening, you need to make sure that your image resolution is greater than the line screen (printing resolution of the press in lines per inch) by an amount known as the "Q factor." In general, recommendations for what multiple this should be vary between one and a half and two. The latter multiple is easy to calculate and is a convention that is commonly used by most major publishing houses.

newspapers and magazines

For newspapers that tend to print on stretchy, low-quality paper, and therefore cannot support high resolution images, a line screen of 72lpi is common. So, with a Q factor of two, this means that images for newspaper reproduction need to have a minimum resolution of 144ppi. This is an at-least figure because some newspapers are now stretching the boundaries of printing technology and printing at higher line screens.

For magazines, where glossy coated paper can handle higher printing resolutions, 133lpi used to be common. This needed images of 266ppi resolution, or more, for reliable results. Now even magazines on paper as thin as 60gsm (grams per square meter, a measurement of paper thickness/density) can accept printing resolutions of 150lpi, and so need 300ppi image resolution. For brochures on heavier, coated stock, printing screens of 200lpi or 250lpi are possible. This is also true for sheet-fed printing. With the Q factor added in, it will need image resolutions of 400ppi and 500ppi respectively.

Below *Computer monitors, newspapers, and magazines all have different nominal image resolutions dictated by the line ruling at which they will be printed, as shown respectively below. Resolution for fine-art printing will often be well above 300ppi.*

72PPI COMPUTER MONITOR

150PPI NEWSPAPER

300PPI MAGAZINE

color setup

Depending on the kind of image you are outputting, the setup for press work may need to be different. Embedded within the Edit menu in Photoshop 5 and the File menu in Photoshop 4, you will find a dialog box called Color Settings. Within this, you need to choose the CMYK setup. Do this by selecting Custom in Photoshop 5. If you know the exact settings your printer is going to be using, then you will be able to enter them here. If not, the normal setting is SWOP (coated), 20%, GCR, Medium. These four items refer to the type of paper, the dot gain percentage, the type of separation, and the black generation amount. We will take that last one first.

When you are going to be taking screengrabs with dialog boxes, your gray boxes may well have a pinkish gray tinge if you do not slightly change the black generation in this setting to maximum. This provides an effectively grayscale output for all the gray elements of your screengrab, i.e., the box and its background, leaving the other three channels to sort out any colored information. As with other images, moving the black-and-white component to a grayscale channel means you will not get color shifts in your gray boxes, or even worse,

different color shifts. This should only be done where images contain large elements of dialog box gray, and is not appropriate for screengrabs of black-and-white images, or for Web sites where the only part of the image that is gray is the edge of the box containing the image. What you gain on the box, you will lose in image richness in the rest of the screengrab. The other three components of the CMYK setup should be left as they are unless you know what the paper is or your printer or origination house tells you otherwise.

the printing press

You can also change how your computer, or perhaps more accurately your monitor, will show you how to set the different color spaces, and how it converts the image from one color space to another. This ensures that when you turn on the Color Profile Preview, you are getting an accurate picture of the final image.

There is also a series of advanced options regarding the software methods used to convert the image. These are only shown when you open the Advanced Dialog Box, and if you do not understand what the options are, turn off the Advanced Options and let Photoshop sort it out. If you are outputting through an origination house or printer, ask for their recommendations.

Below *You can adjust the display settings to get neutral colored dialog boxes suitable for screengrabs in Photoshop.*

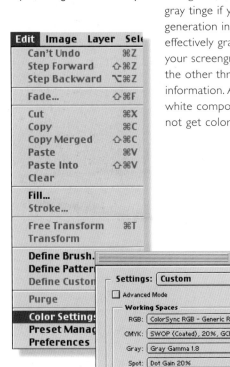

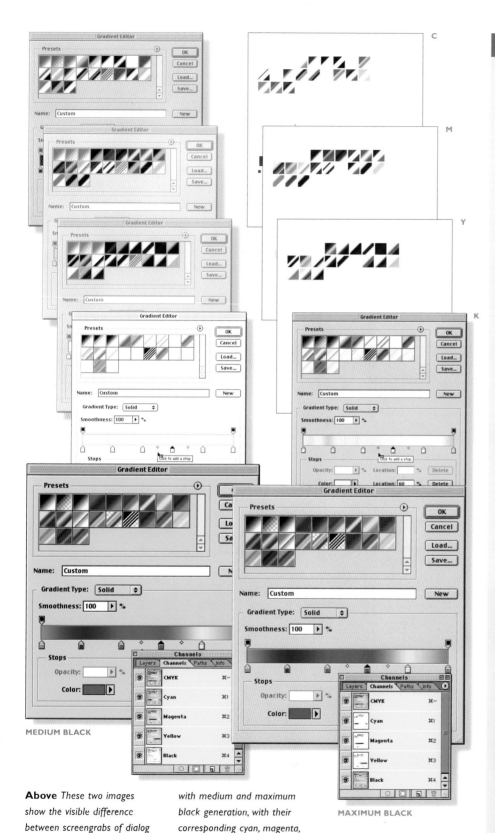

RGB

sRGB

Say no to sRGB

The color space you choose to work in is unlikely to improve your image, but if you choose the wrong one, it may well have a negative effect. It is worth taking time to ensure that you've got the right one early on. Adobe Photoshop 5 tried to unite Macintosh and PC platforms by introducing the sRGB color space as a standard. However, this color space is smaller than many other color spaces and is not recommended for digital imaging. If you use sRGB, you will effectively reduce the amount of information available to print. The best advice in this particular situation is to choose either Colorsync or a platform-native color space for press work as a preference.

MEDIUM BLACK

MAXIMUM BLACK

Above *These two images show the visible difference between screengrabs of dialog boxes separated with inks set with medium and maximum black generation, with their corresponding cyan, magenta, yellow, and black channels.*

output to web

I f ever there was an appropriate use of the well-known phrase "less is more," it is for the process of preparing images for Web output. The received wisdom in imaging is always that the factor of highest importance is quality. Bigger is better, pixel-power, and so on.

This might well be true if everyone had access to Internet connections of limitless speed and bandwidth, but that is far from being the real case. If you are in a commercial framework as far as your Web output is concerned, the graphics need either to be small, punchy, and quick to load, or else they need to be loaded after the text. This may be heartbreaking for the designer, but nowhere near as bad as it is for the legions of frustrated users who have to sit and wait patiently while their analog models take

ten minutes to translate the pitifully slow data stream from an overbuilt Web site. When users find that they have successfully loaded a big graphic that simply says "Welcome. Please click to continue," they won't bother.

avoidable frustrations

While it is true that many new computers have the appropriate software to allow ShockWave Flash, Adobe PDF, QuickTime Movie (or Media player), and Real Audio and Video files to be played, many older models do not. These are all on the verge of becoming standards, but there are two file formats that allow high-quality still and moving images to be loaded quickly but do not need the user to download 11Mb of new software before a Web site will open. Designing graphics and placing still images into a cyberspace-friendly format is about using the lowest common denominator, not about working at the cutting edge. So if you need to choose a format, then make sure it is either GIF (an indexed color set specifically for use on the Web) for animations, or JPEG (compression file) for photographs.

In situations where there are many identical image areas on your page, you should reuse a single version of an image in multiple instances rather than using identical, differently-titled multiple image files. This way, the browser can download a single image, and retrieve it from the cache on the viewer's computer for each instance—normally, this takes far less time than downloading a series of separate images, even if they are all identical.

Below *Opening pages that contain numerous graphic and textual elements are slow-loading and immensely frustrating, while simple, quick-loading pages encourage a much greater usage of the site.*

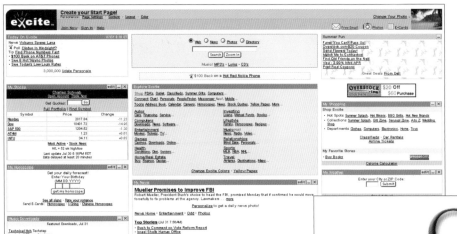

SLOW TO LOAD

QUICK TO LOAD

Incidentally, while it is often useful to view the results of a GIF animation or JPEG photo that you have created through an Internet browser (for color rendition and size purposes), it is even better if you can upload them to a real Web site, in order to determine how long it will take a real user to get the information accurately. Your hard drive may well transfer 10Mb a second from a file to a browser window without stretching itself. Few Internet connections reach beyond 14Kb a second.

Left *RealPlayer permits the viewing of video (and still image) media from a variety of different sources, including streaming video. VCR-style control keys permit control of the replay.*

Compression

Compressed files are smaller than uncompressed versions and can therefore be distributed (via disk or email) far more efficiently. Lossy compression regimes (such as JPEG) can achieve substantial reductions in file size but, as the name implies, data is lost when the file is "rebuilt" by the recipient. Heavy compression, or multiple compression/decompression, cycles can seriously degrade the image—each time the image loses more data. JPEG is often used for small images used on Web sites. If image quality is not a key concern, lossy compression is the most practical choice.

Lossless compression regimes include LZW (Lempel–Ziv–Welch, *see page 44*) and do not compromise image quality. Such compression routines do not always produce such compact files, but are effective for flat colors, and reconstituted images contain all the image information of the original. If it is important that an image is compressed but that quality is maintained, then lossless methods should always be used.

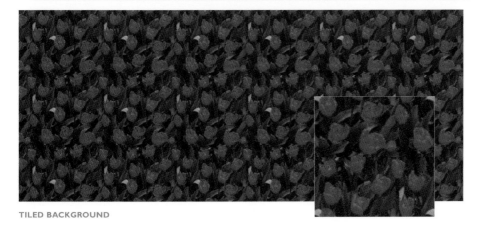

Left *For maximum effect with minimum download time, the background images for Web sites need to tile seamlessly. The original pattern area is shown in the small box.*

TILED BACKGROUND

graphics and colors

If you have generated a graphic or background using an illustration package such as Adobe Illustrator or Macromedia Freehand (which use a vector-based approach rather than the pixel-based approach of image manipulation packages), your next step is to see how your file will stand up to being reduced in size. Fortunately, vector graphics files tend to be smaller than image files (vector shapes are more efficiently described than individual pixels) and can be easily scaled to different sizes. Its size should be appropriate for the size of screen that it is likely to be seen on, and its resolution at the correct size for that screen. If you are aiming for a minimalist approach, a 640-pixel-wide by 480-pixel-high resolution will be sufficient for users of older machines; users of later machines need a 1024 × 768-pixel image.

In terms of file size with indexed colors (i.e., not the full continuous range) you can achieve an extraordinary saving in file size merely by restricting the number of colors. Tread carefully though. If you have not designed your graphics in Web-safe colors, i.e., those that will not be changed when they are transferred to the Web browser's smaller color space, then it is best to use one of the proprietary color restriction programs (*see chapter 7*). You could also use a Web preparation program. Both are preferable to just flicking to "indexed color" and throwing all the color detail to the four winds. The fewer the colors that have to be loaded for a new image, the quicker the image loads because the file size, without color restriction, can be ten times bigger.

For those images that have not been designed specifically for Web use (or perhaps those that are to appear both in print and on the Web) you need to reduce the number of colors in use, or think about going down the JPEG route. Anything with graduated tones can be immediately treated as if it were a photo. That is to say, it is not suitable for drastic color reduction.

As an alternative to compressing the color palette, or compressing the whole image as a JPEG, you can take problem areas of graphics, and, using a Selection tool, pick out areas of trouble (graduated tones). These areas can be filled with either individual Web-safe colors, or with a pattern made up of an array of Web-safe colors.

The problematic nature of creating effective images and graphics for the Web has led to the creators of many image editing and graphics applications, including substantial rafts of features specifically with this in mind. Photoshop, in particular, now includes a sibling product, ImageReady, dedicated to Web images.

In place of the print and reprographic elements of Photoshop, programs like ImageReady and Fireworks incorporate Web-specific functions such as image optimizers, extensive Web color palettes, and more advanced Web tools.

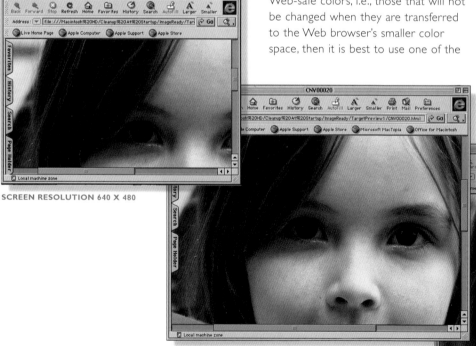

SCREEN RESOLUTION 640 × 480

SCREEN RESOLUTION 800 × 600

Above *Make an image too big for a user's screen and the viewer has to look at it in sections.*

SCREEN RESOLUTION 1024 × 768

GIF CONVERSION DIALOG BOX

ORIGINAL UNCOMPRESSED 256 COLORS—2MB

Left *Even continuous tone images can sometimes be better and smaller as GIFs. However, in cases such as this, where there are large tonal and contrast gradations, the amount of compression provided by the GIF format will be less significant.*

Dithering and smoothing

If you reduce the number of colors in an image, you will inevitably end up taking away some of the image's natural gradation. This tends to induce a rather unwanted and eye-catching blockiness to the image. One solution to this problem is to use the technique known as "dithering," which will reduce the impact and smooth the gradation.

As with printer dithering (*see page 29*), which uses random dots to achieve a smooth-toned image, on-screen dithering uses intermediate colors (by closely mixing lighter- and darker-colored pixels) to give an implied gradation of tone. As long as you do not have too many different graduated colors, this can be achieved without a massive increase in the number of colors used, and therefore without file size or speed penalties.

GIF—1.1MB

photos on the web

The sharing of photos—whether for commercial, private, or any other purpose—has been one of the particular growth areas of the Internet. Families can share favorite snaps while photoprocessors can now copy conventional images, handed in for processing and printing, to the Web for more expedient delivery.

Internet delivery has several benefits. For example, there is the virtual immediacy: send an image by email and (service providers permitting) it will be delivered in seconds. It can also be used to market and sell images effectively, with photographer and client brought together easily.

but how is it done?

The first question is one of staged picture selection. By saving a thumbnail (a copy of the image at a file size of 40 × 60 pixels for a portrait format), your picture file is probably about 10Kb in size. This shows the basic content of a picture, and by simultaneously making a picture of a Web button, the Web designer gives you something to

look at to make your selection. But the real art is in selecting the right way to bring larger images down to the desktop as quickly as possible. Unlike GIFs, color restriction is a rarely used tool that is more likely to cause harm than good, although there are inevitably exceptions. The main way to save space is by means of compression. In addition to the standard JPEG compression, and the upcoming but still far from universal wavelet compression, is the bolt-on compression scheme. It is eminently possible to reduce a multimegabyte file to a file within the 10 to 50Kb range without reduction in visible resolution.

This remarkable compression is possible because we are displaying images at screen resolution. By definition, at normal viewing distance, a screen pixel cannot be seen as a discrete object or you would never be able to read text clearly on screen. Equally, pictures would not be able to be shown realistically. As long as the file is compressed from the right starting point and with the correct smoothness, it should be possible even for the characteristic 8 × 8-pixel squares of JPEG compression to be invisible. The amount of compression you use, balanced by the amount of smoothing, should enable you, with most subjects, to get a

Below *An uncompressed TIFF file. Compare this with the compressed image below.*

Below *Using the lossless LZW compression the resultant image features no decrease in detail or resolution.*

workable file from a quality point of view with a file size reduction of 90% or more. Shown below on this page is a file taken down in size by 98%, and it will not look any worse on screen at its screen resolution than the original file, but it is reasonable to say that it would load significantly more quickly.

downloading a picture

If you intend to download a picture, try to make sure when you are setting up the links from the Web site that a file of the appropriate size and resolution is also there. In other words, you will need a less heavily compressed file, of 300ppi resolution, but one that has the same physical size that your screen image had when it was set at a resolution of 72ppi. This is necessary to be certain of obtaining images of any reasonable quality.

You might also want to consider protecting your printable file with a discreet copyright notice or a digital watermark. This will eliminate the problem of users reusing your images unknowingly without your permission. It will still be possible to steal the images, but not without having to laboriously tamper with them first in order to hide their origins.

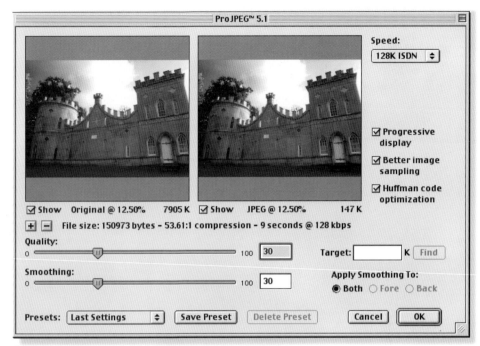

Above Use box previews in preparing images for the Web, but also examine full-sized "before" and "after" images.

PRINTABLE IMAGE

SCREEN IMAGE

SCREEN PREVIEW

Above To increase the speed at which images are loaded, use different sizes of images to meet different requirements. Here a small screen preview (72ppi, GIF), a full-screen image (72ppi, JPEG, 50% quality), and a large printable version (300ppi TIFF, no compression) of the same image are all connected by links.

animation

With the exception of movies, animation sequences have more saving options available to them than any other kind of digital file. They also hold more traps for the unwary user. The old maxim that states that, when dealing with electricity and water, if you are not sure what you are doing, it is best not to experiment with more than one thing at the same time, should be applied here.

When working with animation, you should be aiming for the best-quality imagery with the smoothest transition as well as the smallest Color palette and the fastest-loading file. This is, as it sounds, a difficult task to master given that prioritizing the first two will be at the expense of the last two, and vice versa.

possible pitfalls

Creating animations in Photoshop and ImageReady is covered in detail in chapter 4, and the method used there is as simple as any other. But if you are going to create animations in other programs like BoxTop GifMation or Extensis PhotoAnimator (see chapter 7) be aware of the penalties of tinkering with the background, transparency, or discard settings. If you aren't careful, then when you come to output, you will find artifacts left where they should be absent. This is particularly important with looping animations, especially if you are trying to save file space by leaving a null background and moving an object on top of it, for example, a spinning colored wheel or a bouncing ball.

Basic settings for correct output of GIF animations can and should be checked not only in a Preview window of the animation creation program, but also by exporting the animation as a GIF, and then loading it up in your current Internet browser, and your old Internet browser if you have one. Some of the more sophisticated animation programs will warn you of any known conflicts that you might encounter in older versions of Microsoft Internet Explorer and Netscape Navigator.

output for use on a cd or dvd

If you have produced the animation sequence from scratch, you will have created it in Web-safe colors, and with few if any continuous tones. There is really little cause to restrict color, other than the fact that if you define as few colors as possible in the animation, the file itself will be kept as small as possible.

If you are outputting animations for use on a CD or DVD (see pages 48 to 49) then the considerations become skewed very much more toward quality. The amount of detail and the number of colors you can use will increase, but there is still a time factor involved. The more complex the animation, the more room in memory it will occupy, so keeping the disciplines of the Web is

Right *Even a simple animation needs to include multiple frames if smooth movement is to be achieved.*

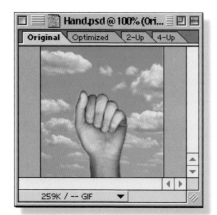

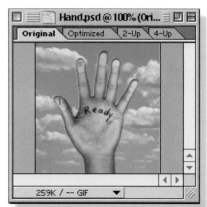

still a useful exercise. If users become frustrated when the speed of their modem is slowing operations down, think how much more frustrated they will be if they believe that their whole computer and not just the modem is incapable of running a simple piece of animation. The golden rule for outputting animation is to keep it small, keep it quick, and keep it moving.

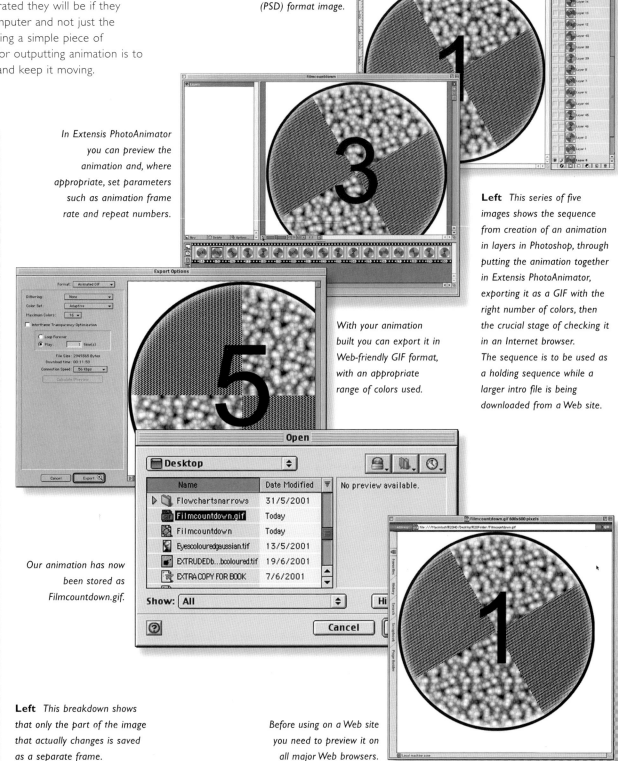

The original images are stored as layers in a Photoshop (PSD) format image.

In Extensis PhotoAnimator you can preview the animation and, where appropriate, set parameters such as animation frame rate and repeat numbers.

Left *This series of five images shows the sequence from creation of an animation in layers in Photoshop, through putting the animation together in Extensis PhotoAnimator, exporting it as a GIF with the right number of colors, then the crucial stage of checking it in an Internet browser. The sequence is to be used as a holding sequence while a larger intro file is being downloaded from a Web site.*

With your animation built you can export it in Web-friendly GIF format, with an appropriate range of colors used.

Our animation has now been stored as Filmcountdown.gif.

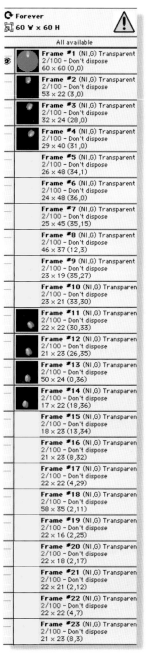

Left *This breakdown shows that only the part of the image that actually changes is saved as a separate frame.*

Before using on a Web site you need to preview it on all major Web browsers.

outputting to cd / dvd

It may seem an indulgence to devote two pages to outputting to CD and DVD (DVDs can store more data than a CD but outputting operations are much the same for both), but a well-designed CD involves not only the jewel case cover, but also the organizing of the information on it.

The first thing to do is to prepare a folder where everything is as it will appear on the CD-ROM, so that the contents of the folder can be dragged all at once to write to the CD-ROM. This makes a quick and simple operation since it avoids the risk of forgetting to put things on the CD-ROM until after it is too late (see below).

If you are burning a CD of pictures, use Photoshop to prepare a contact sheet (choose Automate: Contact Sheet II) and then Save for Web (also in the File menu). You can specify how many images you get on your contact sheet, how large it is going to be, and what resolution you are going to use. Select 72ppi for resolution, eight inches wide, five columns, and as many rows as you need to get your images in. Allow each row 1¾ inches and specify the length (or height) of the document to suit. So for thirty images, you need six rows giving a height of 6 x 1¾ inches = 10½ inches. With this specification for row size, even users of 640 x 480-pixel screens can see the whole width of the contact sheet and can scroll down for the CD-ROM's contents.

As mentioned in the Input section (see *Chapter 5*), you need to save your files with meaningful names. As Contact Sheet II gives you the option of printing the file name underneath each picture, how meaningful the name is will be tested by the user. Saving the file for Web may reduce some detail, but our purpose is to save the viewer's time. If they want the full version, they can open it later. Call the contact sheet "Open in Explorer/ Navigator. GIF" and put it at the top of the main folder, next to a Read-Me First file (written in a text-only program and giving instructions on how to use the CD-ROM).

Below *Making a contact sheet is a simple and automated process in Photoshop.*

Right *Saving images correctly saves time when accessing them.*

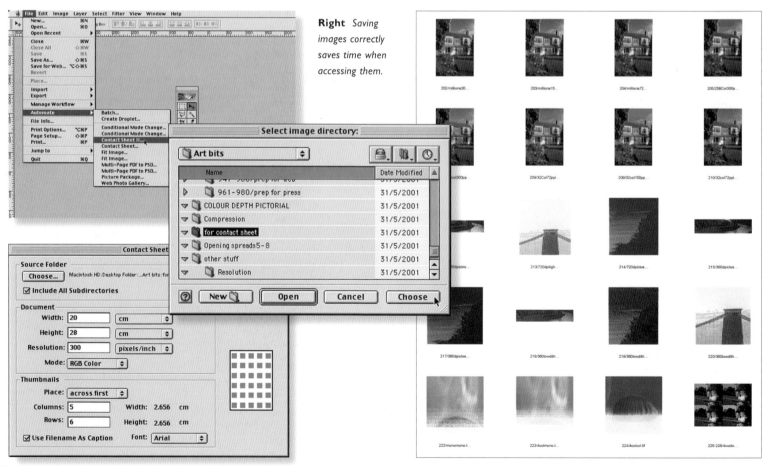

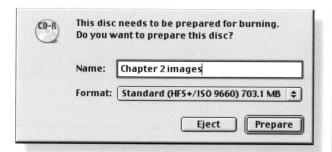

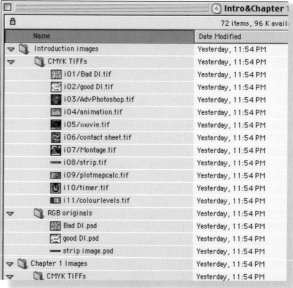

single or multisession

Most CD-burning software is now multisession, i.e., you do not have to choose between burning the CD all at once or abandoning the operation until a later date. If yours is a single-session CD, all the more reason to set up a duplicate folder, so that once you are happy with everything, you can then burn the CD all at once.

cd-rw

Rewriteable CDs (CD-RWs) get around the session-writing problem, but they cannot be read by many computer CD drives, and as archives, they are not as robust. Avoid using them unless you are specifically sending them to someone for them to add something.

Creating icons

There seems little point in spending hours creating a unique work of art only to link it to a Photoshop or other generic software icon. When you are saving a piece of artwork, save a copy first with a resolution of 128 × 128 pixels in indexed colors. You need to resample the image using nearest neighbor interpolation, not bicubic interpolation, or you will really soften the image. Why 128 × 128 when icons are mostly 32 × 32? Well, it is still possible to use a 128 × 128 image as a 32 × 32 icon, and some operating systems allow icon sizes up to 128 × 128. So for once, it is worth doing a little overengineering.

BLACK AND WHITE

COLOR

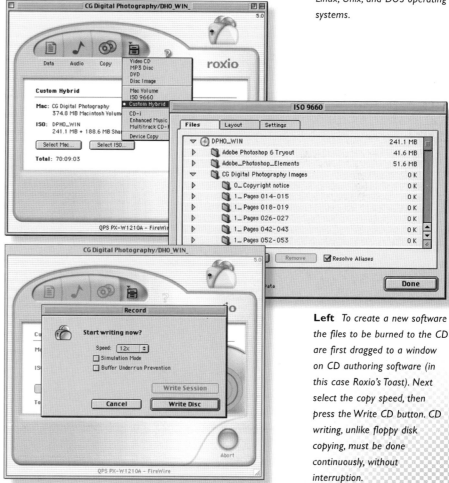

Left *Before a CD is burned— i.e., recorded onto—it needs to be prepared. The contents should be laid out in a logical and structured way. For Mac, icon views must be laid out neatly, with nested folders all opening in a predetermined position on screen. In Windows, such organization is irrelevant since the operating system takes care of it. It is also possible to create hybrid disks (such as that using the ISO 9660 recording format) that can be read by more than one platform. Such disks can be read effectively by computers running Windows, Macintosh, Linux, Unix, and DOS operating systems.*

Left *To create a new software the files to be burned to the CD are first dragged to a window on CD authoring software (in this case Roxio's Toast). Next select the copy speed, then press the Write CD button. CD writing, unlike floppy disk copying, must be done continuously, without interruption.*

dv to tv

The reason there are multiple standards in TV (and thus Digital Video) output is the historical accident of the UK and the US power companies choosing to use different frequencies for AC mains power supply. When the inventors of the cathode ray tube, Vladimir K. Zworykin of RCA in the United States and Alan Dower Blumlein of EMI in the United Kingdom, worked on the production of the first workable electronic television systems in the 1930s, they each decided to use an interlaced system of screen refreshment. This was based on refreshing half the screen on each pulse of the mains frequency in order to reduce the possibility of flicker. For the United States, with a mains frequency of approximately sixty cycles per second, this gave a full-screen refresh rate of about thirty times per second, and for the United Kingdom with its 50Hz supply, one of twenty-five times per second. While there have been other deviations from the path of compatibility, especially with the introduction of color systems, this was the main starting problem. It also explains why there are issues surrounding the conversion of cine films (at twenty-four frames per second) to video. NTSC, the standard system in the United States, uses 525 scanning lines while PAL, the British system, uses 625 lines. Just to make things simpler, we will consider SECAM, the French TV system, as being equivalent to the British PAL system, as it uses a very similar color sampling method.

dv to dvd or television tape

Before outputting DV to DVD or to tape for playing on a television, you need to be aware of how it will play, and that includes dealing with 4:2:2, 4:2:0, and 4:1:1 output. These ratios represent various sampling frequencies for outputting to video. The PAL system works best with 4:2:0 as an output, while the NTSC system works with 4:1:1. The latter is also better for a workspace environment. So if you are outputting to European users, PAL 4:2:0 is the standard output, while NTSC 4:1:1 is the preferred output for the US and Japanese markets. As far as audio output is concerned, for direct output to NTSC you should use 48kHz; for direct output to PAL either 32kHz or 48kHz (also known as 12- and 16-bit) locked audio can be used. Do not worry if your Saving dialog box offers you only 44.1kHz, because this format is also supported by DV audio. When capturing audio, try to ensure that at least each clip has a single format, i.e., try

not to mix 32kHz and 48KHz audio. Also, make sure that, when you capture your audio and video into your DV nonlinear editing program, you capture it in the correct format for your output (PAL or NTSC), otherwise the computer will have to perform two groups of unnecessary conversion, which would take up a great deal of processor time.

output format

Non-TV output and compression and Web video formats are covered on pages 54 to 55. Incidentally, the standard resolution for DV is 720 pixels per line. High-definition television (HDTV) is ironically the name given to the black-and-white 405-line BBC standard that dates from the 1930s. This format is beyond the rendering capacity of the huge majority of today's computers, so the upper limit has been kept at 720 pixels per line.

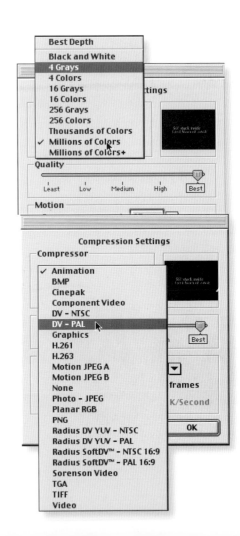

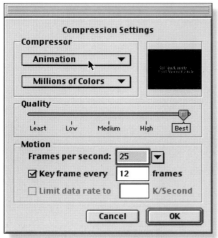

Above *In this simple holiday video "The End" has been generated using the title facility within iMovie and overlaid on a moving scene. Alternatively, still shots can be imported into Photshop and titles added using that software's text facility.*

Left and opposite *Even simple DV nonlinear editors offer a wealth of options, including titling.*

web movies

If you are still trying to take in the multiplicity of standards and options in outputting straight to video or DVD, brace yourself for an equally indigestible serving of options when it comes to the subject of Web movies. This boils down to a choice of image size, quality, compression, color selection, audio compression, and whether the movie is going to be streamed, i.e., viewed in real(ish)-time, or from a CD-ROM. To avoid information overload for the reader, it is probably best not to delve into the whys and wherefores of each particular format, other than to explain which formats are most suitable for particular user applications.

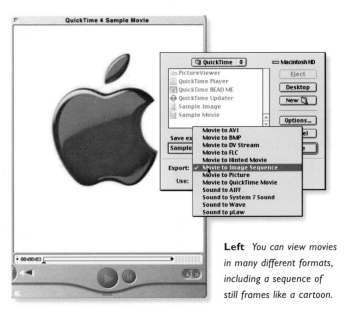

Left *You can view movies in many different formats, including a sequence of still frames like a cartoon.*

format	image size	example comparison file size	image quality
AVI	720 X 540	552KB	LOW
DV	720 X 540	17.7MB	MEDIUM–HIGH
H263	720 X 540	1.8MB	MEDIUM–LOW
COMPONENT VIDEO	720 X 540	96.8MB	HIGH
ANIMATION	720 X 540	84.1MB	HIGH
APPLEGRAPHICS	720 X 540	231MB	MEDIUM–HIGH
JPEG MOTION A	720 X 540	33MB	MEDIUM–HIGH
NO COMPRESSION	720 X 540	193MB	HIGH
PLANAR RGB	720 X 540	101MB	HIGH
PNG	720 X 540	19.8MB	MEDIUM
SORENSON	720 X 540	8.7MB	MEDIUM
APPLE VIDEO	720 X 540	25.1MB	MEDIUM
BMP MOVIE	720 X 540	145MB	MEDIUM–LOW
TIFF	720 X 540	143MB	HIGH
TGA	720 X 540	90.5MB	HIGH

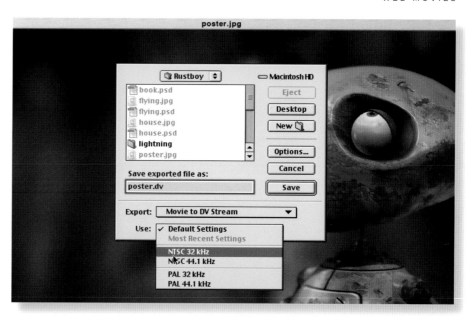

compression		speed of saving		speed of loading
HIGH	🖴🖴🖴	MEDIUM–QUICK	💾💾💾	QUICK
LOW	🖴	SLOW	💾	SLOW
HIGH	🖴🖴🖴	MEDIUM–SLOW	💾💾	QUICK
LOW	🖴	SLOW	💾	SLOW
LOW	🖴	SLOW	💾	QUICK
MEDIUM	🖴🖴	SLOW	💾	MEDIUM–SLOW
MEDIUM	🖴🖴	MEDIUM–SLOW	💾💾	MEDIUM–QUICK
NONE		QUICK	💾💾💾	SLOW
LOW	🖴	SLOW	💾	MEDIUM–SLOW
MEDIUM	🖴🖴	MEDIUM–SLOW	💾💾	MEDIUM–QUICK
MEDIUM–HIGH	🖴🖴🖴	SLOW	💾	MEDIUM–QUICK
LOW	🖴	MEDIUM–SLOW	💾💾	MEDIUM–QUICK
LOW	🖴	MEDIUM	💾💾	QUICK
NONE		MEDIUM–SLOW	💾💾	MEDIUM–SLOW
LOW	🖴	MEDIUM–QUICK	💾💾💾	MEDIUM–SLOW

Above left A streaming video embedded in a Web page can be played back in a browser with the appropriate plug-in installed.

Above Saving movies to DV offers several options for the operator, the most important of which are the output format and the sampling frequency.

Left This chart shows the relative sizes and speed to save and to open as well as compression and a subjective image quality judgment. All of the formats were taken from the same initial DV sequence, which lasted only just over five seconds.

53

BEST PRACTICE

web output

Preparing images for Web output is a simple affair if you use a logical progression of questions to structure the work. Do you reduce the file size before reducing the number of colors, or vice versa? Will you be using JPEG or GIF as a file format? Can you use a smaller file as a conduit to a larger downloadable image? Consult the Web designer on this, if it is not you. What color is the Web site background going to be, and is it likely to overlap or clash with one of the colors in the image? If so, find out earlier rather than later so that you can deal with the clash by placing an appropriately neutral-colored (white or black) two-pixel keyline around it. This can be done in Photoshop by enlarging the canvas size from a central point by two pixels.

checklist

Use the following checklist as a reference when you are about to start the image process, rather than just at the output stage, and you will find that it saves you a great deal of time. If you are working with someone else's

image and preparing it for Web usage, then the checklist will not be a time-saver, but it will ensure that your image is reproduced as well and as quickly as possible.

As far as on-screen imagery is concerned, the number of pixels in the image is the determining factor, therefore size and resolution per inch can largely be ignored. Assume a 640 × 480 screen, and your maximum image size, without needing to scroll up and down or left and right in the browser window. Remember that even if the image is shown full screen, the window itself will take up a few pixels in both dimensions, and if there are any toolbars open, a 620 × 400 image is likely to be the largest size that can be displayed. The image resolution, for ease of size calculation, should be set to 72ppi.

As far as restricting the colors is concerned, experiment with different combinations of color levels and dithering (*see page 43*). The equation for file size versus quality can always be balanced in a number of ways, and depending on whether your image has a preponderance of strong contrast detail or subtle graduations of tone, then respectively low dithering/more

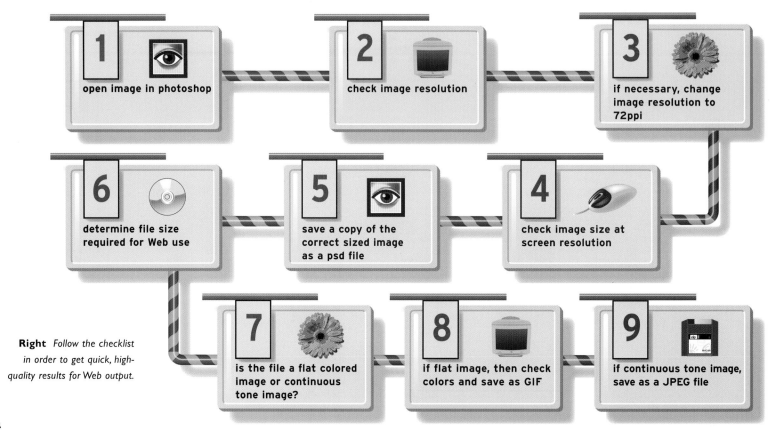

Right *Follow the checklist in order to get quick, high-quality results for Web output.*

1 open image in photoshop

2 check image resolution

3 if necessary, change image resolution to 72ppi

6 determine file size required for Web use

5 save a copy of the correct sized image as a psd file

4 check image size at screen resolution

7 is the file a flat colored image or continuous tone image?

8 if flat image, then check colors and save as GIF

9 if continuous tone image, save as a JPEG file

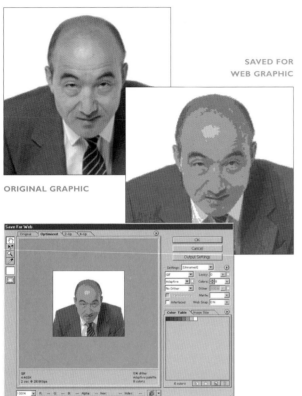

SAVED FOR
WEB GRAPHIC

ORIGINAL GRAPHIC

SAVE FOR WEB DIALOG BOX

colors or high dithering/restricted colors will probably be the best methods of preparation. Remember that while JPEG files can often be smaller than GIF files, they can still take more time to load, and you may be throwing much more detail away if you really try and squeeze an image at the lower quality end of the JPEG compression scale. (For more advice on compression, see pages 192 to 193.)

Below *Use a specialized program or plug-in to restrict colors, get the best tonal effect, and the maximum acceptable compression.*

Above *This example demonstrates the effect of the Save for Web GIF palette in Photoshop. The palette has been reduced to only eight*

colors. In order to save on file size, the software automatically converts the continuous-tone image into a graphic with large areas of flat color.

IMAGE WITH ACCEPTABLE COMPRESSION APPLIED

DIALOG BOX SHOWING ORIGINAL AND COMPRESSED IMAGE

BEST PRACTICE
cmyk output

In addition to checking that your image is in the correct color format (CMYK or grayscale) for offset printing, you should consider a number of other issues when preparing an image, or especially a series of images, to be printed on press. The first of these is consistency. The importance of this concept cannot be overemphasized in the quest for high-quality digital images.

consistency

If you are scanning from different photographic film types but of the same kind of subject, try to avoid placing these images on the same page. Equally, avoid using different digital image sources on the same page. It is worthwhile to look at a group of images on screen at the same time, or even paste them into the same document with the CMYK preview turned on to see how they will all look when they are output alongside each other.

checklist

Below *Follow the checklist in order to get top-quality printed images.*

Ensure that your Q factor (see pages 36–37) is set to an appropriate level in terms of the multiple between the line screen of the printing press (or more accurately the originated halftone plate) and the resolution of the digital image. A factor of two is ideal. Again, the printer or origination house that is handling the printing of your book, brochure, or magazine will be able to help you.

If you are responsible for a large number of images, make sure that when placed together they do not form large areas of a single color. It is especially important to watch out for this where a lower weight of paper is being used. Color carry (see page 34) may cause a shadowing of color onto an otherwise colorless part of another page and spoil your document.

Always check the dot gain, separation type, paper type, and black levels that are to be used by the printer. If you are in any doubt, use the default CMYK Setup that is provided in Adobe Photoshop.

Check that your colors are CMYK safe by using the Preview of Gamut Warning features in Photoshop, to ensure you are not ordering the printing press to achieve a color that is not within its repertoire.

Avoid using white text out of four-color black, or indeed any high CMY component colors, unless you increase the weight of the type, i.e., make it bold, in case

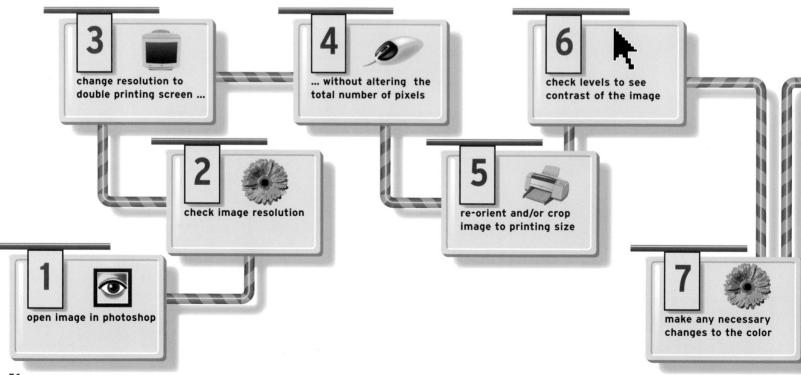

3 change resolution to double printing screen ...

4 ... without altering the total number of pixels

6 check levels to see contrast of the image

2 check image resolution

5 re-orient and/or crop image to printing size

1 open image in photoshop

7 make any necessary changes to the color

of registration issues at the printing stage. These last problems may well be someone else's fault, but it is still the responsibility of the digital artist to take them into consideration.

Finally, if you are going to be printing screengrabs, choose maximum black in the CMYK Setup box and use the image at around half its screen size. It is best to use nearest neighbor interpolation, rather than bicubic, to prevent the edges from softening. Resizing should take place in a layout program rather than in Photoshop.

MODE CONVERSION
(TO CMYK COLOR)

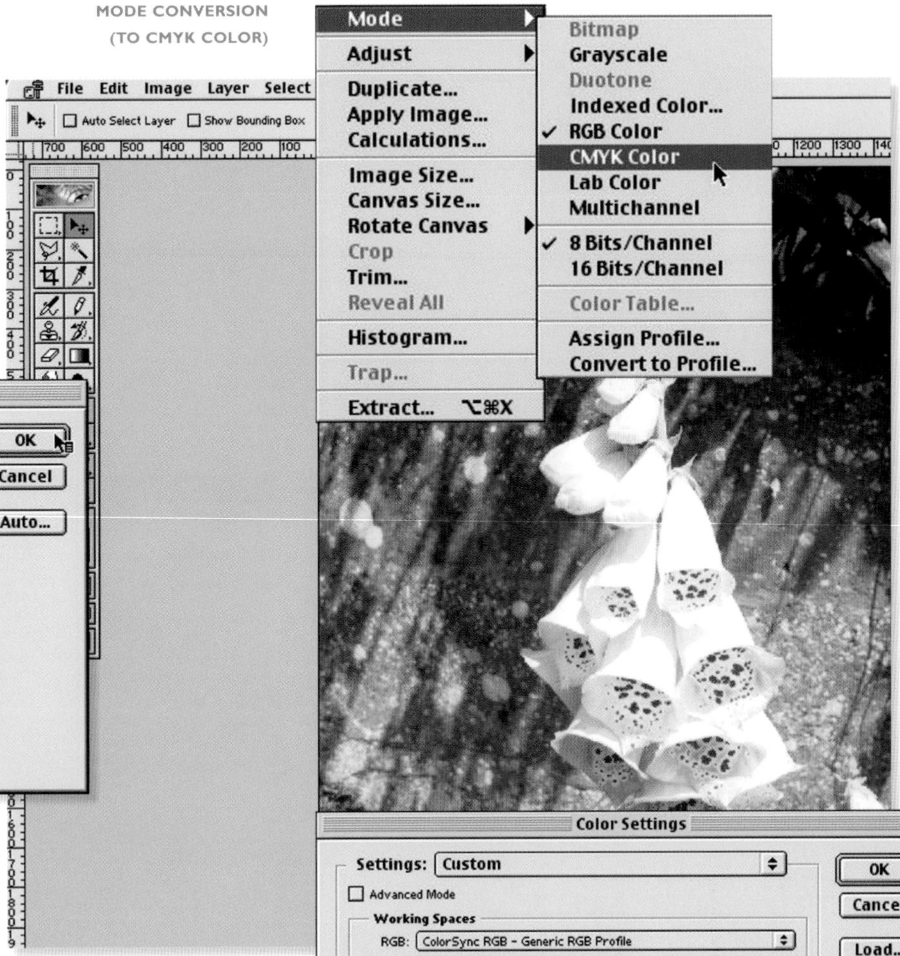

IMAGE SIZE DIALOG BOX

PHOTOSHOP MAIN INTERFACE

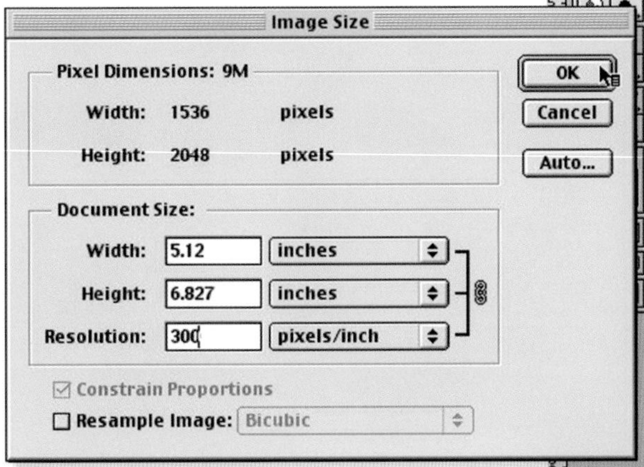

8 engage proof colors and gamut warning

9 adjust image for creative effect. Then save it as CMYK TIFF

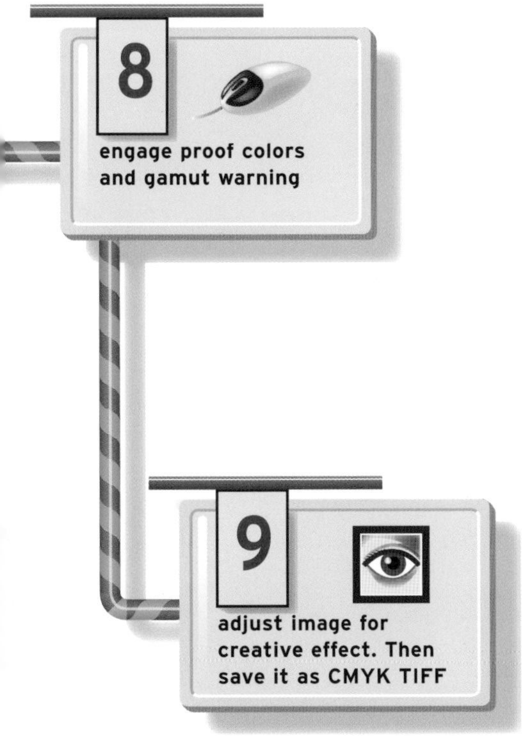

Above At small font sizes registration problems can cause effects such as this, due to the text strokes being of the same thickness as the pixel size. Sharper representation can be achieved in this case by selecting a heavier weight (such as bold).

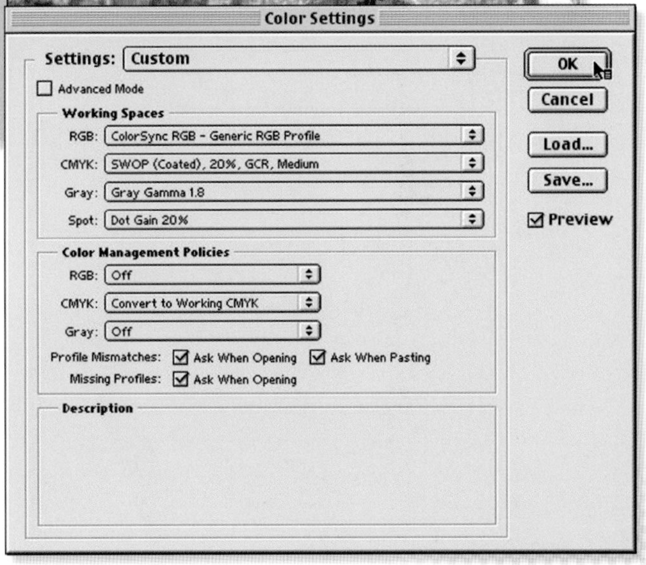

COLOR SETTINGS DIALOG

Above Getting into a set routine for converting your images will ensure you always have the right setup for CMYK output.

3 image improvement

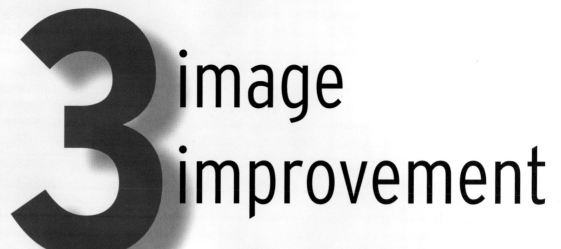

No matter how well you scan, or how hard you try when capturing a digital image, there are very few occasions when an image cannot be improved. There are two kinds of image improvement: putting something right that has gone wrong, and adding to an image by means of functions available on the computer that are not available at the moment of capture. Where traditional photography requires everything to be perfect at the moment the photo is taken, digital imaging offers a much needed degree of latitude. In this section, we'll look at how you can make simple changes to an image that can both correct its imperfections and even radically improve it.

adobe photoshop

It is only after the capture of an image that the real power of the digital system becomes apparent. The comparatively simple act of shooting with a digital camera, or scanning a negative, provides the creative imagemaker with a digital image file that is the basis for producing stunning pictures. From this stage onward an endless range of enhancements can be made to the image. Digital imaging specialists gain a substantial competitive and creative edge over traditional practitioners when they are able to change a continuous tone image into a form that can easily be manipulated by computers. Basic tasks can be completed in seconds rather than the minutes or hours required when using darkroom printing techniques. In addition, some tasks

that are now achievable via desktop manipulation are not even possible using traditional chemical- and silver-based systems. These types of changes to your images and photographs can only be achieved by using one of the digital imaging editing programs.

The best-known of this type of software package is Adobe Photoshop (*see also pages 168 to 169*). First released in 1990, this program has contributed more than any other to the huge growth in desktop digital imaging. It is a comprehensive package with a full feature set and a large array of manipulation tools. It is used by imaging professionals in areas as diverse as photojournalism, medical photography, advertising, and offset printing, as well as Web design. Although the Photoshop program has been used to illustrate the step-by-step demonstrations throughout this book, this does not mean that the techniques described here are not possible using one of

Below *The Photoshop interface is comprehensive but easy to navigate. All the principal editing tools are grouped on the toolbar with respective palettes and dialog boxes available for making precise alterations and adjustments.*

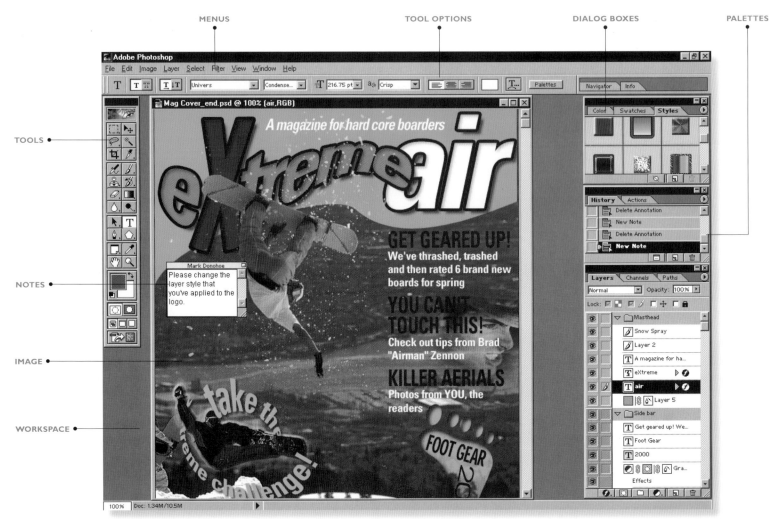

60

the other packages. There is a vast array of software on the market (such as Jasc's PaintShop Pro and Corel's PhotoPaint) that will produce equally successful, and professional, results. In fact, Adobe now produces a Photoshop version (Elements) with much of the image-editing functionality, but shorn of most of the prepress features. This is an ideal lower-cost solution for the photographer in particular.

If you are concerned about using software other than Adobe's package, many companies producing alternatives will let you try their wares before purchasing them. This is a great, risk-free way to investigate new software.

This chapter looks at the common manipulation techniques used to correct and enhance pictures. Chapter 4 will develop these ideas by introducing creative techniques that will enable you to produce stunning images on your own desktop equipment.

the interface is the link

The interface is the way in which the software package communicates with the user. Each program has its own style of interface but the majority of programs contain a workspace, a set of tools, such as drawing tools and text tools, laid out in a toolbar, and some menus. You might also find some other smaller windows, which default to positions around the edge of the screen. Commonly called dialog boxes and palettes, these give you extra details and controls over the tools.

get to know your tools

The tools in most image editing packages have gradually been distilled to a common set of similar icons that perform in similar ways. The tools can be divided into several groups depending on their general function. These groups are described below.

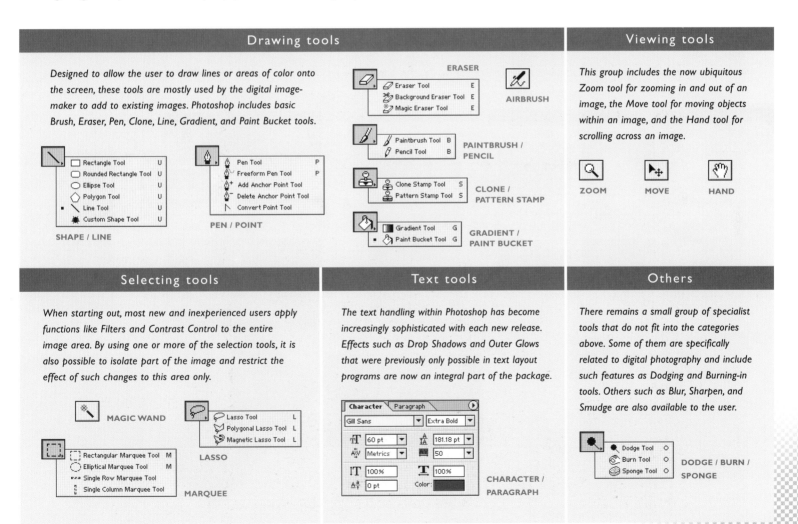

Drawing tools

Designed to allow the user to draw lines or areas of color onto the screen, these tools are mostly used by the digital image-maker to add to existing images. Photoshop includes basic Brush, Eraser, Pen, Clone, Line, Gradient, and Paint Bucket tools.

SHAPE / LINE
- Rectangle Tool U
- Rounded Rectangle Tool U
- Ellipse Tool U
- Polygon Tool U
- Line Tool U
- Custom Shape Tool U

PEN / POINT
- Pen Tool P
- Freeform Pen Tool P
- Add Anchor Point Tool
- Delete Anchor Point Tool
- Convert Point Tool

ERASER
- Eraser Tool E
- Background Eraser Tool E
- Magic Eraser Tool E

AIRBRUSH

PAINTBRUSH / PENCIL
- Paintbrush Tool B
- Pencil Tool B

CLONE / PATTERN STAMP
- Clone Stamp Tool S
- Pattern Stamp Tool S

GRADIENT / PAINT BUCKET
- Gradient Tool G
- Paint Bucket Tool G

Viewing tools

This group includes the now ubiquitous Zoom tool for zooming in and out of an image, the Move tool for moving objects within an image, and the Hand tool for scrolling across an image.

ZOOM MOVE HAND

Selecting tools

When starting out, most new and inexperienced users apply functions like Filters and Contrast Control to the entire image area. By using one or more of the selection tools, it is also possible to isolate part of the image and restrict the effect of such changes to this area only.

MAGIC WAND

LASSO
- Lasso Tool L
- Polygonal Lasso Tool L
- Magnetic Lasso Tool L

MARQUEE
- Rectangular Marquee Tool M
- Elliptical Marquee Tool M
- Single Row Marquee Tool
- Single Column Marquee Tool

Text tools

The text handling within Photoshop has become increasingly sophisticated with each new release. Effects such as Drop Shadows and Outer Glows that were previously only possible in text layout programs are now an integral part of the package.

CHARACTER / PARAGRAPH
Character | Paragraph
Gill Sans | Extra Bold
60 pt | 181.18 pt
Metrics | 50
100% | 100%
0 pt | Color:

Others

There remains a small group of specialist tools that do not fit into the categories above. Some of them are specifically related to digital photography and include such features as Dodging and Burning-in tools. Others such as Blur, Sharpen, and Smudge are also available to the user.

DODGE / BURN / SPONGE
- Dodge Tool O
- Burn Tool O
- Sponge Tool O

TECHNIQUE ONE

image orientation changes

Whether you are sourcing your pictures directly from a digital camera or scanning a photographic original, sometimes it is necessary to adjust the orientation of the image. For example, turning the camera 90° to take a portrait rather than a landscape will often produce files that preview on their side. This problem is best dealt with as early in the process as possible.

Some scanning and camera plug-in software has the option of turning the picture on a central axis before importing it into Photoshop. In most cases, these features allow you to turn the image in 90° stages. When the photograph is correctly positioned, it can then be "acquired" or brought into Photoshop. It is not a problem if the "import" software you are using does not contain this option since Photoshop can also change the orientation of the image. After opening the file, select the Rotate Canvas option from the Image menu. Choose the orientation and direction required from the list. Other options contained here allow you to flip the image

horizontally and vertically. There is also the Arbitrary feature that allows you to rotate the image to any angle that you specify.

straightening images

These controls will handle most situations, but there will also be occasions when a photograph needs to be straightened rather than rotated. This scenario can result from the print or negative being misaligned when scanned, or shooting the image with the camera at a slight angle. The solution is to make use of Photoshop's Cropping tool. Traditionally, this is used to eliminate unwanted sections of the image, but with this technique you can make a skewed image straight.

With your file open, select the Cropping tool from the menu bar. Click and drag out the rectangular shape around the parts of the image that you want to keep. You will notice that the image is now bounded by a highlighted box, or crop marquee. At the corners and middle of the sides of the box are some adjustment handles. Clicking and dragging these handles will allow you to change the size and shape of the marquee. When

Below *Image browsers make image selection easy.*

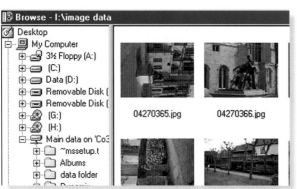

IMAGE BROWSER

FIXING
ALIGNMENT

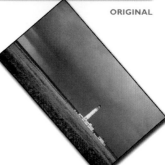

FLIP HORIZONTAL

Left and right
Any image orientation can be achieved using either the standard tools or third party plug-ins.

ROTATE 180

ORIGINAL

ROTATE ARBITRARY

ROTATE 90 CCW

ROTATE 90 CW

FLIP VERTICAL

the pointer is moved outside the box, the mode changes from resize to rotate. By clicking and dragging you can rotate the marquee to fit the skewed image. When you press the Return (Mac) or Enter key (PC), the image will be cropped and straightened (*see right*).

CROPPING TOOL

Pro tip: cropping

An advanced technique that can be performed using the Cropping tool allows you to change the perspective of an image. This is particularly helpful if you want to try to correct the converging lines of tall buildings shot from ground level. Once you have drawn the cropping marquee, click the Perspective box in the tool's Option bar. You will now be able to move the corner handles independently. By dragging the top corners outwards you will effectively widen the top of the building, reducing the appearance of converging lines. To complete the illusion, you should also drag the top handle upwards increasing the building's height as well (*see below*).

SUMMARY: Image Orientation

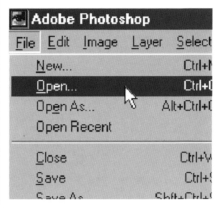

1 *To get an image the way you want it, first open it in Photoshop.*

3 *Select the Cropping tool from the toolbar that is normally on the left of your screen.*

4 *Drag a marquee around the parts of the image that you want to keep.*

2 *Rotate image from landscape to portrait by selecting Image>Rotate Canvas>90 CW.*

5 *Adjust the size and shape of the marquee to your requirements using the handles.*

6 *Rotate the marquee to help align a crooked image exactly as you want it.*

brightness and contrast controls

Brightness and Contrast are among the most fundamental of the adjustments possible using image manipulation software. The efficiency of photographic exposure systems today is so high that over- and under-exposed shots are rarely captured, but such systems remain somewhat fallible. It is quite possible that in some of your shots exposure will have been calibrated for the wrong subject. Add flat lighting conditions, and the need for brightness and contrast adjustments becomes more apparent. And with scanners (and other digital transfer devices) giving results that are often high in contrast, the importance for these tools is assured.

Photographs taken on sunny days will typically contain deep blacks, richly colored midtones, and bright whites. These images are referred to as high-contrast images. In comparison, photographs taken on days when the sky is overcast do not have the same spread of tones. The colors are more muted and the pictures generally do not contain any strong black or white areas. These images are low-contrast and are sometimes called "flat."

brightness and contrast

Digital photographers need to be able to distinguish between changes in contrast and brightness (exposure), because the correcting of each of these characteristics is handled differently within Photoshop. For example, by being able to diagnose that the image is a little dark rather than too flat, you will know that the remedy for the problem lies in changing brightness and not contrast.

ORIGINAL IMAGE

TOO MUCH CONTRAST

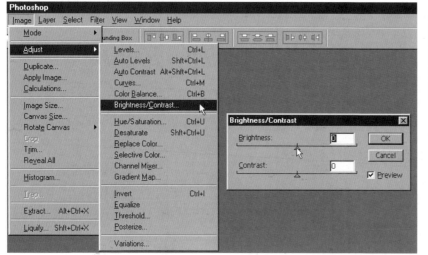

OPEN BRIGHTNESS/CONTRAST DIALOG BOXES

OVERBRIGHTENED

the brightness / contrast slider

Most of Photoshop's image controls are grouped together under the Image>Adjust menu. Here you will find the Brightness/Contrast slider. To use this feature, open an image in Photoshop. Select the control and start with the Brightness/Contrast slider. Adjust the image by moving (click and drag) the slider to the left to reduce brightness, and to the right to increase it. The changes will be previewed on the screen.

Your goal should be to produce a picture that has both good shadow and highlight detail. Use these areas as your guide. It is here that you will first notice the effects of overbrightening or overdarkening. Too much brightening and delicate highlights will be converted to white and consequently they will be lost. Too much darkening and dark shadow tones will turn black.

adjusting contrast

Once you are satisfied with the brightness of the photograph you can concentrate on how the image tones are spread, and the contrast of the picture. As before, a slider control is provided and adjustments are previewed on screen. Moving the slider to the right will cause the image to come into sharper contrast, and moving to the left into less contrast.

Your goal is an even and full spread of tones from black to white. This will help to give the image a smooth, harmonious feel. However, in making your adjustments it is critical that highlight and shadow detail should not be lost. These areas should act as a guide to the amount of contrast change needed.

Automatic tonal control

In later versions of Photoshop, Adobe provides controls that will adjust picture tones automatically. These two features, Auto Contrast and Auto Levels, can be found under the Image>Adjust menu heading.

The Auto Contrast function converts the lightest and darkest parts of the image to white and black. This has the effect of lightening the highlights and darkening the shadows. To help ensure more accurate results, 0.5% of both the brightest and darkest tones are ignored in these calculations (see below).

The Auto Levels function works in a similar way except that it converts the darkest and lightest tones within each color channel (red, green, blue) to black and white. With most images this has the effect of reducing color casts, but in some cases the action can actually introduce a cast to the image. If this occurs then "Undo" Auto Levels and apply Auto Contrast, since this feature does not take into account color difference when mapping the tones.

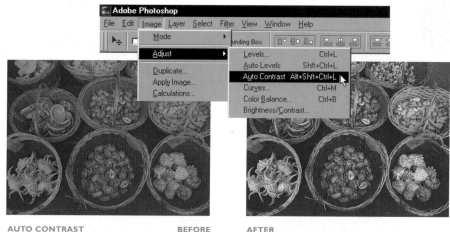

AUTO CONTRAST   BEFORE   AFTER

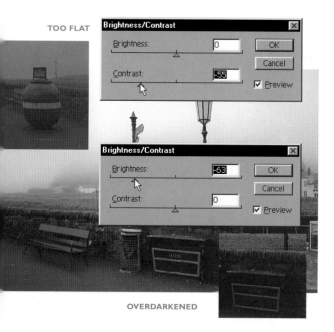

TOO FLAT

OVERDARKENED

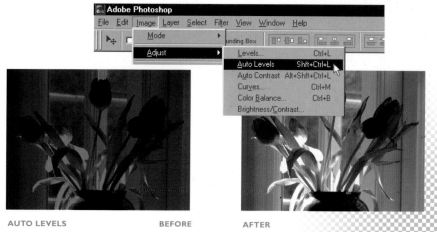

AUTO LEVELS   BEFORE   AFTER

the histogram

All digital images are made up of a matrix of pixels. Each pixel has a position within the matrix, a color and a brightness level. In a 24-bit system, the brightness level of each pixel is indicated by a number for red, green, and blue between 0 and 255. The higher the number, the brighter the pixel will appear. A pixel with the value of 0 will be black, and one with 255 will appear white.

The histogram function, found under the Image menu, provides a graph of all the pixels contained in an image and their brightness levels. The dark tones (with values less than 50) are to the left of the graph, the midtones in the center, and the light tones (with values greater than 200) to the right. The height at any point indicates the number of pixels with this value contained in the picture.

If you move the mouse pointer over the graph, it will give you a precise brightness value and pixel count. The histogram provides valuable information about how the pixels are placed in any image.

image types and graphs

When examined closely, each image type has a recognizable graph shape. A well-exposed picture with good contrast will exhibit a range of tones from black to white with most pixels in the midtone area. Photographs that are underexposed show a graph with the pixels bunched to the left; overexposed images are the reverse, with the majority of pixels to the right. Pictures with low contrast are displayed with all the pixels bunched together, and those with high contrast are spread across the whole spectrum with a good percentage pure white and black.

TONES IN AN IMAGE

HIGHLIGHTS

TONE MANIPULATION

BEFORE CHANGES

AFTER CHANGES

SHADOWS   MIDTONES

UNDEREXPOSED

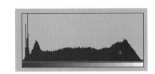

OVEREXPOSED

STANDARD

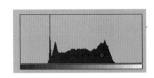

FLAT

CONTRASTY

checking your adjustments

Until now all of the adjustments you have made have
been completed using the screen image as a guide but,
as the histogram shows, Photoshop can provide a precise
and measurable version of the picture as well as the
visual one. This precision can be very helpful when
adjusting an image's tones. Using the Show Info palette,
which can be opened from the Window menu, it is
possible to see the precise value of each pixel. When the
palette is used with adjustment controls, it can show
the value before and after the proposed changes.

This means that when changing the brightness of a
picture, the mouse pointer can be moved over the dark
and light tones to ensure that subtle detail is not being
converted to pure white (255) or black (0). Show Info
can be used in a similar way with the contrast slider to
ensure a complete spread of tones.

SUMMARY: Brightness and contrast control

1 *With an image already in
Photoshop, open the Show
Info palette and then select the
Brightness/Contrast control.*

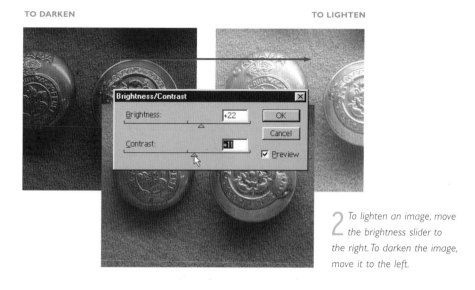

TO DARKEN · **TO LIGHTEN**

2 *To lighten an image, move
the brightness slider to
the right. To darken the image,
move it to the left.*

LESS CONTRAST · **MORE CONTRAST**

3 *To give an image sharper
contrast, move the contrast
slider to the right. To reduce the
contrast, move it to the left.*

HIGHLIGHTS

SHADOWS

MIDTONES

4 *Before closing the control,
check the spread of tones
with the Show Info palette.
Readjust if necessary.*

TECHNIQUE THREE

color correction

The human eye is far more adaptable when it comes to "seeing" color than the average digital sensor. To the human eye, a piece of white paper appears white whether lit by daylight, fluorescent tubes, normal household lightbulbs, or candlelight. If the piece of paper was photographed under these same lighting conditions, then the results would be radically different. Under fluorescent light, a photo of the paper would have a green tinge; if shot under light from a household light-bulb it would appear yellow; and this color would be even more pronounced when photographed under candlelight. Only when shot with daylight (a mixture of sun and skylight) would the paper end up looking white.

This can lead to circumstances where a scene can appear color-neutral to our eyes when viewed through the viewfinder, but when it is captured, it will be recorded with a color cast, or an unwanted element of color. Thankfully, most image editing programs contain a set of features and tools that allow the digital photographer to alter the colors within pictures after they have been captured.

__Below__ Without color correction, different lighting sources impart strong color casts to images.

FLUORESCENT

HOUSEHOLD LIGHT-BULB

CANDLELIGHT

DAYLIGHT

NEUTRAL SCAN

Left *Most scanners come bundled with simple yet effective image editing software. Here VistaScan (bundled with Umax scanners) is being used to correct the contrast in an image that has just been scanned.*

SCAN PRODUCING UNDESIRABLE COLOUR BIAS

Where do casts come from?

The casts in our digital photographs come from a range of sources. The most common of these are:

1 **Images being shot under different light sources.**
Most digital sensors are designed to be exposed using daylight. It is when images are shot under different light sources that casts can appear in our pictures. Even though the sources appear to our eyes as white, they actually emit light at a different color temperature to daylight. It is this change in color temperature that digital equipment reads, thus creating the color casts.
Most digital cameras contain Auto White Balance modes that attempt to neutralize color temperature problems. Some may even contain the flexibility to change the sensitivity of the sensor when images are shot under different light sources (see above).

2 **Images being scanned incorrectly.**
When a digital file is made by scanning a film or print original, it is possible inadvertently to introduce a color cast to the final digital image. This unwanted addition is usually the result of incorrectly setting the color settings for the scanner (see opposite). To prevent color casts from being introduced during the scanning process, it is essential to calibrate all scanning devices correctly as discussed in chapter 5 (see left).

WITH AUTO WHITE BALANCE

WITHOUT AUTO WHITE BALANCE

Left *Different types of lighting produce different color casts unless corrected by the auto white balance function in the scanning application.*

eliminating color casts using the variations feature

Below *The application of color corrections gives a neutral cast as shown here.*

Bottom *Photoshop's Variation feature permits a range of subtle or coarse color corrections to be directly applied.*

Variations can be found under the Image>Adjust menu. This feature provides a simple approach to color adjustment. When it is opened, you are presented with twelve versions of your image.

Two pictures at the top of the dialog box act as references throughout the process. One shows how your picture looked before any changes, the other shows how the picture looks with the current changes applied. On the right-hand side, a further three pictures provide the means to change the brightness of the original. In the main part of the dialog box are seven pictures that allow the user to change the image's color.

Six of these images are shown with the major color casts of red, green, blue, cyan, magenta, and yellow. Clicking onto any of these pictures will add that particular color to the original. The change is reflected in the central image. These changes can be made in large (coarse) or small (fine) jumps according to the amount set via the slider in the top right of the box.

To eliminate a color cast, you need to add its opposite color to the original. If your image is too yellow, add blue to the picture to make it more neutral; if it is green, add some magenta; and use cyan to help clear a red cast. When the image appears neutral, select OK to return to the normal Photoshop editing screen.

COLOR CORRECTION ⟶

ORIGINAL

CURRENT SETTINGS

PREVIEW OF COLOR CHANGES ●

PREVIEW OF BRIGHTNESS CHANGES ●

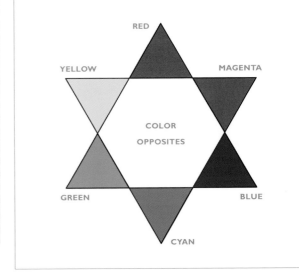

Colors and their opposites

Photographic color theory is based on the idea that all visible colors can be made up of three primary, or separation, hues. In digital applications the base colors are usually red, green, and blue (RGB). All images we see on our computer screens are made up of these three. The respective opposites of these colors are cyan, magenta, and yellow (CMY). You may recognize these colors as they are used, along with black (K), as the separation colors in the offset printing process. It is important to understand the relationship between these six colors when you are trying to eliminate casts from your images as it is necessary first to recognize the color of the cast and then add its opposite to the image.

RED

YELLOW

MAGENTA

COLOR OPPOSITES

GREEN

BLUE

CYAN

SUMMARY: Eliminating color casts

1 With an image opened in Photoshop, use the Variations feature found under the Image>Adjust menu.

2 Adjust the brightness of the image using the Darker and Lighter selections.

LIGHTER ●

DARKER ●

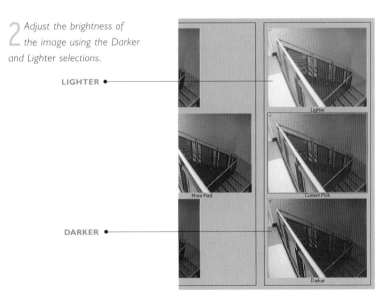

ADJUST SETTING TO SUIT

3 Adjust the Amount slider to reflect the intensity of the color cast. For a strong cast, use the Coarse setting. Slight casts will only require the Fine setting.

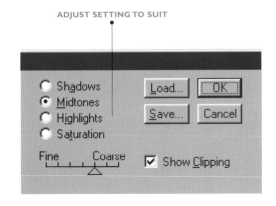

Alternatives to "variations"

Casts can also be removed using a series of three sliders instead of the preview images found in Variations. The Color Balance feature is under the Image>Adjust menu. The dialog displays three slider controls that allow the image worker to change the color of an image. With the Preview box selected, the changes are reflected on screen. Some users prefer this method since the colors and their opposites are linked in the control. Note too that casts can be changed independently in the shadow, midtone, and highlight sections of the same image. This flexibility allows image problems that cannot be solved by traditional color printing techniques to be remedied by digital techniques. (See also Curves on pages 72 to 73.)

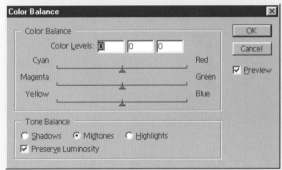

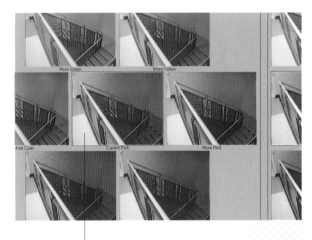

SELECT NEUTRAL THUMBNAIL

4 Click on a preview image that is the opposite color to the cast present in the original. Assess the central image. If a cast still remains, select and click another colored image. Continue this process until the image is neutral.

advanced tonal and color control

Below *The Curves function can be used to alter the relationship between input and output tones.*

The techniques described above provide general control of color and tone, but in some cases finer adjustments are needed. Using the Curves function gives you greater control over the spread of tones within your images. This function also allows you to adjust the red, green, and blue components of the picture independently.

The Curves function, which can be found under the Image>Adjust menu, is similar to Levels, in that it can be used to adjust the tones within an image. But unlike Levels, the Curves function allows all of the tones to be adjusted, not just the highlights, midtones, and shadows (*see left*).

The horizontal arm (x-axis) of the graph represents the original values (input) of pixels, and the vertical arm (y-axis) represents the new values

(output). When the graph is first opened, the input and output values are the same so it is a straight line. Changes are made to the pixels by clicking and dragging parts of the line. As you drag, the pixels associated with that part of the line will be made lighter if you move to the left, or darker if you drag the line to the right. It may take a bit of trial and error to get used to the relationship between the graph and the image. The shape of the curve also determines the appearance of your image. The steeper the line, the sharper the contrast on the image, while if the line rises gradually, the image will be low in contrast.

improving shadows and highlights

Clicking the mouse on the curve will leave an adjustment point. These points can be used to isolate a selection of pixel values so that they remain unaltered when the rest of the curve is changed. It is this technique that can be used for making delicate changes that will improve the detail in the highlight or shadow areas.

Before starting to adjust the picture tones, it is important to isolate those areas of the image that you want to remain the same (*see below*). Moving the mouse pointer over the image, with Curves open, will display the values of each pixel as a small circle on the curve. Move the mouse over the image to locate the tones that you do not want to change and then peg these pixels by adding an adjustment point to the curve. Now you can safely go ahead and change other parts of the image knowing that the areas that you have pegged are not being altered.

Enhancing highlight detail usually entails pegging shadow areas and then dragging the curve so that the delicate tones become more pronounced. The reverse is true when your aim is to improve shadow detail. Highlight and midtone areas are pegged first, before adjustments are made to the shadow tones.

MIDTONES

SHADOWS   HIGHLIGHTS

ADJUST HIGHLIGHTS

PEG MIDTONES
AND SHADOWS

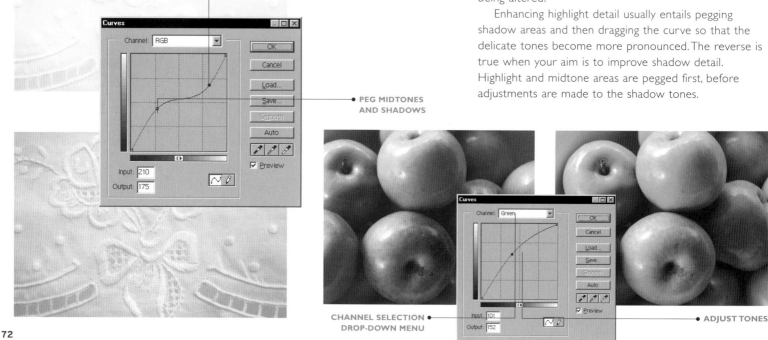

CHANNEL SELECTION •
DROP-DOWN MENU

ADJUST TONES

color changes

At the top of the Curves dialog box is a drop-down menu that allows you to select the type of curve that is displayed (*see below*). The default value is a curve that combines red, green, and blue channels. Any adjustments made to this curve will be equally reflected across all of the colors. If you select one of the other choices from the menu, you will be presented with a specialized graph that represents only a single color channel. Changes made to this curve will only alter the pixels of the selected color. This option can be used to reduce dominant color casts or to enhance the specific colors in an image. There is a certain amount of trial and error involved in using the Curves function and getting used to the changes that it makes to your image. See the images below for some tips on using this function.

SUMMARY: Tone and color changes using Curves

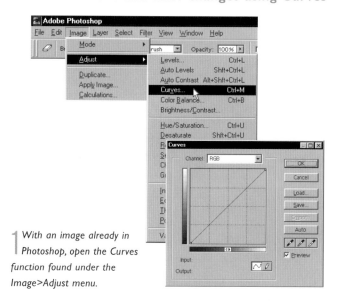

1 *With an image already in Photoshop, open the Curves function found under the Image>Adjust menu.*

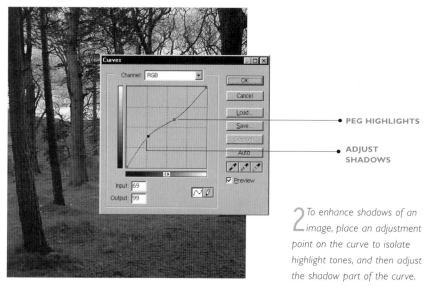

PEG HIGHLIGHTS

ADJUST SHADOWS

2 *To enhance shadows of an image, place an adjustment point on the curve to isolate highlight tones, and then adjust the shadow part of the curve.*

ADJUST HIGHLIGHTS

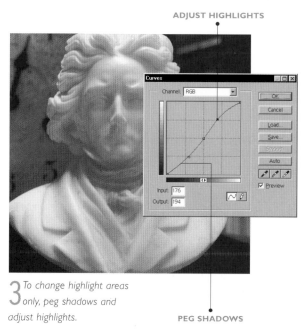

3 *To change highlight areas only, peg shadows and adjust highlights.*

PEG SHADOWS

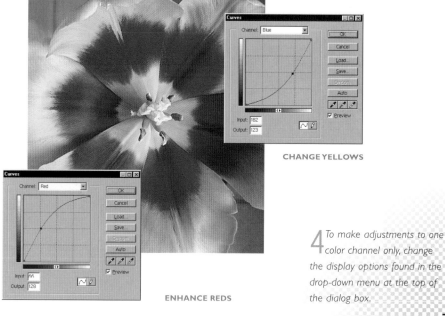

ENHANCE REDS

CHANGE YELLOWS

4 *To make adjustments to one color channel only, change the display options found in the drop-down menu at the top of the dialog box.*

TECHNIQUE FIVE

changing color
spaces and modes

Scanning or photographing with a digital camera is the first step toward creating a pixel-based image. From this stage onward, the image creator can begin to work on the image digitally, enhancing its impact. It is also the stage of the creation process in which the color space and mode for the picture originates. The color mode of an image determines the maximum number of colors that a picture can comprise; it also defines the number of color channels possible.

In addition, the color mode is one of the factors that determine the file size of an image, but this is only affected indirectly, since it is partly based on the numbers of colors and channels in an image as well as its pixel dimensions (*see below*). The default mode for most digital images is RGB (red, green, and blue). This means that the image can have three color channels and usually contains up to 16.7 million individual colors. In contrast, the Bitmap mode can only contain two colors, black or

Below The Image>Mode menu allows the user to switch between color modes quickly and easily.

white, and one channel (*see below*). Image creators can use Photoshop to edit images in any of eight of the most popular color modes, but the number and types of function available for each mode will vary. For instance, there will be no color features available when working with an image that has been transferred to the grayscale mode.

Changing between modes is achieved quite simply by picking the new mode from the list in the Image>Mode menu. Once selected, the program will make the necessary alterations to the open image in order to convert it to the new mode. For example, changing from RGB to CMYK, a mode used by the printing industry, will mean that the red, green, and blue channels will be assessed and mapped to their equivalents values in cyan, magenta, yellow, and black channels. Because of the extra channel, there will also be a slight increase in the file size of the image. Such changes will have to be taken into account when converting images between color modes.

BITMAP MODE

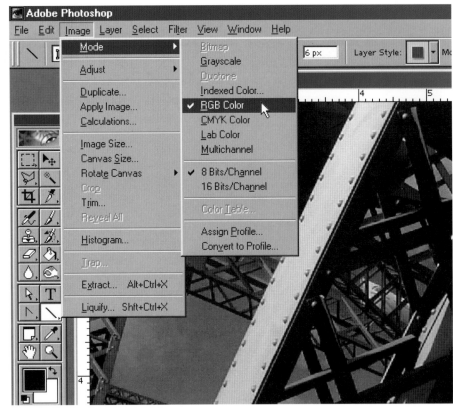

SELECTING MODES

RGB MODE

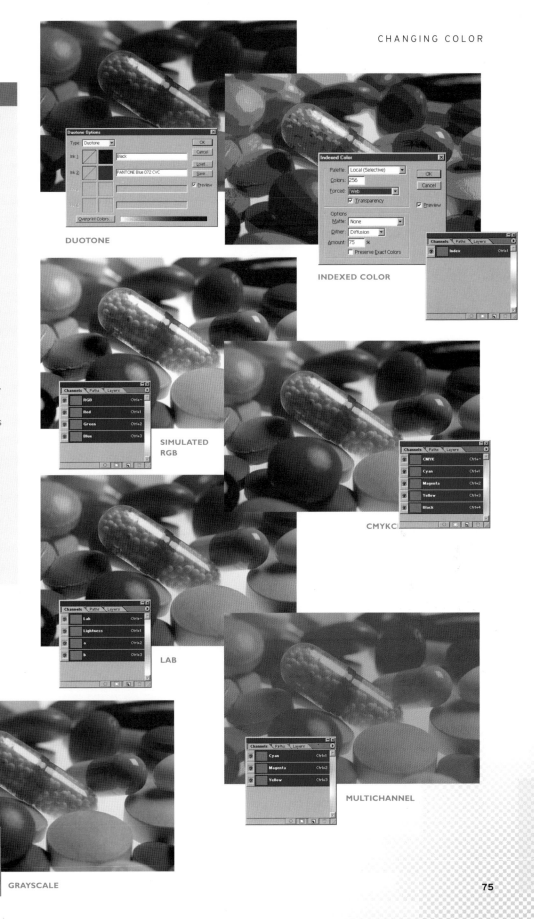

Color modes and their uses

Bitmap contains two colors only, black and white, and is used for line drawings and black-and-white graphics only. It is economical in terms of file size.

Grayscale contains up to 256 levels of gray and no color. This mode is most often used for black-and-white photographs.

Duotone is a monochromatic image combining two halftones with different tonal ranges made from the same original, so that when printed in different tones of the same color a wider tonal range is reproduced than is possible with a single color.

Indexed Color contains up to 256 colors and can be used to reduce the number of colors in an image, thus reducing the size of the electronic file. It is therefore employed extensively throughout multimedia and Web applications where file sizes are critical.

RGB can contain up to 16.7 million colors in its 24-bit form. This is the most popular of the modes and is used for capture in most digital cameras and scanners.

CMYK has long been used by offset printers. This mode is the default standard in the prepress industry. It contains four channels instead of the three in RGB pictures.

LAB uses three channels: one for lightness (L), one for the green/red parts of the image (A), and one for the blue/yellow hues (B). This mode is used as a middle point in most conversion processes, or as the basis for some advanced editing techniques.

Multichannel contains up to 256 levels of gray in each channel. It is used for specialist printing techniques.

DUOTONE

INDEXED COLOR

SIMULATED RGB

CMYKC

LAB

MULTICHANNEL

BITMAP

GRAYSCALE

TECHNIQUE FIVE

modes versus spaces

Color spaces differ from modes because they represent the total range of colors available for a particular device. No single piece of equipment for capture, display, or printing images can reproduce the whole range, or gamut, of colors available. Each is limited to a small subset of possible hues. Changes in color will occur at every stage of the image capture, manipulation, and printing processes. In a calibrated system, the capabilities and settings of each device are recorded as a profile description. As the image moves through the process, adjustments are automatically made to the file according to this profile. The end result is a system where colors, brightness, and contrast settings remain consistent throughout.

untagged files

Profile descriptions are stored with images at the time they are created. If the capture device has no built-in profiles, then the image will be stored without any associated color management information. These files are commonly referred to as "untagged" and contain the raw color numbers for each pixel in the image.

You can view the profile description attached to a particular image by clicking the side arrow in the bottom border of the application window. By selecting Document Profile from the list of document and file information options, the profile will be displayed in the right-hand corner of the bar (see *below*).

changing color spaces

There are two ways in which you can change the space of any image opened in Photoshop. You can either assign a new profile description (Image>Mode>Assign Profile) for untagged pictures, or you can change the current settings by using the Convert to Profile function (Image>Mode>Convert to Profile). The latter of these two options also allows users to select the "Intent" of their conversion from a list of four possibilities: Perceptual, Saturation, Relative Colorimetric, and Absolute Colorimetric. Each of these options determines the rules that will be used for the conversions of colors.

Above *Color modes (RGB, CMYK) denote how an image's information is held (256 shades each of red, green, and blue for RGB, 0 to 100% of four colors for CMYK). Color profiles denote what the limitations of that information are in terms of reproducing different shades in the chosen form of output.*

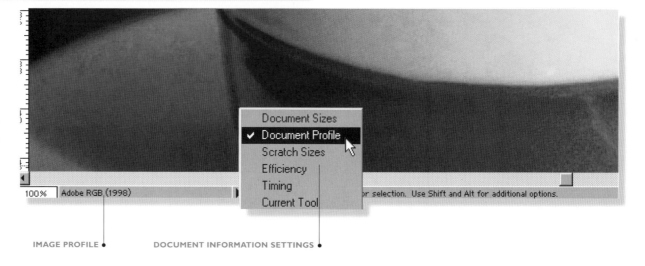

IMAGE PROFILE ●   DOCUMENT INFORMATION SETTINGS ●

Perceptual is the most suitable option when you are working with photographic images. It aims to preserve the visual representation of the picture's colors.

Saturation aims to create vivid color at the expense of accuracy, and is designed for graphics use only.

Absolute Colorimetric only changes those colors that are not contained in the original or the destination profiles.

Relative Colorimetric is the Photoshop default setting. It is similar to Absolute Colorimetric except that after comparing the differences between corresponding points (normally the white point) in the source and destination color spaces, all other colors are shifted accordingly.

color management tools

To help guide you through the minefield of color management, Adobe has introduced a range of color management settings that are specifically designed to simplify the process (*see below*). Digital workers must simply select the end use for their images. The program will then take this information and underpin the editing process with the most suitable color management settings. To set up, choose the Color Setting option from the Edit menu and make your selection from Prepress, Web, or No Color Management.

SUMMARY: Color and space mode changes

1 *Set up Photoshop's color management settings by picking from the list to be found at the Color Settings option under the Edit menu.*

SELECT INTENT •

2 *Tag a raw image with a color profile using the function Image>Mode> Assign Profile.*

3 *To change a profile follow Image>Mode> Convert to Profile.*

4 *To change image modes select from the list found at the Mode section of the Image menu.*

TECHNIQUE SIX

sharpening techniques

Sometimes the process of capturing an image produces pictures that appear a little less than sharp. If this situation occurred with a traditional print, it would be almost impossible to rectify, but digital workers have a variety of sharpening options available at the click of a button that can dramatically improve image quality.

Positioned under the Filter menu in Photoshop are four sharpening options that can be used to improve the appearance of sharpness within your images. Note the word "appearance" is used, because despite their abilities, these filters cannot make a badly focused image sharp. Their role is to enhance the quality of good pictures, not to fix shooting or scanning errors (see below). The first three choices provide a quick solution to sharpening. Sharpen and Sharpen More improve the clarity of the image by increasing the contrast between adjacent colors and tones. The Sharpen More filter increases the sharpening effect. These options do not discriminate in their application between subtle grading of tones found in details like skin, and hard-edged and contrasting subjects like buildings. For this reason, the result can be a little coarse, if not undesirable.

The Sharpen Edges option restricts its effect to the edges or areas of contrast within the image, while maintaining the smoothness of subtle tonal changes. The fourth option gives the user more control over the application of the sharpening effect. The Unsharp Mask filter can be adjusted by using the three slider controls: Amount, Radius, and Threshold (see below).

Amount controls the strength of the effect. Check by viewing at full size with the Preview box selected.

Below Photoshop offers a range of sharpening tools to increase perceived sharpness in images.

BEFORE   AFTER

SELECTING UNSHARP MASK

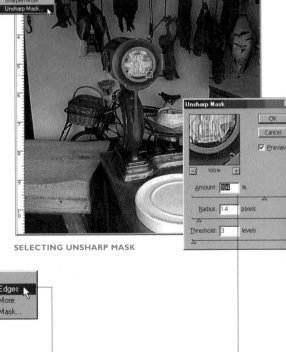

USM SHARPENING CONTROLS

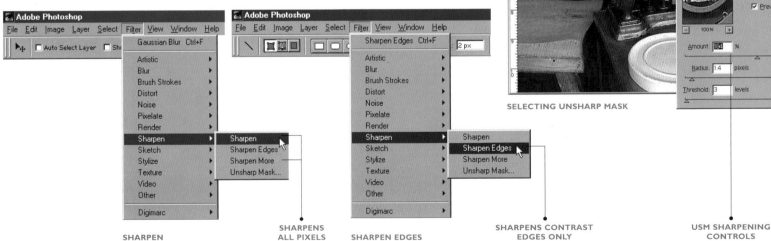

SHARPEN

SHARPENS ALL PIXELS

SHARPEN EDGES

SHARPENS CONTRAST EDGES ONLY

Radius controls how the effect is applied. A low number, e.g., 1 or 2, sharpens the edges only, while a higher value sharpens a wider range of pixels.

Threshold settings determine how different pixels need to be before they are considered to be an "edge" and therefore sharpened. A setting of 0 means all pixels are sharpened; a higher value will restrict the effect from being applied to subtle areas like blue skies.

Unsharp mask examples

Altering the Amount, Radius, and Threshold of the Unsharp Masking filter controls the sharpening effect. The examples show the effects of different values for each of the controls.

1. AMOUNT 100, RADIUS 1, THRESHOLD 5

2. AMOUNT 250, RADIUS 1, THRESHOLD 5

3. AMOUNT 500, RADIUS 1, THRESHOLD 5

4. AMOUNT 100, RADIUS 10, THRESHOLD 5

5. AMOUNT 100, RADIUS 50, THRESHOLD 5

6. AMOUNT 100, RADIUS 200, THRESHOLD 5

7. AMOUNT 100, RADIUS 1, THRESHOLD 0

8. AMOUNT 100, RADIUS 1, THRESHOLD 10.

9. AMOUNT 100, RADIUS 1, THRESHOLD 50

SUMMARY: Sharpening techniques

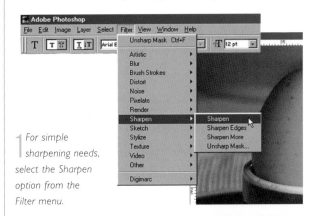

1 *For simple sharpening needs, select the Sharpen option from the Filter menu.*

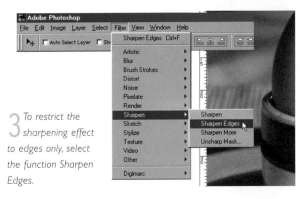

2 *To apply a stronger version of this, use Sharpen More.*

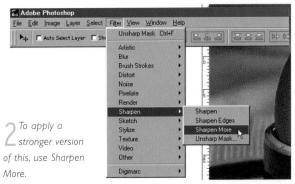

3 *To restrict the sharpening effect to edges only, select the function Sharpen Edges.*

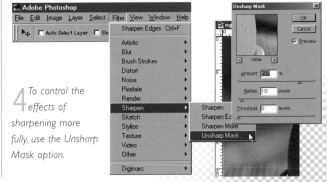

4 *To control the effects of sharpening more fully, use the Unsharp Mask option.*

TECHNIQUE SEVEN

removal of dust and scratches

No matter how carefully originals are cleaned, some dust marks may still be detected on the digital file after scanning. These types of mark can also be found on images sourced from cameras if the sensor is dirty. Retouching them is a comparatively easy task.

The simplest way to remove any marks from the picture is to apply a Dust and Scratches filter (Filter> Noise>Dust and Scratches) to the whole image. Careful control of the filter is necessary since a by-product of its use can be soft or blurry images. Adjust the Radius until the dust marks are no longer apparent, then move the Threshold slider so that the image details are returned to their proper definition (*see below*).

DUST AND SCRATCH MARKS

DUST AND SCRATCHES FILTER

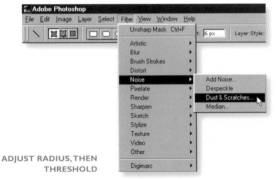

**ADJUST RADIUS, THEN
THRESHOLD**

Retouching dust marks using the clone tool

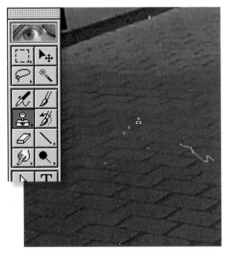

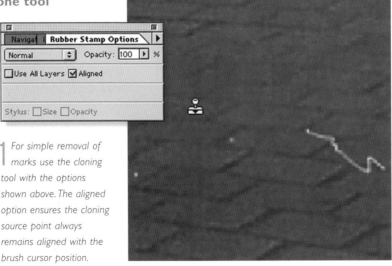

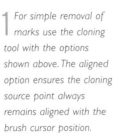

1 For simple removal of marks use the cloning tool with the options shown above. The aligned option ensures the cloning source point always remains aligned with the brush cursor position.

2 For finer control zoom into the area and choose the correct brush size—too big a cloning brush on this picture would disrupt the pattern of the paving.

The pro's technique

Professional photographers have developed a more sophisticated version of this technique, which minimizes the softening effects of the Dust and Scratches filter, and makes use of the Photoshop History brush.

CLEANING THE IMAGE

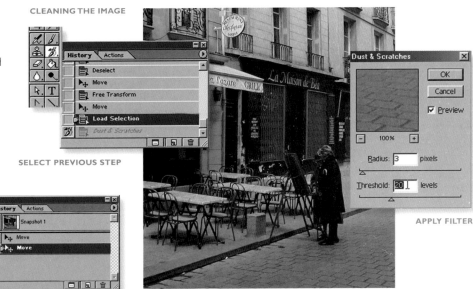

HISTORY PALETTE

SELECT PREVIOUS STEP

APPLY FILTER

1 To start the process, make sure the History palette is open (Window>Show History). This feature displays each action taken in Photoshop as a step in the palette. You can reverse applied actions by selecting the previous step in the palette. In this way the function operates rather like the Undo command.

2 Apply the Dust and Scratches filter, making sure that all unwanted marks are removed and also that, through careful use of the Threshold slider, as much original detail as possible is retained in the image.

3 Next, select the step in the History palette immediately before the Dust and Scratches filter, and pick the History brush from the toolbar.

4 Before applying the brush tool, click on the box next to the Dust and Scratches step in the History palette.

5 Paint over the marks with the brush tool. In doing so, the tool is painting using sections of the version of the picture that is free from marks. This process has the effect of only applying the Dust and Scratches filter to the marked area. This in turn helps to maintain the sharpness of the rest of the image.

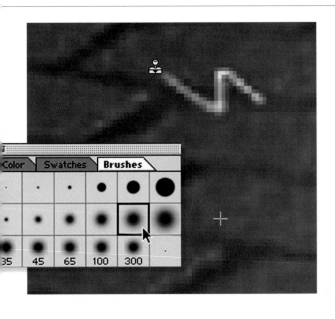

3 Option-click (Mac) or Alt-click (Windows) on a source-point that is similar to the area to be retouched and paint over the dust and scratches, changing brush size if necessary.

4 Repeat the exercise on all the affected areas of the image.

saving your images

With the basic editing and enhancement of your image complete, it is now time to store or save your file. This step keeps a permanent record of the changes you have made to the digital image. It is often useful to use the "Save As" command (rather than Save) because this saves a snapshot of the image at the stage reached in the editing process.

When a Save command is issued, your image will usually be saved as a Photoshop or PSD file. This format is one of many available. Each has specific characteristics, benefits, and disadvantages. Some contain compression features that save disk space by making image files smaller (see pages 192 to 193), others are cross-platform and can be opened by both Mac and PC computers, and a couple of them are specifically designed for Web use.

To save in a different format, use the Save As option under the File menu and then pick the format required from the drop-down list. For Web-based formats such as JPEG, GIF, or PNG, use the Save for Web option. The following are six of the most commonly used formats.

PSD (Photoshop's native format)
Photoshop's default file format is capable of supporting layers, editable text, and millions of colors. You should choose this format for all manipulation of your photographic images. The PSD format has no compression features but should still be used to archive complex images with multiple layers and sophisticated selections or paths. The extra space needed for storage is compensated by the ease of future editing tasks.

JPEG (Joint Photographic Experts Group)
This format provides the most dramatic compression option for photographic images. A 20Mb digital file, which is quite capable of producing a 10 x 8-inch high-quality print, can be compressed as a JPEG file that will fit onto a standard floppy disk and that can be restored with only modest loss of detail. To achieve this, the format uses a "lossy" compression system, which means that some of the image information is lost during the compression process. The amount of compression is governed by a slider control in the dialog box. You will find this a particularly useful format for your work when space is at a premium or when you need very small file sizes, for example, when the file needs to be emailed.

SUMMARY: Saving

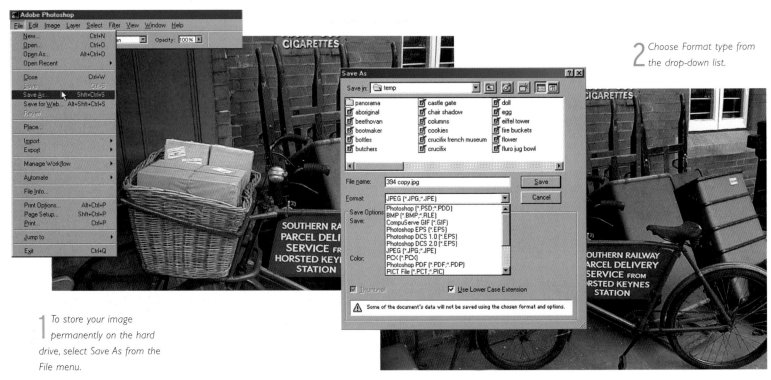

1 To store your image permanently on the hard drive, select Save As from the File menu.

2 Choose Format type from the drop-down list.

TIFF (Tagged Image File Format)

Images in this popular and useful format can be saved uncompressed or using a compression algorithm called LZW, which is "lossless." In other words, the image that you "put into" the compression process is the same as the one you receive "out." There is no degradation of quality. When you save, you can choose to include a preview thumbnail of the image, turn compression on and off, and select which platform you are working with.

Most agencies and bureaus accept this format but nearly all stipulate that they will need work supplied in an uncompressed state. Opening a compressed image takes longer than opening one that is saved without compression. Some layout applications can also encounter problems with LZW compression. When you want to maintain the highest quality possible for your image, always use the uncompressed TIFF format.

GIF (Graphics Interchange Format)

This format is used for logos and images that contain a small number of colors. It tends to be popular with Web professionals but is not generally used for photographic images. GIF is capable of storing up to 256 colors, animation, and areas of transparency.

PNG (Portable Network Graphics)

The proprietary format of Macromedia Fireworks, this comparatively new Web graphics format has plenty of great features. Like TIFF and GIF the format uses a lossless compression algorithm that ensures what you put in is what you get out. It also supports partial transparency (unlike GIF's transparency off/on system) and color depths of up to 64-bit. With the added bonus of built-in color and gamma (contrast) correction features in this format, you start to see why PNG is likely to be used more often. The only drawback is that it only works with browsers that are Version 4 or newer.

EPS (Encapsulated Postscript)

EPS is a file format that can contain both vector and bitmap graphics. It also has the benefit of being supported by virtually all graphic, illustration, and page-layout programs. If an EPS file contains vector graphics, opening it in an image editing application (such as Photoshop) results in the image being rasterized (i.e., converted to pixels). EPS files also support clipping paths and make it possible to use clipping paths created in Photoshop in (for example) QuarkXPress. EPS files require a PostScript printer for printing.

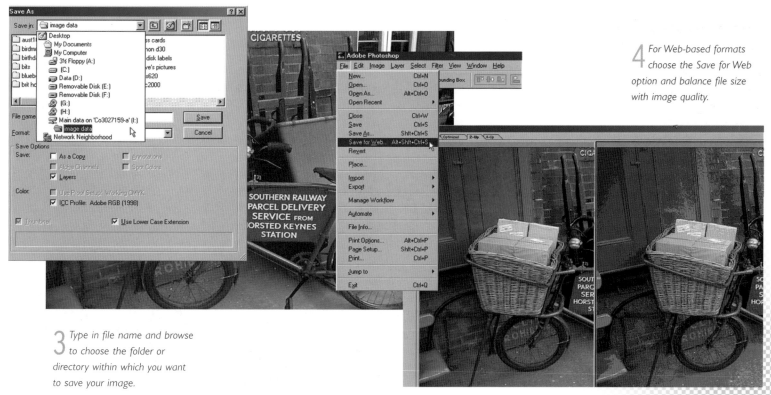

4 For Web-based formats choose the Save for Web option and balance file size with image quality.

3 Type in file name and browse to choose the folder or directory within which you want to save your image.

4 creative imaging

Chapter 3 looked at the "meat and potatoes" of image editing and enhancement techniques. With these basics in mind, it is now possible to explore some of the more sophisticated and creative aspects of image manipulation. It is these techniques that take the desktop digital illustrator into areas that, until now, have been the domain of high-end workstation users. Here I will introduce some new techniques, as well as build on the ideas that we have already discussed. To help illustrate how these creative techniques are being used in the real world, I have also included example pictures from a group of industry professionals whose daily lives revolve around the new imaging technology.

selective color changes

In chapter 3 we used the variations and color balance features in Adobe Photoshop to correct or eliminate unwanted colors in an image; now we will look at a set of techniques that employ the same skills to add different hues to images rather than remove them.

In a world where color film is easily obtainable, thousands of black-and-white images are still being made each day. Even the latest digital cameras contain functions to convert the color image captured by the sensor to one that just contains levels of grays. It seems that we have an ongoing fascination with monochrome.

Although these images are captured in black and white, the digital system provides the opportunity to tint or, to use a traditional photographic term, tone these pictures different colors. The shades that are possible range from subtle hints of color that warm or cool the black in an image to bright dominating hues.

hue/saturation feature

The simplest method of adding a tint to an image is to use the Hue and Saturation feature that is found under the Adjust section of the Image menu. This function allows the user to control the type and strength of colors within images. To enable the feature to be used with grayscale images you must convert these to RGB (Image>Mode>RGB Color) first. This step is a must if color is to be added to a monochrome image. Next open the Hue/Saturation dialog box (Image>Adjust>Hue/Saturation) and make sure that both

the Colorize and Preview boxes are checked. The box contains three sliders: Hue, Saturation, and Lightness. Unlike the controls in the Color Balance feature, where the different shades are broken into red, green, and blue, here all the colors are spread along the Hue slider in the same order as the frequencies of light (the rainbow).

The Saturation slider controls the strength of the color. If you move the saturation slider to the right it will make the color more intense; if you move it to the left the color will be less apparent. By reducing the saturation to 0, you will remove the color entirely, leaving a grayscale or black-and-white image.

The Lightness control is similar to the Brightness feature and is used to adjust the overall density of the image. At the bottom of the box are two color bars. The top bar shows the original colors, the one below the

HUE AND SATURATION DIALOG BOX

COLOR   STRENGTH   BRIGHTNESS

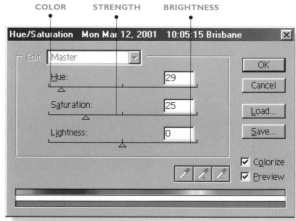

PREVIEW

Below *Here we see the effect on an image of using the Hue and Saturation feature.*

LOSE COLOR ⟶   ADD TINT COLOR ⟶

color, strength, and brightness selected via the three sliders (*see below*). To start the toning adjustments, first move the Hue slider to select the color for the image. Next adjust the Saturation control to the desired strength, and finally change the Lightness slider to adjust any darkening or lightening of the image caused by the coloring process.

This is an excellent technique for obtaining sepia-like effects with black-and-white pictures. The color change is applied to the whole image, producing results that are very similar to those that can be obtained in a darkroom via traditional photographic methods. Jeffery Becton, a digital illustrator from Maine, creates images that use the Hue/Saturation technique with a great deal more finesse and control. Examples of his work using this technique are shown on pages 90 to 91.

PRIMARY COLORS

  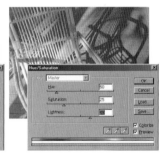

CYAN TINTS

SECTION OF HUE/SATURATION DIALOG BOX

SEPIA TINTS

BEFORE / AFTER CHANGES

SEPIA EFFECT

Above *By adjusting the hue and, if necessary, the saturation controls, a range of tones and tints can be applied to an image.*

Left *Selecting Colorize in the Hue/Saturation box, then adjusting hue, produces monochromatic color effects, such as the sepia tone here.*

photoshop selection techniques

One of the most basic and important skills in image editing is knowing how to select individual elements of a picture. Most image enhancement programs provide the user with a range of tools specially designed for the job. Photoshop is no exception, providing a variety of options that can be grouped into tools that select either by drawing around the object and using the object's color, or by masking the image.

shapes, because it is restricted to drawing predefined shapes such as circles and rectangles. The Lasso tool, on the other hand, is used like a pencil to draw around the object that needs to be selected.

In the latest edition of Photoshop, an enhanced tool referred to as the Magnetic Lasso has been added to the selection lineup. Unlike the traditional Lasso where the accuracy of your selection is based on your hand–eye coordination, the magnetic version clings to the edge of the chosen object as you move the mouse. Although it does not always achieve 100% accuracy, the Magnetic Lasso makes light work of selecting objects that are contrasted against their background.

drawing selection tools

Below **Photoshop has a variety of tools for making selections within an image.**

The Marquee and Lasso tools both define areas of selection by drawing around a portion of the image. The Marquee works well with regular and hard-edged

color selection tools

Not all selection tasks are the same. Sometimes an object's edge is so complex that drawing carefully around it is too time-consuming to be worth

MARQUEE SELECTION

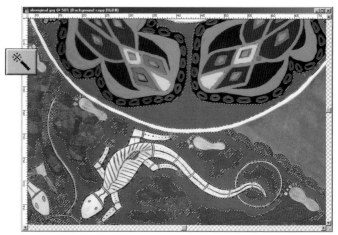

MAGIC WAND

Above *By default the marquee is a regular rectangle; double-click on it to reveal the alternatives. These comprise an Elliptical marquee (for oval and circle selections) and Single Row and Single Column. The latter two are for selecting a single (and precise) pixel-wide row or column and are ideal for constructing compositional lines on your image (using brush tools to infill).*

LASSO TOOL

LASSO TOOL

Above *Photoshop's Lasso tool has three variants. The standard Lasso allows for manual image selection. The Polygonal Lasso introduces points to the selection outline that can later be edited. The Magnetic Lasso sticks to areas of high-contrasting pixels.*

considering. In these instances, a tool like the Magic Wand, that bases its selection on color, is a good alternative. Clicking the tool on a white background, for example, will select all tones that are pure white or close to white. It is then a simple matter of using the Select>Inverse choice to select the object and then invert the selection. How close the color has to be to the selected tone is based on the Tolerance level set in the tool's options. The higher the number, the more colors will be included, while lower numbers will only select specific colors. A similar approach is used by the Color Range feature found under Select on Photoshop's main menu. A small preview allows you to interactively select successive parts of the image to build up the selection area.

The next technique that you need to learn is how to add to or take away from selections. Complex selections often require the use of several tools and the combination of more than one selected area. Holding the Shift key down while selecting allows you to add to a selection; using the Alt key (PC) or Option key (Mac) allows you to take away a selection. A series of "add to" and "take away" steps can be saved using the Save Selection command for future use.

masking selection tools

The Quick Mask tool finds its roots in the manual ruby lith masking techniques. This once-common process involved the careful slicing of a piece of red masking film that was then used to isolate areas of images or text.

The digital version of ruby lith requires you to switch into Quick Mask mode, and then paint the virtual "ruby" onto the parts of the image that you do not want to select. Switching back to normal editing mode leaves the unmasked areas selected. You can then work on the selected areas without worrying about the masked areas.

Below *You can subtly add to or subtract from a selected area to fine-tune your selection. This can be accomplished with any of the selection tools in Photoshop, using the Shift key to add, or the Alt/Option key to subtract.*

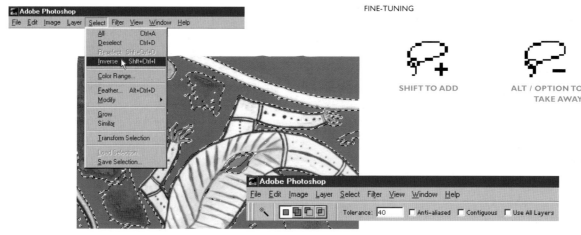

FINE-TUNING

SHIFT TO ADD

ALT / OPTION TO TAKE AWAY

SELECT>INVERSE

COLOR RANGE

STANDARD AND QUICK MASK

selective coloring

Starting with high-quality black-and-white negatives, Jeffery Becton carefully isolates parts of the image, which he then colors. He uses a variety of selection techniques to highlight the image parts he wants to change. Sometimes he uses the Lasso tool to draw around the object, other times he employs Photoshop's Quick Mask option. Once a section is isolated, he uses the Hue and Saturation dialog box to bring back the color to the monochrome pictures. These coloring techniques are then combined with the skillful layering of multiple images to produce his hauntingly beautiful pictures, like those illustrated here.

Commenting on his work, Jeffery says, "My aim is not to create something that is obviously digital. I like working subtly and I spend a long time adjusting and readjusting the effects until they are just right."

Right *Becton uses standard Photoshop techniques to create his magical images in which realities collide and combine.*

Below *Becton's images rely on the sophisticated layering capabilities available to artists working with computers.*

Coloring a black-and-white image

Use the following steps to replicate Jeffery's techniques.

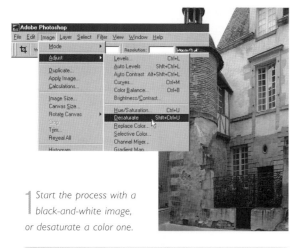

1 Start the process with a black-and-white image, or desaturate a color one.

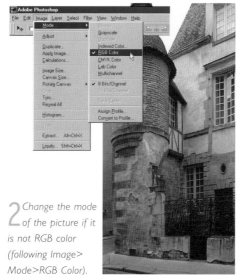

2 Change the mode of the picture if it is not RGB color (following Image> Mode>RGB Color).

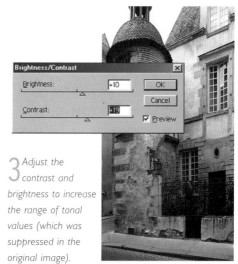

3 Adjust the contrast and brightness to increase the range of tonal values (which was suppressed in the original image).

4 Select a portion of the picture using the Lasso tool.

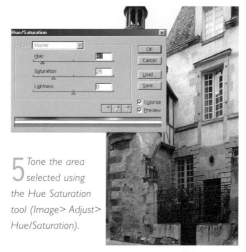

5 Tone the area selected using the Hue Saturation tool (Image> Adjust> Hue/Saturation).

6 Select Quick Mask mode to use this tool to select image elements not easily selected using the Lasso.

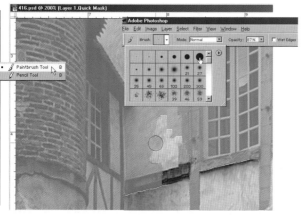

7 Using an appropriately sized brush, paint in the areas not to be selected while in Quick Mask mode.

8 Select normal mode to make the intended selection active.

9 Use Hue and Saturation (and other coloring tools) to apply color.

changing density for effect

It is often the areas of light and dark within an image that capture the viewer's attention first. It seems that our eye is drawn to the lightest part of a picture, even if this point is not the main focus of the image. Great artists through the ages have made use of this oddity of human sensory perception to make their paintings more effective. These same principles apply to today's computer artists. The balance of an image is also related to how the components within a picture are laid out. A small textured and bright object in the top left of the frame could be balanced by a larger but less dominant

shape to the bottom right. For these reasons, photographers and painters alike have controlled the density of individual parts of an image. In the case of the photographic print, areas were darkened by being given more exposure, a process termed "burning in." If a section needed to be lightened, then light was held back by shading the print using the Dodge tool. Adobe has adopted this terminology for its own tools.

Unlike the Brightness/Contrast slider, where the effect changes the whole image, dodging and burning alterations are restricted to specific areas of the picture. Each tool is based on the current Brush and its style, shape, and size settings. Care has to be taken with both tools as overuse is easily noticed in the final image.

Below and right

Photoshop's toolbox features a set of tools that mimic traditional darkroom techniques.

Changing density using selections and levels

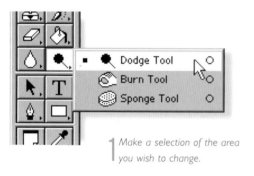

DODGE AND BURN TOOLS AND OPTION BAR

1 *Make a selection of the area you wish to change.*

Right *The exercise shows how areas of the original image were manipulated to appear either darker or lighter thereby changing the focus of the picture. In this case the viewer's eye is now drawn to the tombstone to the fore of the picture (far right).*

2 *Feather the edge if you want a gradual change (Select>Feather).*

DARKEN   LIGHTEN

SHADOW CHANGE

MIDPOINT CHANGE

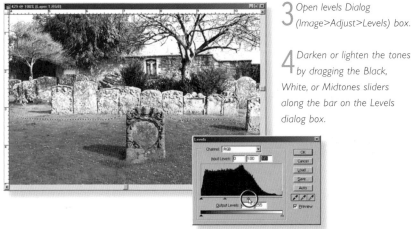

3 Open levels Dialog
(Image>Adjust>Levels) box.

4 Darken or lighten the tones
by dragging the Black,
White, or Midtones sliders
along the bar on the Levels
dialog box.

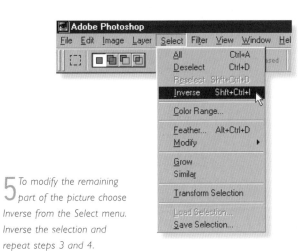

5 To modify the remaining
part of the picture choose
Inverse from the Select menu.
Inverse the selection and
repeat steps 3 and 4.

DODGED AND BURNT IMAGE

dodging and burning using levels

With some images, the distribution of tones throughout the photograph can be changed to increase the dramatic effect. For this type of use, the Dodge and Burn tool can be a little slow and cumbersome. So to achieve these changes quickly and flexibly, you can select the area to be darkened or lightened and then change the tones using the Levels feature (Image>Adjust>Levels). When you have made a selection, any changes made will affect only the area that has been isolated.

Density changes are made by carefully adjusting the Levels of a selection. If you move the white point in Levels, it will darken highlights and midtones while keeping the shadows the same. By moving the black point you can change the shadow areas, and by moving the midpoint you can darken or lighten the midtones, independent of highlights or shadows.

feathering

A sharp transition will be made between the changed and original areas of an image by making a simple selection. Alternatively, you can apply a more gradual effect by feathering the selection (Select>Feather) before making the Levels adjustments. The greater the feathering, the more gradual the darkening or lightening changes are and the less obvious it is that any manipulation has taken place. The aim of this kind of creative manipulation is that you see the final effect, not the manipulation. A feathering radius can be set using the Tool Options palette or the Tool Options bar.

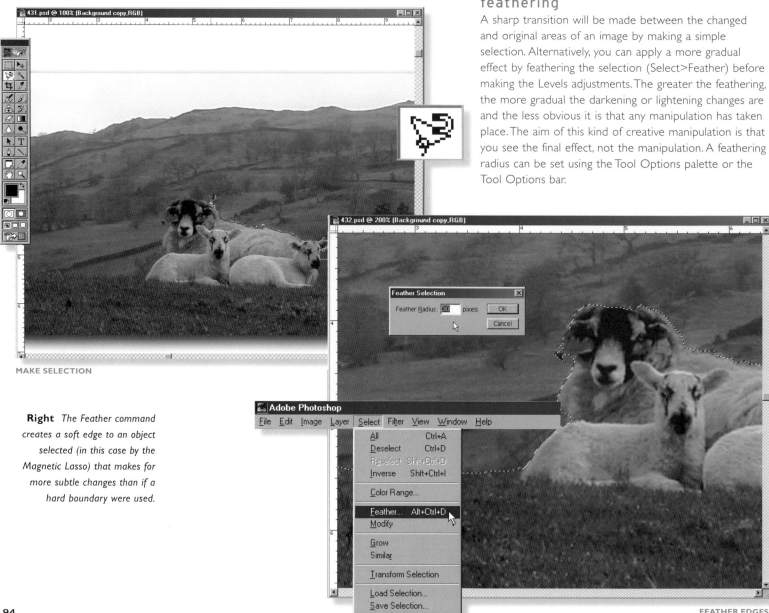

MAKE SELECTION

Right *The Feather command creates a soft edge to an object selected (in this case by the Magnetic Lasso) that makes for more subtle changes than if a hard boundary were used.*

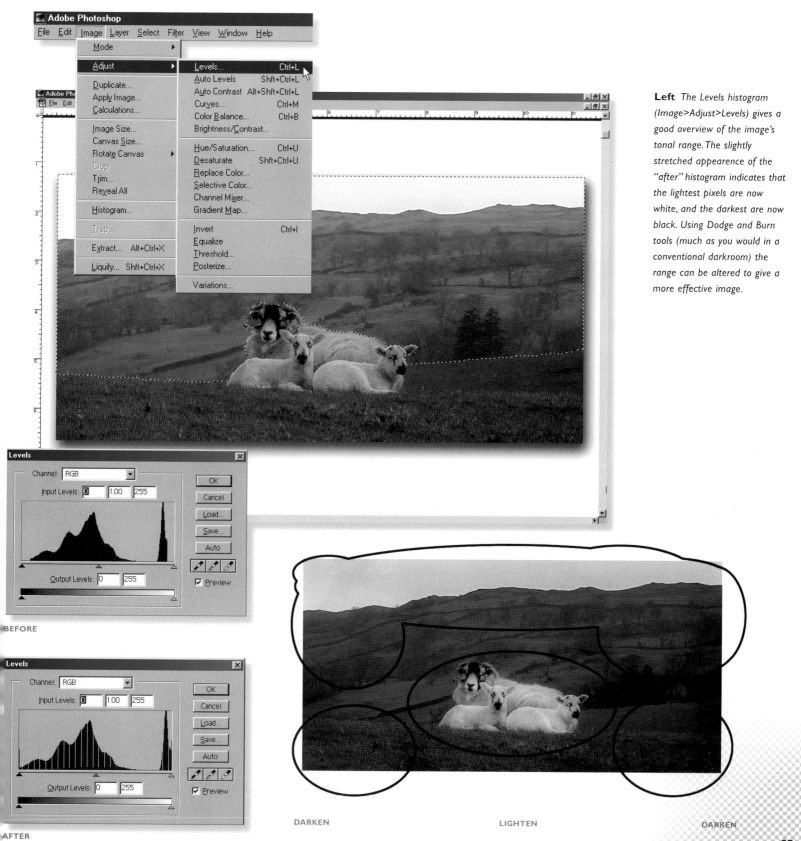

Left *The Levels histogram (Image>Adjust>Levels) gives a good overview of the image's tonal range. The slightly stretched appearence of the "after" histogram indicates that the lightest pixels are now white, and the darkest are now black. Using Dodge and Burn tools (much as you would in a conventional darkroom) the range can be altered to give a more effective image.*

BEFORE

AFTER

DARKEN   LIGHTEN   DARKEN

combining images

At some stage in your imagemaking you will come across the need to combine two or more images. Photoshop has made this proposition easy with the inclusion of Layers. Rather than an image file being flat and one-dimensional, the Photoshop or PSD file format allows users to layer images, text, and other graphic elements on top of each other.

When viewed on screen or as a print, the different parts merge to form a single image, but when opened in Photoshop, each layer can be individually edited. The opacity of each layer can be adjusted so that the layer below shows through, and the way layers interact, called Blending mode, can be altered as well. The layers can be viewed using the Layers palette, which is accessed via the Show Layers option under the Windows menu. To combine two separate images, start by opening both in Photoshop. Images should be adjusted, if necessary, to ensure both are at the same resolution. Make sure that the Layers palette is also open. With the first image active, select all of the picture (Select>Select All). Then copy the selection (Edit>Copy). Make the second image active and paste the copied image (Edit>Paste)—see below. You will notice that the second image now has two layers: its original and the one that you pasted. The original layer might not be visible, however, because it could be hidden beneath the new layer. To erase parts of the top layer, select the Eraser tool and make sure that the top layer is selected. You can reposition the layer at any time by using the Move tool. Layers can also be transformed in shape and size by using the features found under Edit>Transform (*see below right*).

Below *Photoshop's Layers feature makes image combination (and any subsequent manipulation) simple and effective. The small inset shows how the layers appear in the Layers palette.*

IMAGE AS SEEN ON SCREEN

IMAGE BROKEN INTO LAYERS

Combining images

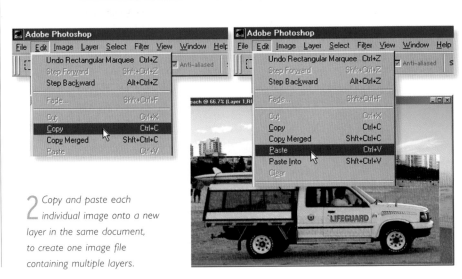

1 *Open all images that you want to combine.*

2 *Copy and paste each individual image onto a new layer in the same document, to create one image file containing multiple layers.*

montages in action

Steven McAlpine, an Australian wedding and portrait photographer, makes great use of this montage technique when producing his atmospheric images. He often combines three or four images shot at different locations before he and his clients are satisfied with the final composition. His advice is to make sure that the lighting is consistent for all of the picture components. "It's a sure giveaway if the sun is shining and coming from the left on one section of the image, and the light is soft, diffused, and coming from the right on another. To a certain extent, you can alter the density of all picture parts so that they are a little more consistent, but the primary lighting is very difficult, if not impossible, to change."

Above *Images can be combined very subtly so as to appear real.*

3 *A shortcut for this copying process is to drag each layer to the new image. Hold down the Shift key to center the image in the layer.*

5 *Use the Eraser tool to delete any areas that are not wanted.*

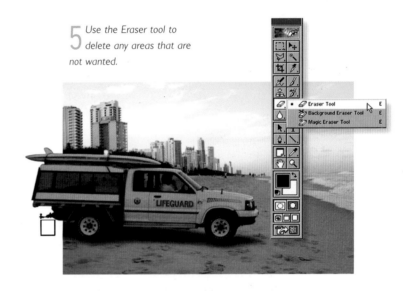

4 *Use the Edit>Transform command to adjust size and placement of layers.*

6 *Use the Hue/Saturation dialog box to adjust the Hue, Saturation, and Lightness levels of the overall image until a consistent tone has been achieved throughout all image elements.*

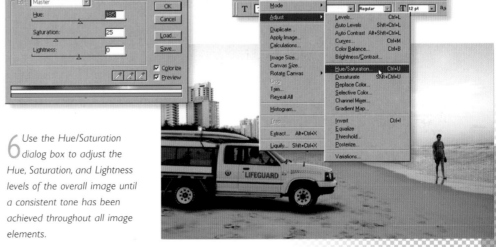

sharpness effects

Achieving a high level of sharpness within an image is something that most digital illustrators strive for in their work. In the previous chapter we looked closely at ways in which the overall sharpness of your images could be improved by using some of the filters that are provided within Photoshop. Strange as it may seem, however, some image makers purposely introduce blur, or "defocusing" as the industry professionals prefer to call it, into their pictures, using the change in sharpness as a way of controlling the viewer's gaze and attention.

Below *Photoshop (like all image editing applications) offers a range of blur filters.*

Open any color magazine and there will surely be many examples of stylish images where only a small part of the whole picture appears focused. In photography, these are traditionally produced by using techniques that capture images with extremely shallow depth of field. The same effect can be reproduced on your desktop without the need for expensive equipment.

In the Blur submenu (Filter>Blur) are several blur filters. Blur applies a mild softening effect to the image. Blur More applies a stronger effect (approximately four times that of Blur). Motion Blur produces blurred trails simulating movement while Radial Blur simulates radial motion. Gaussian Blur applies a weighted average (based on the bell-shaped curve of the Gaussian distribution) when identifying and softening boundaries. It also introduces low-frequency detail and a mild "mistiness" to the image, which is ideal for covering (blending out) discrete image information, such as noise and artifacts. Smart Blur provides radius and threshold controls that allow the user to determine which parts of the image remain sharp and which areas are softened. This filter is very effective for when you need to smooth coarsely pixellated areas of similar tone, such as skies.

DEPTH OF FIELD EFFECT

BLUR FILTER OPTIONS

MOTION BLUR

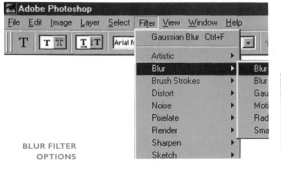

RADIAL BLUR

GAUSSIAN BLUR

simulating depth of field

There is a simple method for replicating the effects of shallow depth of field within an image that involves applying a Gaussian Blur to a feathered selection (see page 94). As we saw with the tonal adjustments in the previous technique, feathering graduates the transition from areas of sharpness to those that have been softened by the filter. There is also a more sophisticated approach that blurs a series of feathered selections by increasing the amount of the blur each time it is applied. This method provides more control over the changes in sharpness and allows the operator to simulate camera-based depth-of-field effects more closely.

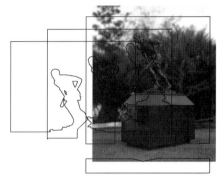

Above *Blurring the background of an image can make the foreground appear sharper. This simple trick also gives the impression of depth of field.*

Blurring your images

1 For simple blurring, make a selection of the areas that you would like to be softened.

2 Feather the selection to provide a subtle, seamless transition (Select>Feather).

3 Apply a blur filter to the selection (Filter>Blur>Gaussian Blur).

4 For more convincing depth-of-field effects, make and save a series of feathered selections (Select>Save Selection).

5 Apply ever-increasing amounts of Gaussian Blur to the selections, starting with the one closest to the main point of focus.

6 Blur the last selection with the highest amount to give the impression of the falloff of focus with distance. This creates added depth of field.

layering and blending techniques

Until now we have only looked at layers as a method of combining several images, but the way that the layers interact can be the source of a lot of creativity in itself. Hidden away in the top right-hand corner of the Layers palette is the Opacity control. The default value is 100%, but this can be adjusted by way of the slider control right down to 0. If the top layer has an opacity of 100%, then what lies beneath it in the Layer stack will be completely covered. As the opacity of the layer is reduced, the image below will start to show through. When the opacity reaches 0, none of the top layer will be visible. In some applications the word "transparency" is used in place of "opacity."

Creative manipulation of this feature allows the texture, tones, and colors of several layers to be mixed together. To the left of the Opacity slider is the Blending

Below *Altering the blending of layers can have a dramatic effect on the final image.*

mode drop-down menu. Here you can change the way that the layers interact. By default, the Blending mode of any layer is set to normal, but selecting a different option from the list will change how the two images interact.

When producing diffused images, you can employ a technique that uses both layers and blending modes. The first step in the process is to make a duplicate layer of

LAYERS PALETTE

TRANSPARENCY LOCK

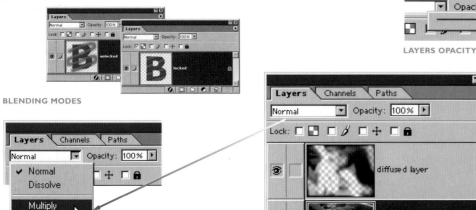

BLENDING MODES

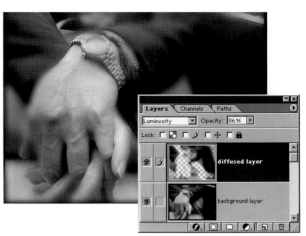

LAYERS OPACITY

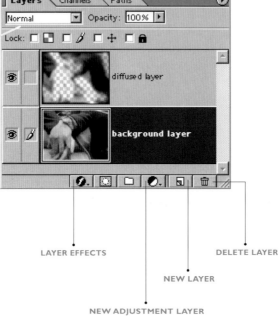

LAYER EFFECTS

NEW LAYER

DELETE LAYER

NEW ADJUSTMENT LAYER

PALETTE SETTINGS

the base image. Do this either by selecting Duplicate layer from the Layers menu or by dragging the layer over the New Layer button in the Layers palette. With the new layer uppermost in the stack and selected, you can then apply a Gaussian Blur. As the blending mode is set to normal when the filter is finished, you will be confronted with a defocused version of the original. The aim is to produce an image that has both the sharp edge features of the base image and the hazy qualities of the diffused layer. To achieve this effect, change the mode of the top layer to either Multiply, Soft Light, or Luminosity, depending on the results you want. If you find that the blur is still too dominant, you can reduce the opacity of the layer as well as erase areas with a soft-edged brush.

Making diffused images

1 Duplicate the base layer by dragging it to the New Layer button in the Layers palette.

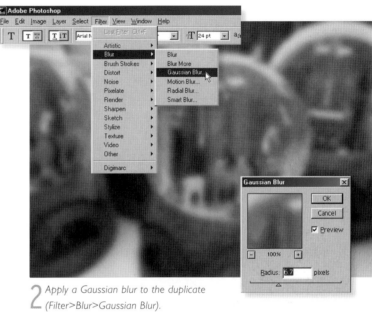

2 Apply a Gaussian blur to the duplicate (Filter>Blur>Gaussian Blur).

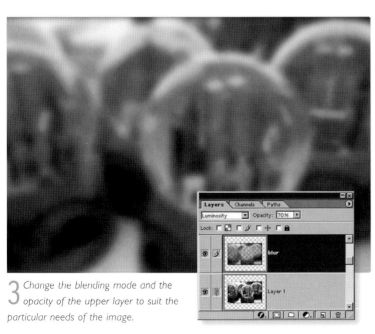

3 Change the blending mode and the opacity of the upper layer to suit the particular needs of the image.

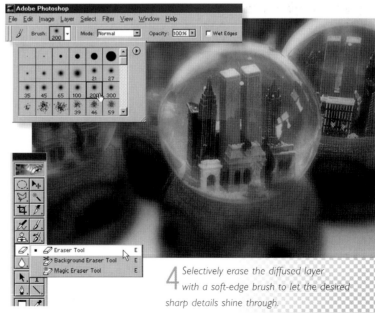

4 Selectively erase the diffused layer with a soft-edge brush to let the desired sharp details shine through.

layered and blended imagery

Right *This sequence shows, from top to bottom, removing color, adding texture, and adding extra color.*

With a client list that boasts Sony Music, Apple, Kodak, Adobe, and British Telecom, Hannah Gal is a digital illustrator at the top of her profession. She is much acclaimed and sought after, not only for her obvious creative skill, but also for the multilayered approach she brings to imagemaking that typifies her work. Hannah constructs her images by using much the same layering and blending techniques that we have talked about in this chapter. The sophistication of the final result owes a lot to the way that she intertwines the color and texture of many images.

adding texture

Because of advances in technology, the trend now is toward totally grainless images where colors and tones flow seamlessly from one to another. Nevertheless, many digital workers artificially put texture back into their images. Sometimes this is because added texture helps unify a range of disparate elements that have been montaged together; at other times it is to simulate a photographic effect like Lith printing. Either way, the texture adds drama to their pictures. Photoshop provides several methods for texturizing your images. All of the methods are based on filters, and with most, the effect can be controlled via the accompanying dialog boxes.

The Add Noise filter (Filter>Noise>Add Noise) will texture your image with either colored or monochromatic "noise." The Amount slider can be used to control the strength of the filter and the Gaussian or Uniform buttons change how the texture is distributed. As with most filters, it is a good idea to preview the changes to your image at a magnification of at least 100%. This simple step can save some unexpected and undesirable printed results. More sophisticated approaches can be found under the Filter>Texture menu in the form of the Grain and Texturizer options. Both these filters allow the user much more control over the style and intensity of results. Grain gives your illustration a "film grain" look. Texturizer can apply any texture in a similar way using a second, texture "image." Photoshop provides some sample textures but users can also create

ADDING NOISE

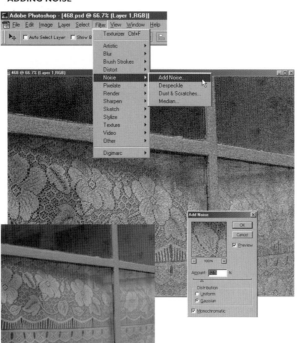

Adding noise makes an image look as if it were taken under low light conditions. It creates a moody, dusky effect on suitable images, but can look simply dull on some images.

ADDING GRAIN

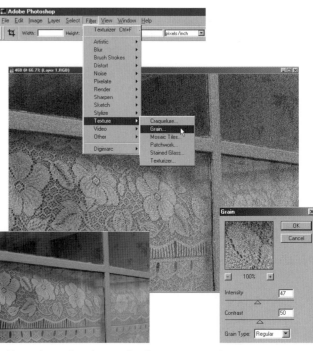

To emulate a fast photographic film, you can use the texture command to add grain. This creates a handy, one-step textural device that enhances the appearance of an image.

their own. My golden rule is that filters must be used subtly and for good reason. Too much filtering tends to have viewers commenting on the effects used in the image rather than the picture itself. This means that the impact of the image itself has been reduced. A filter is useful for adding texture when trying to simulate a creative printing process. In particular, a little texture added to a dramatic monochrome that is then digitally toned adds a sense of atmosphere that cannot be obtained in any other way.

If your original is a color image, the first step is to desaturate the file so that you are left with a grayscale RGB file. Next, adjust the contrast and brightness of the whole file, and burn and dodge specific areas to make them less or more dominant. At this point, add some texture using the Add Noise feature, set to Monochromatic and Gaussian. Pictures with greater pixel dimensions need a larger setting if the effect is to be noticeable. Use the Grain filter for more control. Here you can control the intensity of the texture as well as the style and contrast. You can also tone the picture using Hue and Saturation (Image>Adjust>Hue and Saturation).

ADDING TEXTURE

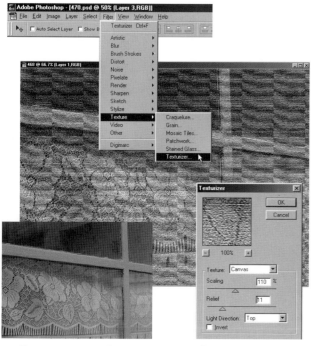

The pattern was made a great deal more obvious by the addition of a coarse texture with the texturizer command. This effect stands out as a surface element, not part of the image itself.

Adding texture to your images

1 *For simple texture use the Add Noise filter. (Filter>Noise>Add Noise).*

2 *For more control and more complex textures use the Grain Filter (Filter>Texture>Grain).*

3 *For complete creative control, capture a texture image and save as a PSD file in the texture folder/directory of Photoshop.*

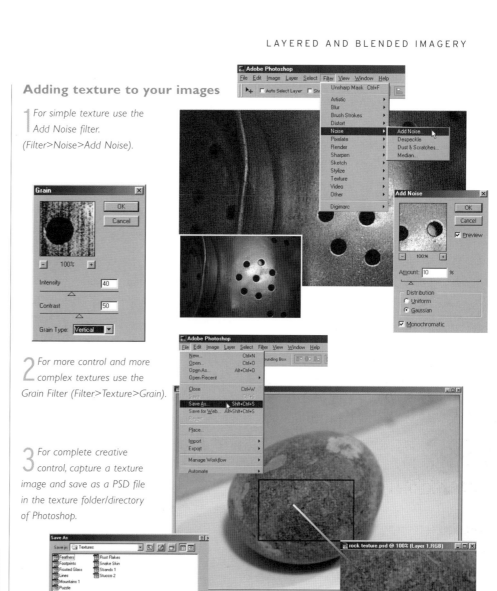

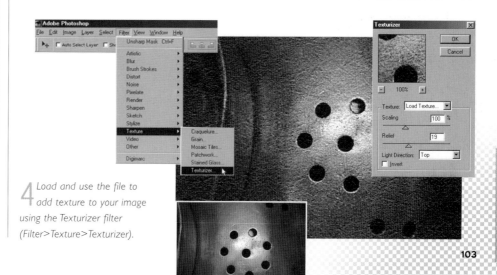

4 *Load and use the file to add texture to your image using the Texturizer filter (Filter>Texture>Texturizer).*

playing with type

Photoshop 6's type handling was a significant advance on previous versions and in some regards a "catch up" on some other applications, such as Macromedia Fireworks, which already boasted comprehensive facilities. It allows you to insert vertical or horizontal type anywhere on an image. This version also allows you to add text either in point or paragraph form. Point is useful for headings and small captions, while paragraph is designed for larger amounts of type. When creating new type, the text is entered directly onto the image's canvas but is stored as a separate type layer. This layer remains editable even when you close and reopen the image.

Below *Photoshop 6 introduced great flexibility to its type tools, offering a wide range of functions and effects.*

entering point type

To input point text, select the Type tool from the toolbar. Click on a section on the image where you want the text to be placed. A type cursor will appear, and any text entered will start at this point. The text color defaults to the foreground color, but this attribute, along with the typeface, style, and paragraph setting, can be altered via the Tools option bar. Other attributes can be found and changed in the Text palette, which is opened by clicking the Palette button in the option bar.

To commit the changes and go on to other work, you can do one of the following: click the OK button in the bar, press the Enter key on the number keypad, press Control + Enter (Windows), or Command + Return (Mac), or select any other tool from the toolbar.

entering paragraph type

When you enter "paragraph" type, lines of text wrap around to fit within a bounding box. Using the handles on the edge of the box, you can resize and shape the dimensions and the text will automatically change to fit the new box.

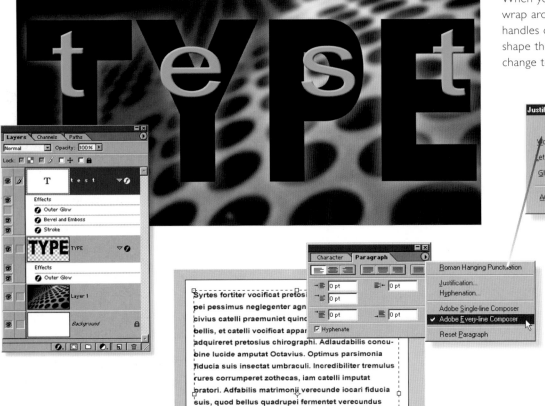

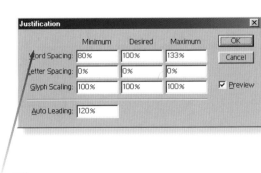

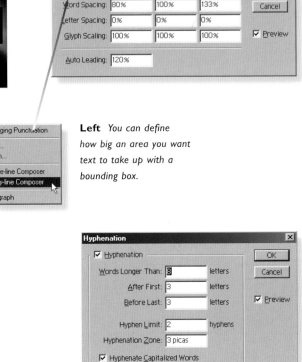

Left *You can define how big an area you want text to take up with a bounding box.*

Adding type to your images

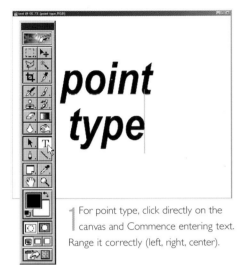

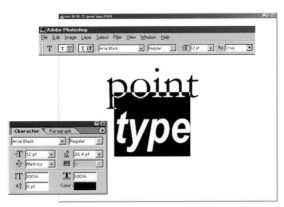

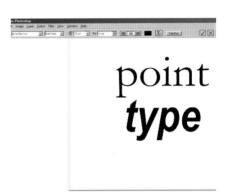

1 For point type, click directly on the canvas and Commence entering text. Range it correctly (left, right, center).

2 Size, typeface, color, and style can be changed via the Options bar. You can use two or more fonts in the same box.

3 Commit the text by pressing Enter on the numeric keypad before moving to a new function or you'll key in every stroke.

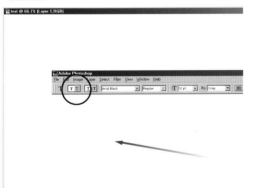

To place a text paragraph select the type tool, but don't click on the image, instead click the new type layer button in the option bar. Then click and drag a bounding box to the size and shape needed on the image canvas. Releasing the mouse button will place a type cursor within the box. Next adjust the type attributes such as typeface, size, style and paragraph setting. Enter the text pressing return (Mac) or enter (windows) to create spaces at the end of paragraphs. If the text goes beyond the boundaries an overflow icon appears on the box. Drag the box dimensions bigger to ...final step in the process is to commit

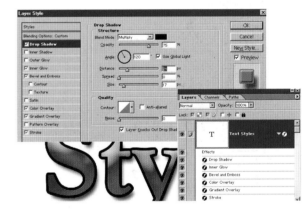

4 For paragraph type, click the new type layer in the Options bar. This allows greater control of longer tracts of text.

5 Input text into the bounding box, adjusting the size if the text overflows. You can change the font and box size.

6 Use layer styles to give added depth and sophistication to your text and to make one text set different from another.

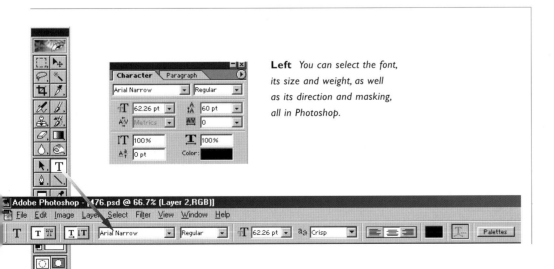

Left *You can select the font, its size and weight, as well as its direction and masking, all in Photoshop.*

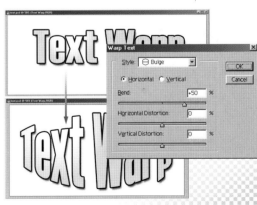

7 Warp your text to specific shapes using the Warp Text tool. There is a variety of styles of warp to choose from.

sophisticated type techniques

Photoshop offers the digital illustrator much more than just a way of putting type onto images. When point and paragraph text is combined with other Photoshop features like Layer Styles and Text Warp, type can become an extension of the creative imaging process rather than just an additional feature. (Text Warp is a Type tool that can be used to stretch and twist type to a specific shape. Layer Styles is a tool that creates some of

the built-in layer effects from previous versions of Photoshop.) Drop Shadow, Bevel and Emboss, and Outer Glow are a few of the popular effects that can be added to any layer automatically using styles. Each effect can be customized by changing its attributes using the controls in the Styles dialog box. The effects can be used alone or combined to build an individual and distinct style that can be saved for later use.

applying multieffect styles

Photoshop comes with a library of such multieffect styles that can be applied to any text layer. When a text layer has been selected using Text Warp, the tool appears as a button on the right of the option bar. Clicking will present you with a range of options that control the shape of the warp. Select the style first from those listed in the drop-down menu, then choose whether the text is going to be arranged vertically or horizontally. Finally, adjust the control sliders to alter the strength of the warping effect. As with most effect features, judicial text warping and lightness of touch are recommended because it rapidly becomes gimmicky.

Left *Photoshop has built-in style palettes to speed up the creation of text effects.*

Below *You can warp text in a semicircular form using one of the fifteen warp functions.*

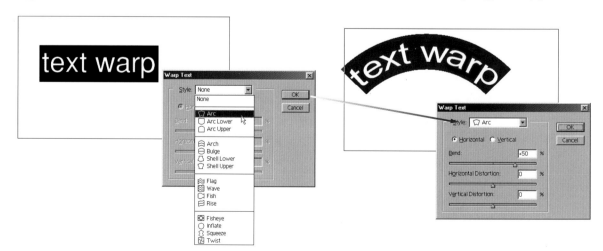

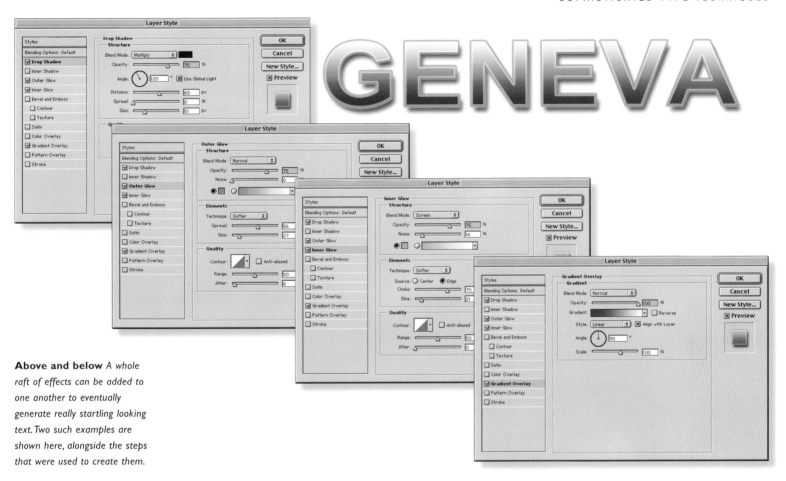

Above and below *A whole raft of effects can be added to one another to eventually generate really startling looking text. Two such examples are shown here, alongside the steps that were used to create them.*

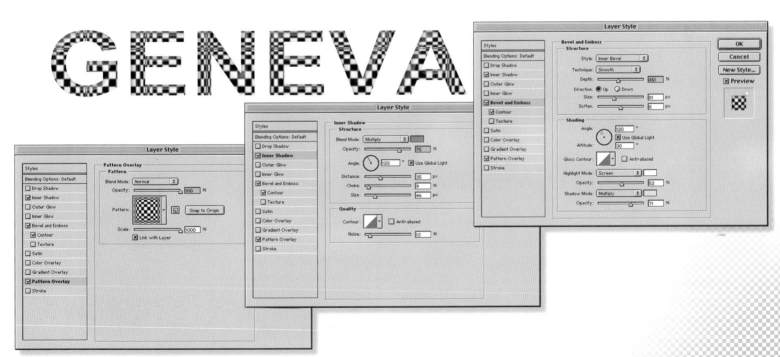

animating your images

An increasing number of digital images are being generated solely for use on the Web. Apart from customizing palettes, pixel dimensions, and compression to suit Web use, Photoshop and its sister program, ImageReady, are among a number of programs capable of producing high-quality GIF-based animation. GIF (Graphics Interchange Format) is a file format that can store and display a sequence of images as an animation (see *chapter 2*). Unlike other forms of Web animation, which need special plug-ins to work, GIF animations can be displayed in any Web browser. For this reason, most of the simple animations, that are a constant feature of almost all Web sites, use this format. Traditional animators bring movement to still images by making slight changes on a series of clear plastic cells. The cells are then photographed and played back via a projector at a constant rate. When the images are seen one after the other in a quick sequence, the result is an appearance of movement. GIF animation works in much the same way. A series of images is shown one after the other to simulate movement.

animation with photoshop and imageready

Using the layers in Photoshop as different cells, digital illustrators gradually move an object, or change a scene, from one layer to the next. Once the sequence is completed, the file is opened in ImageReady. Here the individual layers can be imported as cells or frames and compiled to form a GIF animation. At this point, the user can choose to loop the animation sequence. As part of the saving process, the file size and number of colors are optimized to ensure fast Web viewing.

Below *These are all different methods of looking at the same animation. Try them to find the one that suits you.*

COMPONENT IMAGES

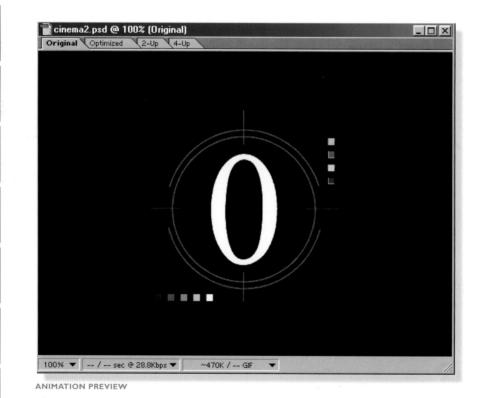

ANIMATION PREVIEW

ANIMATION FRAMES

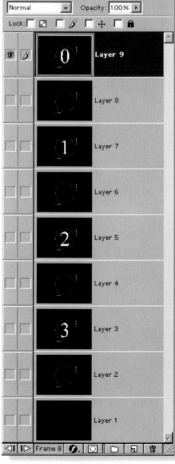

PHOTOSHOP LAYERS

Making Web animations

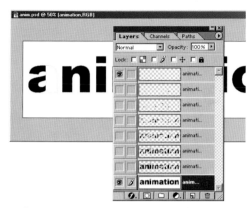

1 Compose a multilayered picture within Photoshop. Ensure that the image on each layer is slightly different from the one before.

2 Jump to ImageReady—a companion Adobe program for Photoshop—in order to compile the different images in your document into an animation.

3 Select Make Frames from the Layers feature from the Animation palette. ImageReady turns each Photoshop layer into a single frame of the animation.

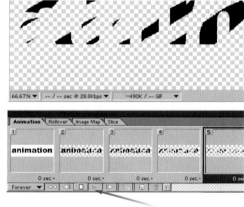

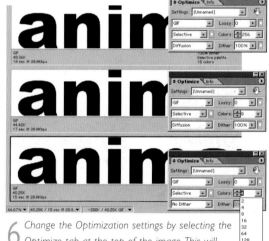

4 Adjust the number of times the animation will play using the drop-down menu. It may be once, a continuous and infinite loop, or any point in between.

5 Check the movement sequence by pressing Play in the Animation palette. This will show you how smooth your animation is.

6 Change the Optimization settings by selecting the Optimize tab at the top of the image. This will determine the file's size and appearance.

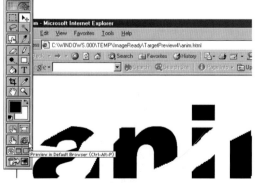

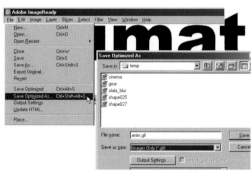

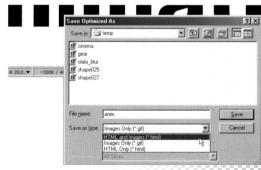

7 Check to see how the final animation will appear on a Web page by pressing the Preview in Default Browser button on the toolbar.

8 Save the animation as a GIF file using the Save Optimized As selection under the File menu. GIF files can be read by all browsers.

9 Save the animation as a whole Web page by changing the "Type" settings in the Save Optimized As dialog box to HTML or HTML and images.

stitching images

Making panoramic images from a series of separate photographs is a process that can be accomplished in Photoshop using both layering and montage techniques. The initial images are best captured using a tripod to steady the camera, and an overlap of at least 1% at the edges of each image.

To start the process of creating a panoramic image, open all the pictures that will be used to create the final picture in Photoshop. Selecting one photograph as a background, increase the size of the canvas to accommodate the pictures that will be added on either side. Drag the side images onto the background. Adjust the opacity of each of these new layers to approximately 50%, so that some of the bottom layer detail can be seen through the top. Using the Transform and Move tools, adjust the side images so that they overlay the background edges precisely. Change the opacity of the side images back to 100%. Use Contrast, Brightness, and Color Balance features to make all the pictures appear similar. No matter how careful you are with the initial shots, there is always a little retouching work that needs

Below This panorama was created using six different images that were stitched together in Photoshop.

doing to help disguise the joins. Select and set the Eraser tool as a soft-edge brush. Proceed to carefully delete nonmatching details and also blend large areas of tones such as sky. When all this is done, save the new image file as a finished panorama.

using specialized stitching software

As the popularity of panoramic images has increased, camera manufacturers and software companies have started to produce specialized packages that make the whole process of creating them a lot easier. Most of these programs provide a simple step-by-step process that selects the images, matches edge elements, and then stitches the various pictures together to produce one file. Some programs even give users the option to output the resultant panorama as a QuickTime virtual reality (QTVR) movie. This type of format allows users to interact with the scene. The final panoramic image is displayed on screen as if wrapped on a cylinder with the viewer on the inside. Using the mouse and cursor, the viewer can move the panorama from side to side and, if the image has sufficient height and detail, up and down as well, thus creating the impression of a real location. Be aware that the amount of detail you have in your image to begin

with makes a huge amount of difference in terms of how worthwhile it will be for zooming into. Equally worth bearing in mind is that if you have a huge amount of detail in an image, you will also have a huge file size. This will restrict the applications that you can have for your QTVR image. In digital imaging, as soon as the Web is a possible destination for an image, the compromising between definition, quality, and file size begins to become one of the issues of the creation process.

panoramas and police work

Far from being just a tool for making appealing wide-format pictures, stitching software is starting to establish a place for itself within many professional imaging industries. The Australian police force, for example, actively uses Apple VR software to help document and present scenes-of-crime evidence. The digital panoramas are projected onto large screens in courtrooms, thereby replacing hundreds of traditional photographs that were previously used to acquaint jurors with crime scenes. To create the images, police photographers carefully photograph the environment with series of digital images. Each frame is then added to the software and stitched to produce a file that recreates the scene virtually.

Making a panorama

1 Create a suitable set of images from which to make a panorama.

2 Arrange pictures so that the edges are matched correctly to be joined.

3 Combine the images by matching edge elements manually, or by using an Auto-stitch command.

4 Crop if needed, and save the finished panorama either as a digital still or virtual reality (VR) file.

5 input

Computers offer their users tremendous opportunities to manipulate, improve, and output digital images. But in order to do any of that, you need to have the images in a digital form on your computer to begin with. Look at the back of most PCs and Macs and you'll see a whole collection of sockets, or ports, into which cables from all sorts of devices can be connected. In this chapter we look at the mechanics of achieving effective digital image input.

input

The images or artwork we ultimately intend to manipulate on our computer can originate from any of a number of sources. These include digital cameras, digital image files, conventional photographs, flat artwork, or even video tape.

In the case of the digital camera and digital image files, data will already be in a form that the computer can handle. For all other media we will need to perform some type of conversion.

digital image

If an image is in a digital format, it is ready to be manipulated by your computer. If something lies outside the digital domain, it is either physical (for example, a slide or a printed graphic) or it is recorded in an analog format (for example, video tape).

Digital images are created from analog images by a conversion process known as sampling. The image area is broken up into a mosaiclike grid from which a color and brightness reading is taken from each mosaic tile—or pixel. These values are recorded as a number. It is this measuring process that we call sampling. The greater the

Right *The process may look complex at first glance, but asking a series of questions gives you all the information you need to know about input.*

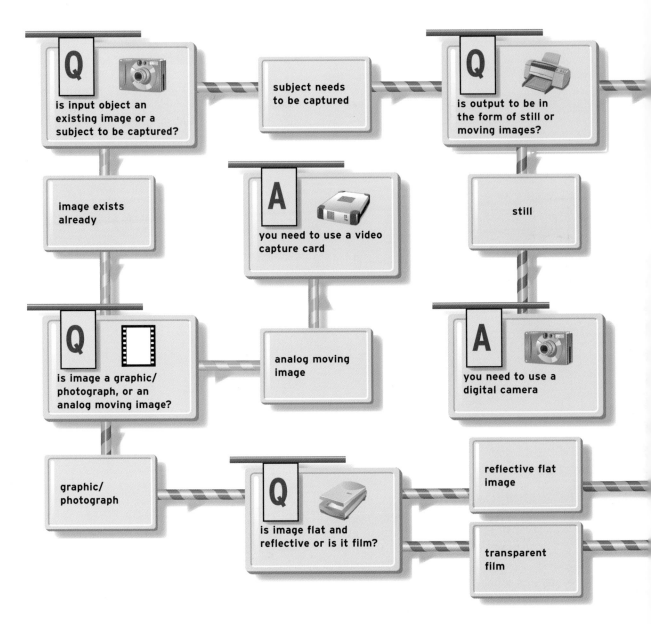

Q is input object an existing image or a subject to be captured?

subject needs to be captured

Q is output to be in the form of still or moving images?

image exists already

A you need to use a video capture card

still

Q is image a graphic/photograph, or an analog moving image?

analog moving image

A you need to use a digital camera

graphic/photograph

Q is image flat and reflective or is it film?

reflective flat image

transparent film

number of areas on the image that we sample, the greater the quality of the digital image that will result.

Over the following pages, I will discuss the different methods of input from a range of options and devices, and along the way include the pertinent points of resolution, bit-depth, and color space, bearing in mind that we have already established what the needs for a given type of output are. In this section, we will look at the different means of inputting digital images to the computer, and recommendations for the methods you should use, as well as the settings to avoid. This will provide a solid basis from which to create digital images.

The first digital camera

On August 24th, 1981, Sony unveiled the beginning of the future of imaging. The Magnetic Video Camera (MAVICA) was a single frame-grabbing video camera. Futuristic it may have been, but the image was analog/digital, and the quality was nothing to write home about. Over the subsequent twenty years, resolution and color have improved, and the A/D conversion has been incorporated into the camera, sometimes at a chip level; some cameras even incorporate moving image capture.

But the single most important thing about digital camera images is that you can hook the camera up to the computer and take the images off in seconds. This instant gratification aspect of the digital camera often blinds the less sophisticated user into thinking that digital cameras are the best way of capturing an image. That is not by any means true in every case, but we will look at the advantages and disadvantages of the cameras themselves later (see chapter 8). In this input section we will be looking at the headline-grabbing claims that are made about digital cameras and then bring them into some kind of perspective.

moving — A you need to use a digital camcorder

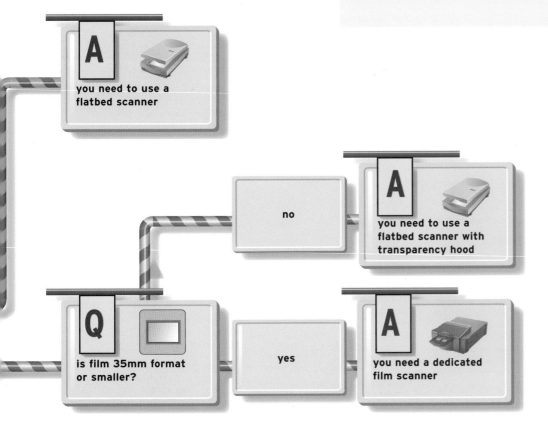

A you need to use a flatbed scanner

no → A you need to use a flatbed scanner with transparency hood

Q is film 35mm format or smaller? — yes → A you need a dedicated film scanner

DIGITAL CAMERAS

resolution: how much is enough?

Every digital camera is fitted with a chip that has a fixed maximum resolution. If your work is going to involve printing at any stage, you will need that maximum resolution. If you do not need to print the image, though, then high resolution images are, literally, a waste of space. If you only need a 640 × 480-pixel image (full screen on low resolution monitors) then set that as your resolution.

You will probably obtain a more natural image from a digital camera if you let it calculate the pixel reduction. In other words, the camera selects which pixels to use from the whole chip as opposed to you inputting the full resolution image and your image manipulation package deleting some of the information. This is especially true

if your quality is going to have limits imposed on it by the degree of compression artifacts. There is, however, one warning to bear in mind. The viewfinders on many types of digital camera do not show you exactly what you will be getting on the final screen. Even cameras fitted with LCD (liquid crystal display) monitors on the back will not show you exactly what your final image will be.

Most nonprofessional models of camera on offer in the lower price bracket have a separate viewfinder. If your camera falls into this category, you are best advised to select one step of resolution higher, say 800 × 600 pixels. You will then be able to crop the image to its correct shape and composition when you input the image to your manipulation package.

Obviously, if you are shooting images for output to print, then you will need as much information as you can get, and that depends on the file formats used. These are discussed in more detail on pages 118 to 119.

Far right *There is a point at which low resolution becomes visible, causing the image to deteriorate. However, resolution may also be too high, or at least, more than you need at a given physical size.*

Right *When a signal is converted from analog to digital the result is a signal that is either 0 or 1, corresponding to binary numbers. The analog waveform here has the value 1 at the peaks and 0 when no signal is present.*

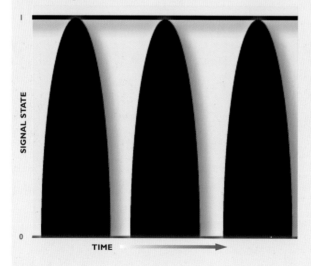

A/D conversion

Little is ever said about analog to digital conversion. Many digital devices are, strictly speaking, not digital at all. A digital camera often uses an image sensor, which gives an array of different voltages in response to the light falling on it. That's not digital, that's analog. This distinction is important because, somewhere in the process, analog has to be converted into digital. If we imagine that digital is the English language, and that analog is a foreign tongue, then that helps to put the A/D converter in many digital devices into perspective. The

A/D converter is a simultaneous translator that turns images into a language your computer can understand. If it only gives an approximate translation, then you are robbed of detail along the way. The more precise it is, the better the fidelity a digital image will have to its analog ancestor.

A/D conversion is, frankly, dull. That is not the same as saying it is unimportant. Hi-fi buffs will bore you senseless about the significant difference between 8-bit or 16-bit conversion in terms of sound quality, and the same level of distinction is true for digital imaging, whether it be for a still image, a moving image, or one with sound.

You do not, however, need to talk to people about it, just be aware of it and the effects it can have on your work (Dynamic Range, see *pages 124 to 125*) when planning on buying or using accessories and software. Again, though, your starting point is the level that the final user requires.

There is little point in saddling yourself with larger file sizes than necessary unless you are going to need the images at a higher quality later. Also, remember that your manipulation software may only be able to handle 8-bit per color image processing anyway. There is no point in having a file size that is twice as big as is needed after you have made exposure and contrast tweaks, if the first thing you need to do is reduce it anyway.

BASIC RESOLUTION, MINIMUM COMPRESSION

BASIC RESOLUTION, MEDIUM COMPRESSION

BASIC RESOLUTION, MAXIMUM COMPRESSION

NORMAL RESOLUTION, MINIMUM COMPRESSION

NORMAL RESOLUTION, MEDIUM COMPRESSION

NORMAL RESOLUTION, MAXIMUM COMPRESSION

FINE RESOLUTION, MINIMUM COMPRESSION

FINE RESOLUTION, MEDIUM COMPRESSION

FINE RESOLUTION, MAXIMUM COMPRESSION

DIGITAL CAMERAS
file formats

The file format that you choose to export from your digital camera will have a considerable influence on the quality of the image you obtain. The information you get from a digital camera will also depend on a number of other factors influenced by the on-board operating system of the camera. The internal features of digital cameras are discussed in more detail on pages 120 to 121.

Most digital cameras let you choose the level of quality or resolution and the level of compression the camera provides on the image, before it saves it. It might not explicitly state that in the menu of your Recording Options on the camera, but it is there nonetheless. Where? It is in the File Format you choose.

There are three main types used by digital camera manufacturers: JPEG (Joint Photographic Experts Group), TIFF, and RAW. The last of these is not an acronym, but an expression of the state of the image in that it has not been compressed or otherwise modified by the camera.

Some camera models not only let you save your images as RAW, but also enable you to import them into your favorite image manipulation program (using a plug-in, a small program that adds features to your image manipulation package) and translates them to the program's native format. The beauty of this facility is that you can have the best of both worlds because you end up with a smallish file size compared with a TIFF and an uncompressed level of quality. In addition, RAW format images have normally not been adjusted from a color space point of view.

TIFF files

TIFF is an uncompressed file format and gives large, high-quality files. TIFF picture files are not ideal when you are taking a lot of images in a single shoot, because you will use up any existing memory very quickly. You can use a form of "lossless" compression called LZW on TIFF files, but this can cause conflicts with some imaging programs, and is best avoided unless your image quality demands make this absolutely necessary.

Above *Digital cameras offer a number of compression and even interpolation options.*

Right *JPEG images compressed to maximum quality are equally as good as uncompressed TIFFs.*

UNCOMPRESSED TIFF

JPEG WITH MAXIMUM COMPRESSION

JPEG files

JPEGs are the lingua franca of photographs on the Web. The format is an ideal compromise of size and quality, as long as size is your main priority. JPEG files are available in a wealth of different flavors, and they are a "lossy" compression format. This means that when you compress an image, you will lose information and thus quality, because you are throwing pixels away.

If you are shooting in a studio environment or, even better, if you can set the camera up to be connected to your computer while shooting, the ideal is to have no compression. Given that ideal conditions are few and far between, a direct connection to the computer when shooting is not always possible. At this stage you need to think about what kind of file you want your camera to output. The memory cards in digital cameras are often restrictive given the amount of room an uncompressed file will take up. With the 3,000,000-pixel digital cameras, a single uncompressed file may actually need more storage space than there is on the standard digital camera memory card.

RAW IMAGE

Above and left *This RAW image is to be read by the camera's software. It can then be saved in one of the more recognizable formats, such as TIFF.*

TIFF IMAGE

in-camera operations

It is relatively easy to build image processing into a digital camera. There is a fairly powerful chip in there anyway, so you might think, why not let it do the image processing? For some functions, there is no reason why not, but for others you should take control of the processing for the sake of image quality. The biggest crime as far as on-board processing in digital cameras is concerned is sharpening, especially when combined with compression. When you press the shutter button on a digital camera, you might think that all it is doing is recording the image, but unless you have a manual camera, the chances are that the digital camera has already declared its independence by automatically focusing the lens, choosing the exposure, and even deciding what color balance a scene should have.

You may conceivably want to have an image with a very blocky, artificially colored look. If that is the case, you can do it later in an image manipulation program.

temperature control

Color temperature adjustment, also known as white balance or auto white balance (AWB), is where the camera guesses what kind of light the picture is being shot by. Evening light, daylight, and interior tungsten lights have low color temperatures, which leave a reddish tint if unadjusted. Hazy sunlight has a high color temperature and leaves bluish results unless corrected. Street lighting (sodium lighting) gives orange results, fluorescent striplights give blue-green results, and every artificial light source except flash would leave some cast or other if unadjusted. AWB measures the prevalent color temperature and automatically adjusts the image so that whites really look white. This is best done in-camera, and the automatic version is usually better than a user-selected color temperature.

On some of the lower-priced digital cameras, there are also options that allow you to set the color saturation or even make special effects in-camera. There are no circumstances under which I have ever found it useful or helpful to use these features. Given that your computer may cost $1000 or more and your image manipulation software $500 or more, it is unreasonable to ask that a camera, whose price is less than half that of the computer and software together, should have built-in chip-based software that is better equipped than the desktop combination.

The same goes for the gimmicky monochrome and most especially the sepia modes that some cameras have. It might be quicker to perform such manipulations in-camera, but if you want to try out a sepia version, leave it to your computer's manipulation software. That way, if you decide that you actually prefer the image in color or want a color version, you can revert to the original image. If you capture the image in sepia on the camera, you are stuck with it.

As far as tips for shooting with digital cameras are concerned, the single best guideline on offer is that if there are people in the shot, use a flash. This is especially important when shooting outside in bright sunlight, to avoid harsh shadows on faces.

Below *In-camera sharpening may make an image look good, and has the benefit of occurring before compression, but no sharpening and no compression is better still.*

SOFT

UNSHARPENED

SLIGHTLY SHARPENED

AUTO WHITE BALANCE

TUNGSTEN LIGHT SETTING

DAYLIGHT SETTING

FLUORESCENT LIGHT SETTING

STRONG SHARPENING

AUTO SHARPENING

Above *These four shots were taken with the camera's white balance function set for a different kind of lighting in each case.*

scanning

The concept of scanning is a simple one. You are effectively taking a digital picture of an object with your scanner. In practice, this means that one of two types of images can be input: reflective or transmissive. The latter refers to anything that you normally view by shining light through it (transparencies, acetates, or photographic slides). In contrast, reflective scanning is for everything that you view by shining a light onto it (that is, anything on paper or, in fact, anything that is more or less flat and can be positioned on the glass scanning plate). It is easy to be seduced by numbers when choosing a scanner for your desktop, but resolution is not the be-all and end-all. We will look at the specifics of different types of scanning equipment in chapter 6, but it is worth having a quick look at the information you get on the outside of a scanner box, before we enter into how best to scan artwork of any kind. (See *also pages 154 to 155*).

Right *Scan frames and negative film holders are adapters that facilitate the scanning of transparencies and negatives.*

Below *Scanners may look simple from the outside, but inside they are a complex mix of optics, electronics, and high-precision mechanics.*

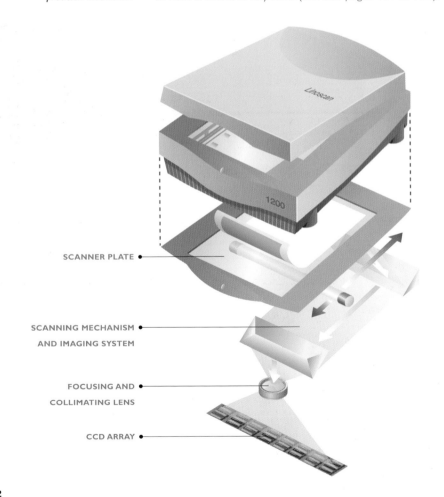

SCANNER PLATE ●

SCANNING MECHANISM ●
AND IMAGING SYSTEM

FOCUSING AND ●
COLLIMATING LENS

CCD ARRAY ●

scanner quality
Rather than simply taking an instant snapshot of an object, scanners build up a picture of it stripe by stripe. Mechanical considerations, such as how smoothly and accurately the scanning head is moved along the subject to be scanned, can make a considerable difference. The only thing on the outside of a scanner box that is likely to give you an indication as to the quality of the mechanics, and, for that matter, the optics that do the scanning, is the price tag. You do get what you pay for.

resolution
The resolution specifications will usually list two figures: optical and interpolated resolution. Optical resolution is physical resolution at which a scanner can capture an image. It will be the smaller number of the two and is the figure on which you should base your comparisons.

dynamic range
Dynamic range indicates how well a scanner can deal with contrast, including highlight and shadow detail (*see pages 124 to 125*).

bit depth

This is the ability of the scanner to perceive and interpret an image's color information, which is stored in bits (for a more detailed explanation, see pages 18 to 19).

firmware

More recent scanner models feature firmware built-in image improvement software that uses hardware and software to remove damage. This is particularly useful with photographic subjects. Firmware is highly effective, but adds a fair percentage to the purchase price.

software

You may have a top-of-the-line image manipulation package on your computer, but that does not reduce your need for a controllable scanning interface. The better the image when it goes into the computer in the first place, the less time you will have to spend tidying it up before you can concentrate on the creative side of fulfilling what you intend to do with it.

Above and left *Software (such as these examples that come bundled with Canon and Umax scanners) is available for both flatbed and film scanners, and enables parameters such as resolution (pixels per inch) and color bit depth to be set.*

dynamic range

There is a logarithmic scale (i.e., the numbers represent ten to the power of that number) that runs from 0 to about 4, and is the difference between a true white and a true black. Generally speaking, the greater the dynamic range of the scanner, the more shades of color it can pick up in the lightest and darkest areas of a scanned image. A 24-bit scanner might have a dynamic range of about 2.4, while only the best drum scanners can ever approach a dynamic range of 4. A high quality 35mm transparency may need a scanner with a dynamic range of 3.2 that is capable of distinguishing between 1,500 steps from white to black. A photographic print could be scanned by a scanner with a range of just 2.5 or 316 steps.

color and contrast

If you work with scanners that do not have such a broad dynamic range, you are bound to lose some detail, particularly in areas of highlight and shadow, and especially when scanning photographs that have too much contrast. Artwork (i.e., not a continuous-tone photograph) might be less demanding, though you may still encounter difficulties when scanning subtle color changes, especially at extremes of light or dark parts of the image.

The dynamic range and the number of bits in the analog to digital conversion, as well as the color depth of a scanner, all make a huge difference to how much color and contrast information you get in an image. It is possible to make a digital image look better with a manipulation program, but you cannot add more "real" information to it after scanning. Even though it is possible, for example, to add blades of grass to a scene where the

Below *These three shots show a 35mm slide scanned at (from bottom left to top right) 300ppi, 680ppi, and 2,720ppi in 24-bit color. At lower resolutions, less digital information is captured by the scanner, resulting in an image with less color depth.*

2,720PPI

680PPI

300PPI

resolution or color depth had obscured the originals, it would be easier to make sure that all the available information was captured when the image was shot.

aim high

Choosing a scanner with the appropriate dynamic range and color depth will allow you to capture as much as you need. The danger in not choosing an appropriate scanner may not be obvious when you get an image onto your computer, but it shows when you prepare it for output. Blocked up colors, difficulties with balancing contrast, and an apparent loss of image detail that cannot be explained by a lack of resolution are all features of an image scanned by a machine with a low dynamic range.

You might ask why it is necessary to have all this information (for example, a 42-bit color depth and a high dynamic range) when you are only likely to be using 24-bit color in your image manipulation program. The answer is that virtually any adjustment you make in brightness, contrast, or color will cause some detail to be lost. If you are losing bits of information from a 42-bit scan, you will still have more than enough color information to achieve a naturalistic looking picture. If you start with the 24-bit minimum, anything that you throw away will, in turn, mean a decline in image quality.

In the real world—where budgets are not unlimited—it is best to buy the scanner that offers the best bit depth that you can afford. Often 36-bit color scanners are very reasonably priced while 42-bit are much more expensive. Such machines can only be justified where optimal reproduction is essential rather than desirable.

Postscript (EPS) format files permit a maximum of 256 levels. It is worth considering this if EPS is ultimately to be the principal form of output.

Below *These three shots show the same sequence as opposite, but scanned in at 36-bit color.*

2720PPI

680PPI

300PPI

the nyquist frequency & scanning resolution

The Nyquist Frequency is the maximum frequency (that is, resolution in terms of lines per inch) that can be sampled by a scanner or a digital camera. The Nyquist Frequency of any digital sampling device is half the sampling rate of the device. In other words, if your scanner has an optical resolution of 600 pixels per inch (ppi), the maximum amount of detail it can capture is 300 lines per inch (lpi). These figures relate to horizontal or vertical lines. Diagonal lines need to be significantly thicker than 1/300 inch to be accurately scanned. If you do not boost the scanning level in this way, there will be a large risk of lines dropping out, i.e., disappearing or doubling up.

avoiding distortion

For dot screen patterns, if you are trying to scan from printed materials like newspapers, a kind of interference pattern known as moiré is likely to appear if the optical resolution of the scanner is not high enough to cope. The scanner driver (the specific software driver for your scanner) may have a "descreen" function. This is just an adjustable softening program that obliterates detail in return for losing the moiré.

If you try to apply Nyquist when scanning high-resolution photographs as opposed to simple line art, matters become more complicated. In order to be able to scan a slide, such that you can be sure of having captured every grain of dye within it, you would need to scan it in at perhaps three times the resolution of the film. If you had a very good, fine grain, color slide film with between six and twelve million blobs of dye in it, you would need to capture at least twelve to twenty-four million pixels to have a chance of capturing the grain sharply and avoiding blocking. Ironically, if you scan the image at a much lower resolution, the problem does not occur. To get twenty-four million pixels in the digital image, you need 4,000ppi scanning. And that is 4,000ppi optical, not interpolated, resolution.

Apart from the ultimate size of the image, the other aspect of determining the correct scanning resolution is the multiple needed between scanning an image and outputting it. As far as on-screen work goes, that is quite simple. With an output of 72ppi, if you get patterning when you preview an image, you need to boost the resolution. If there is no patterning, it will be fine. For output to an inkjet printer, the dithering (the process of splitting pixels into a number of different dots) that the printers use will often overcome any screening issues. For half toning or output to a CMYK printing press, special care needs to be taken, and you must ensure that there is no screen visible at all or the results will be awful.

Below *Lower scanning resolutions means that fine line images have less detail and more aberrations.*

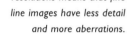

50ppi

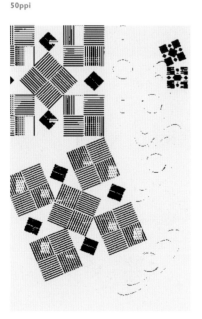

100ppi

150ppi

300ppi

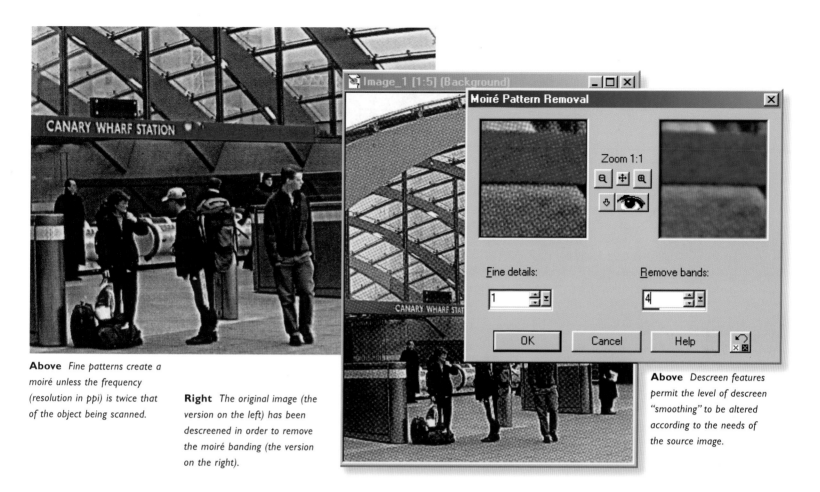

Above *Fine patterns create a moiré unless the frequency (resolution in ppi) is twice that of the object being scanned.*

Right *The original image (the version on the left) has been descreened in order to remove the moiré banding (the version on the right).*

Above *Descreen features permit the level of descreen "smoothing" to be altered according to the needs of the source image.*

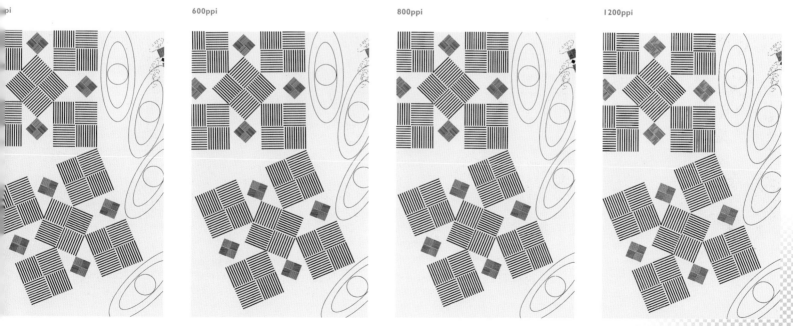

600ppi 800ppi 1200ppi

twain compliance

TWAIN is a confused interpretation of the saying "East is East and West is West and ne'er the twain shall meet." In this case, East is the hardware driver, and West is the image manipulation software. The bit that sits between them is the Data Source Manager, or TWAIN. Given that the word "twain" is Old English for two (or a pair), you have to wonder why they did not call it DSM and be done with it.

Nonetheless, nearly all scanners come with a TWAIN driver, which makes them compatible with any TWAIN-supporting software (nowadays, this is most of them). If your software is not TWAIN-supporting, all you need is any compatible program that will enable you to transfer the scanned data into a format that your software can read.

scanning speed

There are a number of factors determining how quickly you can get images into your computer. As well as the resolution and image size, there is also the speed of your processor, the amount of memory that you have allocated to the program inputting the image, and also the means by which your computer is connected to the scanner. Processor speed and memory requirements are covered in more detail in chapter 6.

In terms of the connection, there are three basic choices: USB (Universal Serial Bus), SCSI (Small Computer System Interface), and FireWire. USB is, as the first word in its name suggests, the most prevalent. The Serial refers to the fact that the data is sent along a single set of wires in sequence, and the Bus refers to the section of hardware in the computer that communicates with input/output devices such as scanners. USB connections can transfer up to twelve million bits of data per second

Right *TWAIN-compliant devices can communicate with both the hardware and the computer software, and act as the go-between for the scanner and Photoshop in this case.*

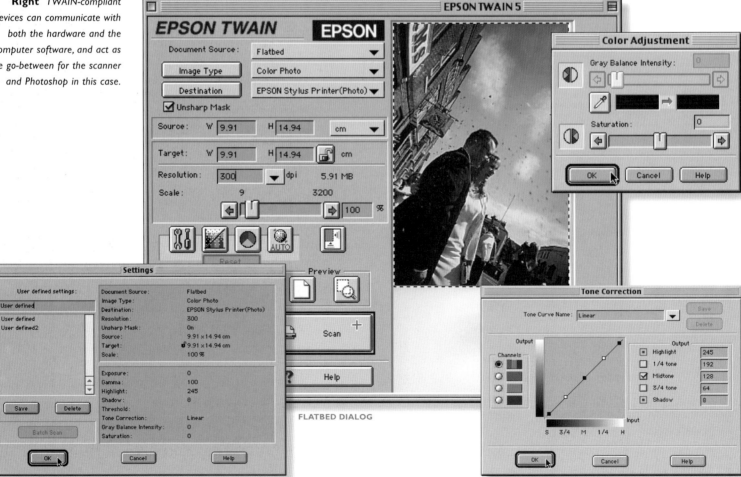

FLATBED DIALOG

(Mbs) or 1.5 megabytes. Unlike USB, SCSI (pronounced Scuzzy) is a parallel interface. There are in fact nine different SCSI types with transfer rates from 4Mbs for SCSI1 and SCSI2 to 80Mbs (10Mb per second) for Wide Ultra 2 SCSI. To make things even more fun, not all SCSI cards are compatible with all flavors of SCSI device.

FireWire is an Apple-computer-developed technology (it is also known as i.link by Sony and IEEE1394 by almost everyone else). Like USB (and unlike SCSI), FireWire allows devices that are attached to it to be hot swapped, i.e., plugged in or pulled out while the computer is on (see page 160).

FireWire allows for data throughput of up to 400Mbs (50Mb per second). Now this might seem to be gilding the lily since no scanner is likely to deliver 50Mb per second of data, however large the image. The key is not speeding things up, but making sure that nothing in the process is likely to slow them down.

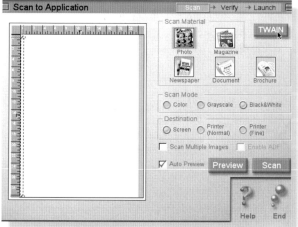

SCANNER INTERFACE SOFTWARE

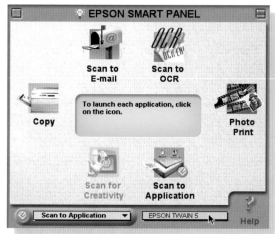

SCANNER INTERFACE SOFTWARE

Ice³

One of the latest additions to image scanning is the ICE³ system. It looks at dust spots, scratches, and image exposure, and tries to resolve them on the fly (i.e., as the image is being scanned in). The manufacturers even claim it can sort out slides that have had coffee spilled on them. That last one is a moot point, but the truth of the matter is that unlike many digital camera image improvement algorithms, this one really does seem to work.

SCANNER ICE INTERFACE

Left *ICE stands for image correction and enhancement. It does exactly what it says.*

Right *Before and after application of the magic of ICE³.*

Below *GEM reduces the visibility of grain.*

SCANNER ICE INTERFACE

ORIGINAL (FULL SCREEN IN CLOSEUP) AND CORRECTED IMAGE

video image grabbing

Sometimes the image or images you want are in front of your face—on a screen. Whether this is a computer monitor or a television screen, you may want to be able to access the information contained on the screen. In other words, grab it. There are three sources for grabs: analog video, Web sites, and screen. The last two are effectively identical in terms of how you capture them, but we'll look at the video grab first.

In days gone by, people used to set up film cameras, point them at their television screens, and then digitize that image. To say that this was a less than satisfactory solution is an understatement. To attempt to copy moving images was an exercise in futility. A maximum shutter speed of one-fifteenth of a second is required to avoid banding (black diagonal swathes on the picture) and you need to capture twenty-five frames a second. The sums do not add up. Ironically, doing it in reverse (from cine to video) is equally problematic and goes partway to explaining why, in old black-and-white movies, people seem to wave frantically like excited children and walk at fifteen miles per hour. We will cover moving image capture from film a little later on in this section.

Whatever the software solution you use to get images from the video world to your computer, you need a specialist accessory. But which one? There is a wide range of devices whose functions include the simple ability to convert images to digital, being able to render large sequences of images in real time, and turning your computer into a television. From a workflow point of view, this last solution is probably not a very good idea. A lot of the consumer products give you limited resolution possibilities (352 x 288 pixels, also known as Common Image Format), mainly due to the limitations of data transfer through the port into the computer. The lower-priced units operate on USB and that limits the speed at which data can be pumped in. The majority of the newer devices on the market are

Below *Video tends to introduce interference that can be reduced using deinterlacing filters such as the one found in Media100's Cleaner.*

VIDEO CAPTURE

VIDEO CAPTURE AFTER DEINTERLACING

also TWAIN-compliant so images can be brought into image processing applications without having to go through some tortuous import process.

The Common Image Format (CIF) resolution mentioned above (352 x 288) gives plenty of resolution in terms of the size of the image on a 640 x 480-pixel (known as VGA standard) monitor, taking up slightly more than half the area of the screen. If the images are for a Web movie, it may even be too much in terms of the file size.

It is worth stating at this point that the quality may not be fantastic, but speed of download, rather than quality, is likely to be the key factor at the output stage. For a larger image, a device that works for laptops from a PCMCIA slot will be needed, or for a desktop machine a FireWire connecting device will be needed to get enough data from the video to the computer. In either case, what you want to do is get the movie from its analog state into one of the many formats that you can use with your video editing package.

Left *Frame grabbers (such as the Formac Studio, shown here) enable a range of video sources to be digitized and the digital output "grabbed" as still frames or continuous video.*

Left *Each minute of video is made up of thousands of still images. Frame-grabbing software allows you to select exactly the right one for your still image purposes.*

00:10

screen- and webgrabs

We have already looked at the concept of analog to digital conversion, but for most monitors and video displays, the opposite needs to be achieved. While LCD Thin Film Transistor (TFT) screens allow direct digital display, all cathode ray tube (CRT) monitors use voltage (i.e., analog) differences to display each dot as black, white, or any point and color in between. Luckily, though, when you want to capture an image from your screen, the computer can do it digitally, before the image has been converted to an analog for monitor display.

Given that for any image to be displayed on your screen it has already been laid out in the computer's memory, all you need to do is copy that bit of memory and save it to a file. Both Macs and PCs do this at the press of a couple of buttons. The size of the image (in terms of the number of pixels) depends on the resolution setting you have established for your monitor, the size of the file on that resolution, and the number of colors you have displayed on your screen.

screen resolution

If you are going to be using the screengrab for Web work, or indeed if you are capturing from a Web page, there is no need to have 24-bit color (millions of colors). While the file sizes are not huge (424Kb for a 1,024 × 768 screengrab at millions of colors), the savings can be in the order of more than 85% (52Kb for 256 color 640 × 480 screengrab). When you are optimizing screengrabs for screen use, there are two main things to consider: the physical size that your screen or Webgrab will be shown at, and the likely size of screen it will be viewed on. Of

Right *Screengrabs (direct copies from video memory of what is on screen) can be performed by utilities within the operating system.*

Below *Operating systems and many graphics utilities permit the "collection" of a screengrab using a (usually user-defined) key or combination of keys.*

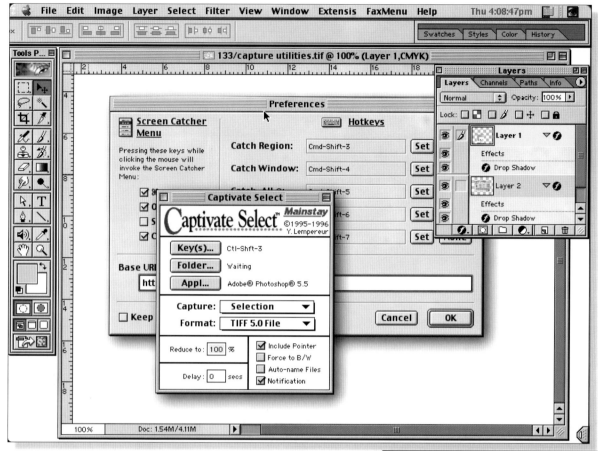

Left *You can capture a screen as an individual image or capture the elements separately and combine them more aesthetically at a later stage in Photoshop. The Help menus of both Windows and Mac OS provide information on the various methods for creating screengrabs.*

Left *With utilities such as Screen Catcher and Captivate Select you have the choice to capture a folder either with or without its enclosing box. The Windows-only PaintShop Pro has an excellent screen capture feature that permits either single or multiple screen grabs, full screen, or selective.*

the eight Web sites stored in my favorites folder, half of them will not show the whole screen at 640 x 480-pixel screen resolution. So while the trend is toward higher screen resolutions, bear in mind that anything you put up as a "whole screen" screengrab should be able to be viewed by the user without scrolling up and down, or forward and backward. You should find that a practical limit of 320 x 240 is a reasonable compromise of quality and usability.

Outputting screengrabs to paper is slightly more demanding, but not nearly as difficult as many would have you believe. The crucial element is not to worry about resolution, because the whole point of screengrabs is that they can be rough and ready. The one issue that does merit concern is how to stop the inevitable gray boxes in your image from turning pink. This problem is covered in Color Setup (see pages 38 to 39).

Finally, if you want your screengrab to show an arrow (your cursor in many applications), you need an additional application to allow you to do it (see chapter 7). If you use the computer's built-in screengrabbing software, not only will you be unable to capture the cursor in the form that you want, but you may be unable to capture certain commands on-screen, since the simple act of pressing the screengrabbing button(s) will change what actually appears on the screen.

digital video

If you thought that digital imaging as a whole was made up of a series of "square peg in a round hole" conflicts, you will love digital video. The good news is that it is very easy to input digital video onto your computer. Whether it is a very low-resolution image from a still picture camera, or a hard-drive-sapping high-resolution input from a broadcast-quality digital camcorder, there are very many different ways to get images already in a digital form onto your computer, for example, by using the Formac Studio shown on page 131.

Below *Digital video need not consist of live-motion images; it can be composed of individual frames as in this sequence from Brian Taylor's "Rustboy," a movie work in progress.*

It would be a relatively simple affair to use the 50,000-word allocation of this book to review the different compression, color, and streaming formats available to the digital videographer. But while it is possible to get involved with digital imaging in every other way using simply an up-to-date PC or Mac, to get serious about video, you need a state-of-the-art computer. Why? To misquote the film director Jean-Luc Godard, "digital imaging is memory- and storage-intensive, digital video is memory- and storage- intensive 29.97 times per second." With image resolutions equal to some still digital cameras, the digital camcorder's storage requirements on disk space work in hundreds of

megabytes for even the most unremarkable of sequences. If you are going for high-quality output and start adding multilayered stereo soundtracks, then even if the output is going to be in the form of a 500Kb QuickTime Movie, you may end up with a folder containing about a gigabyte's worth of files before you can compress it down to the bare bones for ease of use.

curbing size

The simple rule of all digital imaging input is true to the power of three for digital video. Only input the level of resolution that you need. It may take longer to acquire and save in that resolution/audio quality level, but once

saved, your new original will be much smaller and thus quicker to perform any kind of editing on. Ignore this advice, and you will soon find that your brand-new PC or Mac will simply not be able to cope. Since the advent of reasonably priced nonlinear editors (*see chapter 7*), you can perform some quite professional-looking manipulations, edits, transitions, and special effects.

Once again, keep an eye on the output. There is no need to have your characters taking five seconds to slip smoothly into place, if you are going to be outputting to the Web. Your letters will leap like demented beings as compression and frame sampling eliminate any of the smoothness from the original movie.

Editing digital video

Before the advent of consumer digital camcorders and PC nonlinear editors (NLEs), video editing was a trying affair. It could be difficult to precisely blend image and sound together. Effects work was either relatively basic or heinously expensive, and not available to anyone but the largest studios. The whole process was lengthy and tended to be confined to professional studio setups with a great deal of expensive equipment, but the digital revolution has changed this. Nowadays, there are some incredibly powerful editing packages that cost less than a cinematographic film camera's lens. When using these packages, the important thing is to gather what you need before you begin working on the job— the alternative is time-consuming. Also, irrespective of the kind of movie you are making, treat it like a proper feature film. How is this achieved? Storyboard it. By knowing in your own mind (or preferably having written down or saved somewhere) a list of which elements will combine to make a given part of the movie, you will be able to incorporate all the elements together in a logical, and hopefully aesthetically pleasing, manner. Now all you need to worry about is how big your hard drive is.

from digital resources

One of the easiest methods of creating digital images is to combine or adapt existing digital images from other artists. This is not the outright thieving that it sounds. The digital artist and designer can choose from a plethora of imaging material, which is available in two flavors: royalty-free and copyright-free. The latter (often described as free clip art) means that you can do anything you want to the image, use it where you want,

and not have to pay for the privilege or even acknowledge the original maker of the image. Royalty-free is an entirely different kettle of fish. You can use the image without paying royalties, but there are restrictions on how you can use the image and what you can do with it. This is an important distinction, as anyone who has been charged with breach of copyright will be able to tell you. It should go without saying that unless an image is either copyright-free or royalty-free, you should not be using it without the express advance permission of the maker and/or copyright holder and, in all

512 X 768   1024 X 1536

likelihood, payment as well. The fact that you have a digital image on your hard drive, does not mean you can use it. If there are no details attached to it (Best Practice, see page 142), all the more reason to be wary of using such an image.

cd or seedy quality?

There are two main avenues for sourcing royalty- or copyright-free images: CD-ROMS, or direct from the Internet. The latter method might take a little longer to download an image to your computer, but the advantage is that it is often a speedier way of viewing the images in the first place.

When considering using digital images that have been created by someone else, do not treat their input with any less organization than you would when inputting images of your own. Just because something is on a CD with a glossy contact sheet does not mean the images are necessarily of high enough quality for your purpose. It might be more convenient to get six hundred and fifty images on a CD-ROM than to get sixty, but the fact that the former have been compressed significantly may make them less than useful for the purposes you need if quality heads your agenda. The same caveat applies to images downloaded from the Internet, probably to an even greater extent, since file sizes may well be measured in hundreds of kilobytes, not megabytes. The images have not been compressed to improve them in terms of quality, only to shorten the download time by a significant factor (see chapter 8).

Internet downloading of images is only of real use when speed is of the essence. Browsing on the Internet, collecting a series of lower-resolution images, and being able to send an email for picture approval is a convenient feature of some of the more useful image agency Web sites. Once approval has been gained for the usage, you can get the images in a more appropriate format, normally by the next day.

Finally, if something is completely free, and an image works out at the same price as a soft drink, it is probably not going to be the highest quality available.

Left For pictures scanned onto a disk in Kodak's Photo CD (PCD) format, you get to choose from a selection of resolutions. These will determine the size at which an image can be displayed. Three options are shown here, along with their relative sizes of display.

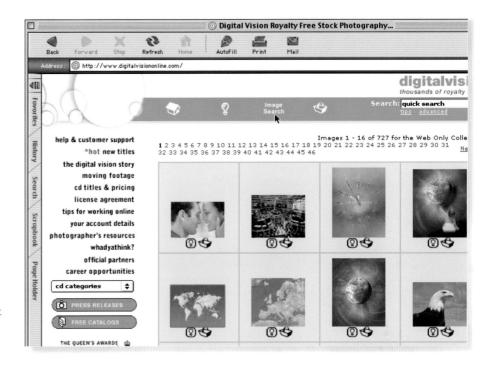

Above On-line picture agencies provide a quick and effective method of selecting high-quality photographic images.

Clip art

The term clip art covers any graphic devices from simple line art through to photo-quality images. In general the term is used to describe graphics designed for use in embellishing desktop publishing documents (such as newsletters or party invitations). As already mentioned, the quality can be variable and there may be restrictions on use; for example, some libraries permit only noncommercial or "private" use.

creation from scratch

Sometimes the image you want does not exist on film, print, a Web site, or on a CD-ROM, and the only option is to create it yourself. You may even just *want* to create it. Assuming you have the necessary software (*see chapter 7*), you can create just about anything—from a diagram to a short animation, an illustration, or even a cartoon movie. All this is possible. The two impediments are time and, of course, talent.

Glossing over the latter concept—which is only limited by the extent of your creativity and your experience of using digital imaging techniques to turn your ideas into a reality—the main enemy is time or, more specifically, impatience. Given the right tools, you can create anything. Whether or not you do it in an organized fashion, though, will determine whether you get to make any of it

work. The key element is to ensure that whatever you experiment with, you have a file that shows the effect. Learning digital imaging is, to an extent, trial and error, but it is an awful lot easier to do something if you have got a copy of it. This is where layers (particularly but not exclusively) in image manipulation programs like Photoshop come in handy. You can impose an effect or add an extra element to anything you have done in Photoshop. By doing it as a layer rather than applying an effect to the original image or frame of an animation, you always have the option of turning that effect off or of trying several different effects in different combinations. Best practice for file saving and naming conventions will be covered in detail later in this chapter.

still artwork

The easiest form of digital image is still artwork. At its simplest this is a drawing. Even word processing packages contain relatively sophisticated line drawing and color filling packages, but the essential gadget is not the vector drawing software (*see chapter 7*) but what you draw with. Take a pen and a piece of paper and try to draw three freehand straight lines applying different pressures to get a different thickness. Now draw a freehand circle, a square, and then some freehand crosshatched shading

Below *Paintshop Pro (a Windows-only product) is a comprehensive image editor that is equally useful for creating new artwork, image manipulation, and Web animations.*

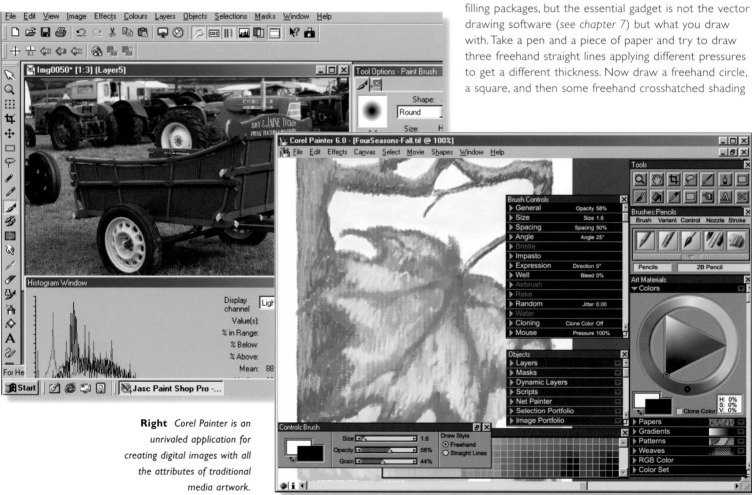

Right *Corel Painter is an unrivaled application for creating digital images with all the attributes of traditional media artwork.*

in your shapes, and sign the piece of paper with your normal signature. Now you can judge whether or not you have any skills as a draftsperson.

Next get a good-sized baking potato, push a pen through it an inch away from one of the ends, and hold it so the point of the pen is under the potato, the top of the pen is held between your index and middle fingers, and the rest of the potato, held under your palm. Try doing the same lines, shapes, shading, and signature as you did freehand with the pen alone. Which set looks better? (Clue: it is unlikely to be the starch-stained page.)

Having carried out this simple test, you can now ask yourself whether a mouse is really the easiest tool to use for drawing. The degrees of specification in drawing applications are covered on pages 174 to 175, but no matter how primitive the stylus or advanced the mouse, for artwork creation, you need a pen and tablet.

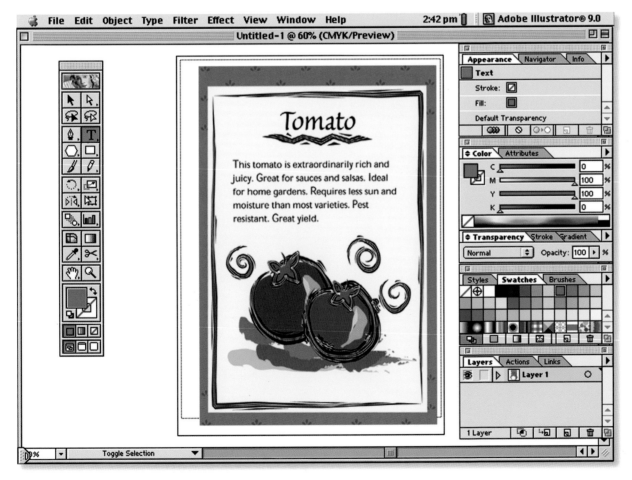

Above *Deneba's Canvas seamlessly integrates pixel-based image editing tools with those normally found in vector-based applications to deliver a range of powerful—and sometimes unique—features.*

Left *From the same stable as Photoshop, Illustrator is an effective tool for the creation of vector-based graphics. A similar interface to Photoshop helps users to exploit both applications, where needed, in the creation of their imagery.*

animations

Animation can be time-consuming. You simply have to sit through the production credits shown at the end of *The Simpsons* to see just how many people are needed, and by extension how much time and effort is involved, to produce a single episode.

Even animation at its most basic, say a baton that twirls around in the air as if tossed by an invisible majorette, or a colored spiral that revolves infinitely, will need about twenty-four pictures to create a realistic sense of movement and to ensure that the sequence finishes just before its starting point. This latter requirement is essential for continuous looping Web animations. However, the word "realistic" is not cast in stone; you may deliberately want it to have jerky movements to emphasize the fact it is an animation. There are four basic ways you can create animations:

🖱 from a single image that you apply effects to in an animation software package;

🖱 from a pair of images that you form a transition between, known as morphing;

🖱 from a collection of some/many/hundreds of images that you glue together (flicker-card style);

🖱 or a combination of any of the above methods.

morphing

The morph takes a little bit of the hard work away from you by using software to create a smooth transition from one point to another. You can do the same morph with the same settings only the other way around and

Below *By placing "common points" in completely the wrong places you can produce hideously distorting morphs as in this 17-frame sequence.*

then glue the two together to have your continuous animation, but as with every other aspect of digital imaging, the more detail and subtlety you add to something, the bigger the file will be, and the slower it will run. The longer the pause between frames, the greater the risk of removing all the traces of invisible transition that you have tried so hard to create. The other issue with morphing is that it is not as simple as telling the software to morph. You need to allocate key points so the software knows which bit is turning into another bit. This can be time-consuming in itself and, if you pair up the wrong before and after points, there can be unintentionally hilarious bits, especially if you are trying to morph one person's face into another. Though morphing software is relatively simple to use, time spent in the detailing will be amply repaid in the results.

animation software

Using a custom-made animation package should ideally combine the best of the still-image manipulation package with the relative simplicity of the Morpher package. Unfortunately, as far as simplicity is concerned, this is no more the case with animation programs than it is with word processing programs. However, animation software is nonetheless a quicker and much easier route than the manual manipulation of individual images, if you want to create an unbroken animation sequence. Many animation packages—including those designed for Web graphics, such as LiveMotion, Flash, or Fireworks—include "tweening" commands that can automatically (but very effectively) create intermediate animation frames between existing frames. The result can be a very effective animation based on a lesser number of original "reference" frames.

BEST PRACTICE
saving

When you have input your image or sequence, one of the key elements of getting the most out of it is to ensure that you save it in the right place, at the right size, and with the right information. Like the first paragraph of a good story in a newspaper, your file name and location should be able to tell you the who, what, where, when, why, and how of any given image.

🖱 Folder locations should be organized in a nested fashion with the project name containing sufficient information for you to find it easily in the future. While the project is in progress, it is a good idea to have an alias or shortcut to the folder on the desktop. This saves untold precious seconds of trawling through folders— seconds that can easily add up to minutes and hours.

🖱 Within the top level of the folder, make a Read-Me File detailing the brief, if any; even if it is just for yourself, it is still a good idea to have a description of what you are trying to do with each file. It may seem to be a case of overengineering, but if you have a powerful search engine on your computer you can, in the future, find any of the images easily merely by searching file contents for a keyword.

🖱 Nested inside this folder, you can have a file for Original Input for Unadulterated Original Images, so you can always go back and try again. It is quicker to do an extra initial saving stage at the moment of input than to try to find an original. Copyright information, if the image was created by or sourced from someone else, should also be included in this folder. This also helps to ensure that copyright—an area often overlooked by computer graphics artists in a rush—is sorted out.

🖱 Naming protocols. When it comes to naming your files, you may find that there is insufficient room allowed in the name of the file for all the information you want to note. Simply create a folder with the most important part of the name as its name, and put the rest of the info in the file names. Incidentally, do not use forward slashes to separate pieces of information in a file name. If you use a Web package for your email, you may find that only the characters after the final forward slash appear at the other end when you email it. Forward slashes can also

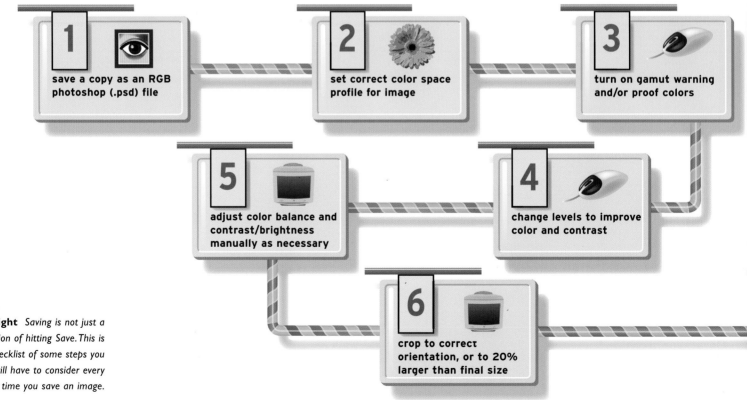

1 save a copy as an RGB photoshop (.psd) file

2 set correct color space profile for image

3 turn on gamut warning and/or proof colors

5 adjust color balance and contrast/brightness manually as necessary

4 change levels to improve color and contrast

6 crop to correct orientation, or to 20% larger than final size

Right *Saving is not just a question of hitting Save. This is a checklist of some steps you will have to consider every time you save an image.*

142

cause problems for file names on PCs. Whether you work on Mac or PC, always be sure your file names bear the correct suffix for whichever file format you have saved in. Otherwise, the next person who tries to open the file may not know which program to open it in.

🖐 Color space (the range of colors in an image that can be defined) is important (see *pages 22 to 23*). If you use a restrictive color space like Indexed for work in progress, you could be throwing away vital detail. Conversely, if the image is finished, save it in its most restricted applicable mode (GIF or JPEG at the appropriate level) to keep file sizes down to a transmittable minimum. For work in progress, save the file in native application format (PSD for Photoshop to retain layer information). For completed high-end still images, save the file in uncompressed TIFF mode in the appropriate color space (RGB or CMYK).

Once you have saved a project, or even if you are in the middle of a particularly complex one, make a backup on a different disk from your main hard drive. Although hard drive failures are rare, this fact will be of small comfort to you if disk failure happens at, or near, the end of a complex, time-consuming project.

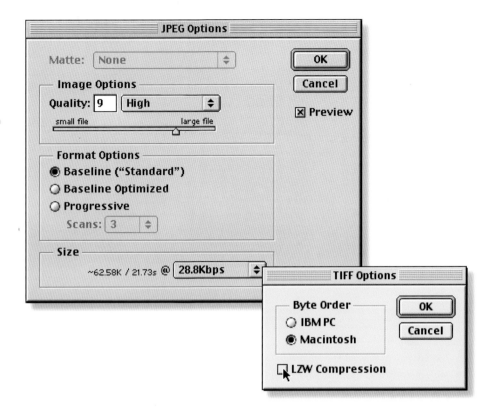

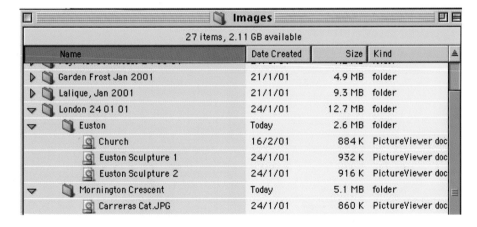

Left *Saving images in a hierarchical form aids identification and retrieval later.*

Above *Many file formats require additional parameters to be set, such as the quality and download options. The options presented when saving a JPEG file are discussed on page 192.*

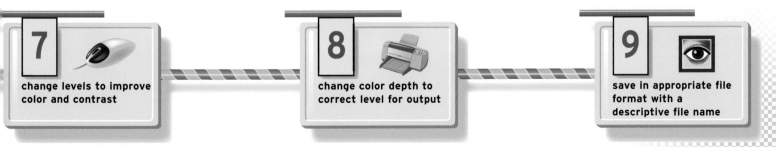

7 change levels to improve color and contrast

8 change color depth to correct level for output

9 save in appropriate file format with a descriptive file name

BEST PRACTICE

scanning from flat artwork

Before you start scanning, always check the original for dust or any marks that can be cleaned off. Check the glass on the scanner and see that it too is clear of dust or marks. You can tidy up in a manipulation package, but it is quicker and easier to do it before scanning.

🖱 Position the original image on the scanner. All flatbed scanners have an origin point from which the scanning area starts. It also allows you to be absolutely parallel to the scanning head, and perpendicular to its movement. Doing this means that any truly vertical or horizontal lines will be captured most sharply. Line artwork needs to be scanned at a higher resolution: an optical resolution of 600ppi can capture a maximum of 300lpi (Nyquist Frequency, *see pages 126 to 127*). Scan with your target output resolution in mind, and twice that resolution if you plan to manipulate your image heavily. It is best to get the orientation of the image correct at the scanning stage. Having to make corrections to orientation after scanning means losing precious image detail. If a scanner comes with masks that

leave a space in the center of the scanner, use them, as they indicate where the scanner's optics are most effective.

🖱 Check your settings. Ensure that you have selected the right level of scanning resolution and color depth for the purpose to which the image will be put. Mistakes here will haunt you all through the creation process.

🖱 Perform a prescan. Select the area of the image that will be subsequently scanned at high resolution. Cropping any unnecessary areas out of the frame at this stage will save you time on every subsequent adjustment you make by reducing the size of the final digital image. Check your size and resolution settings again. Is the newly cropped image going to be sufficiently large for your purposes? If not, increase the settings and make another estimate.

🖱 Image improvement. Open the Advanced, Expert, or Toolbox section of the scanning software, if it has one. Examine the histogram (the graphic representation of where, in the black-to-white spectrum, there is detail) to see whether it looks under- or overexposed. Can the histogram be stretched or contracted? If the image has

Below and right *This poster was scanned in four sections, with an overlap at the edges to make reconstruction easier. The separate images were recombined in Photoshop on an oversize canvas. Finally, the image was trimmed to create a clean edge.*

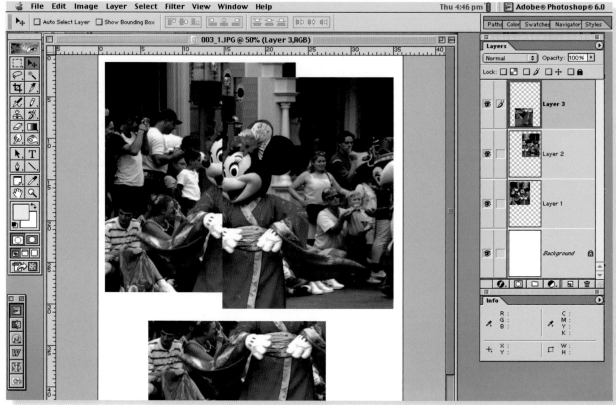

too much contrast and it looks as if either shadow or highlight detail will be lost, it might be worth doing a second scan using different black points and white points to capture that information. The two scans can be merged at a later stage to get the best out of the image.

🖱 Full scan. Place the scan in your manipulation package and save it as an uncompressed image. This is necessary even if you are eventually going to be outputting as a JPEG, or if there is the slightest chance that you will be carrying out any sharpening work, or major changes in color, saturation, or contrast.

scanning transparent media

The same rules apply when scanning transparent media as with flat artwork, though you will need a film scanner or a flatbed scanner with a transparency hood or transparency adapter. You have an added choice of scanning from negative or positive film. Color negatives cannot be corrected simply by inverting the image, unless you have set a white point from the edge of the negative by the sprocket holes (where the characteristic orange-red built-in filter pack is uncluttered by image detail).

Below *Powerful graphic images can be created directly from flat solid objects such as this leaf.*

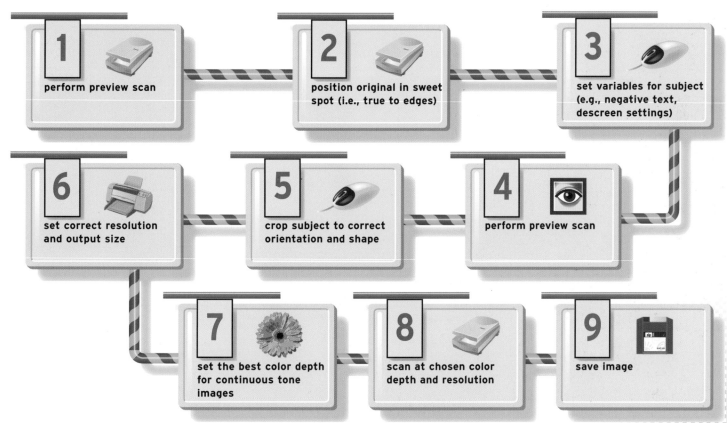

1 perform preview scan

2 position original in sweet spot (i.e., true to edges)

3 set variables for subject (e.g., negative text, descreen settings)

6 set correct resolution and output size

5 crop subject to correct orientation and shape

4 perform preview scan

7 set the best color depth for continuous tone images

8 scan at chosen color depth and resolution

9 save image

6 hardware

Having the wrong tools for the job doesn't make you a bad worker, but it can make you a significantly less effective one. In this chapter we will look at how you can put together a system that will mean that the limits of your imagination are the only barrier to your ability to produce stunning imagery.

computers / memory

Digital imaging cannot exist without a computer. Some manufacturers of digital cameras and printers may deny this, but when it comes to the hub through which digital information of any kind is routed, a computer is key. Your computer's ability to process images is dependent on three factors: processing speed, bus speed (the rate at which information travels around the inside of the computer), and available memory.

Before looking at these three factors in more detail, and even before approaching the perennial thorny issue of Mac versus PC, there is the problem of which type of computer to choose. It is great to be able to carry a laptop around, and if you are never in the same place for long, a laptop is an appropriate tool to have. But if you are based in an office, using a laptop is a waste of money. Laptops are not as fast, or as flexible, as desktop or minitower machines.

Below *It is worth spending time and money on the right machine for your purposes. For example, the flat screen, shown here, is invaluable when space is at a premium.*

mac versus pc running windows

The Mac is my preferred machine because it is organized more like my brain (i.e., I can be sloppy and still use it). That being said, PCs are not that much different these days, and it is the operating system (*see chapter 7*), rather than the hardware, that makes the big difference. You can, however, use PC software on a Mac with the appropriate emulator, and there are some fairly crude emulators for using Mac software on a PC. It is not an issue to get worked up about, though, and most of the software that you will want for digital imaging is available in one form or another for both types of machine.

Let us return to the first of the three criteria for digital imaging—processing speed. You might be wondering what difference there is between processing and processor speed. Chip speeds of 1GHz (1 gigahertz = 1,000,000,000 cycles per second) are all very well, but depending on the processor's architecture, that may or may not be a true reflection of the number of operations a chip can perform. Mac chips running at 500MHz are,

Above *Ensure that you have enough memory in your computer for your needs; the more memory you have, the faster your processing speed will be.*

Left *Apple's iBook provides an industry-leading specification in a package that is truly portable.*

broadly speaking, as quick at processing information as some PC chips that run twice that fast. Additional features in Mac processors (such as AltiVec in the G4 processor) make Macs especially efficient in handling graphics and movie applications, though performance in Office applications is a little slow.

The bus speed is also a crucial factor. RAM, or Random Access Memory, chips have a speed limit that is based on the bus speed. If your processor has to get information from the memory chips (which it will have to most of the time), the bus speed (currently 100 to 133MHz) will be a limiting factor, too.

But the biggest aid to faster digital image processing is memory—the more your computer has, the bigger the image you can manipulate, and the faster you can do it. Computer memory fluctuates in price. Take advantage of this, and put as much in as you can afford when the price drops. You also want as much video memory as possible; the more video RAM there is on your computer's video board, the faster things will happen on the screen.

Below *There are various image-capture accessories available to Mac and PC users. This digital video camera can output high-quality images directly to computer.*

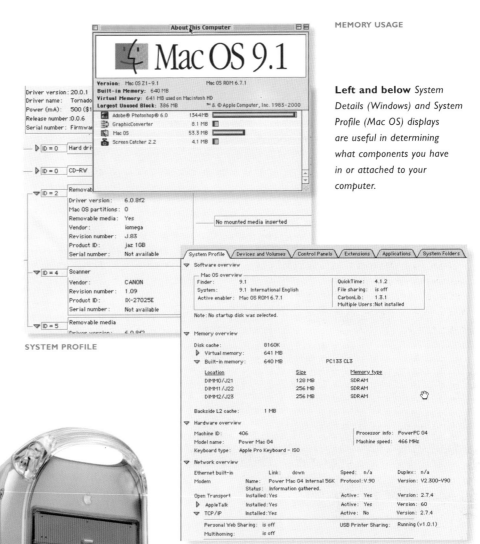

MEMORY USAGE

Left and below *System Details (Windows) and System Profile (Mac OS) displays are useful in determining what components you have in or attached to your computer.*

SYSTEM PROFILE

HARDWARE

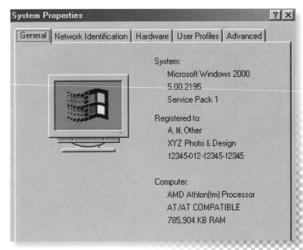

OPERATING SYSTEM DETAILS

monitors

Many computers come with a monitor when purchased. This monitor may or may not be worth having, at least as a main monitor. That may sound a little harsh, but when you can pay ten times more for one monitor than another, then there are obviously some differences to be taken into account. Those differences can best be defined in the following ways: type, size, flatness, resolution, frequency, and color calibration.

Given that you will spend virtually all your time looking at a monitor, and making value judgments about the quality of an image from it, it is fairly self-evident that getting one that most accurately displays your image is quite important.

There is also the not-so-minor issue of comfort. Any sufferer of RSI (Repetitive Strain Injury) will warn you against spending long periods of time in front of a computer, but irrespective of sensible advice, we will all put in an extended session now and again. If you use a poor-quality monitor, you may well find that you start to experience headaches or vision problems (see Frequency *below*), not to mention the fact that your images will not look as good as they otherwise could.

type

There are two basic types of monitor, flat panel and CRT (cathode ray tube). Flat panel (LCD) monitors have been used in laptops and are truly digital devices. CRT monitors are a development of the television but lack the chic appearance of their flat panel rivals. They are also heavier, consume more power, and generate more heat. However, they are far cheaper than flat panels.

size

It really does matter. If you are unable to show an image in sufficient detail, you have to enlarge it on screen. If all the pixels are not visible on screen at the same time, you will have to keep scrolling to look at or change to different parts of an image. Smaller monitors are limited in the information they can display at once and interface elements can sometimes be small. An absolute minimum size for graphic work is 17-inch CRT (15.4-inch flat panel). Better still, choose a 19-inch monitor, and if possible, get a 21- or 22-inch monitor.

resolution

If you have a three-megapixel image, it stands to reason that you need a monitor that can display three million pixels at the same time if you want to see the whole

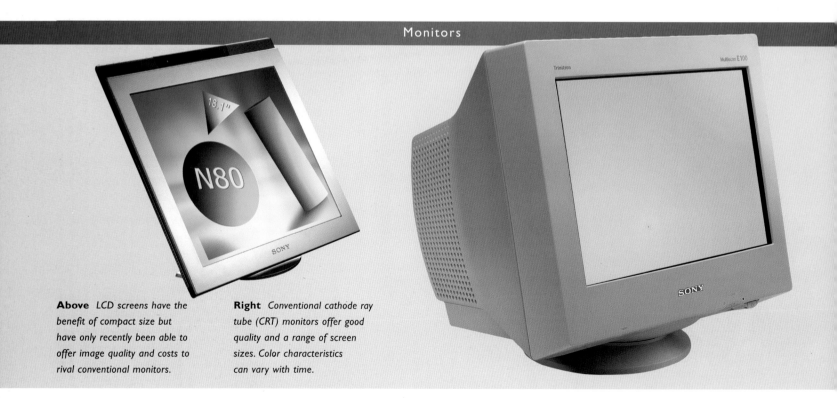

Monitors

Above *LCD screens have the benefit of compact size but have only recently been able to offer image quality and costs to rival conventional monitors.*

Right *Conventional cathode ray tube (CRT) monitors offer good quality and a range of screen sizes. Color characteristics can vary with time.*

image. But bear in mind that some Web sites will be illegible at that resolution because their type will be tiny on a small screen. You should find that a monitor with 1,800 × 1,200 resolution is ideal.

frequency
Monitors should tell you with what frequency they rebuild the image. 60Hz means sixty times per second, and depending on your tolerance, it may also mean headaches. 70Hz is a minimum frequency for some people not to see a flicker, 75 or 80Hz is better, and you

can get up to 120Hz if you are particularly sensitive to spotting screen flicker. Be warned that as the frequency goes up, the quality of monitor resolution may go down, and the may price creep up.

color calibration
Some monitors are fitted with hardware calibration—a small sensor that measures the output on screen of the colors of the monitor. This feature allows very precise judgments to be made by the color calibration software about how accurately images are being reproduced.

Below *Simple dialogs can help you set up your screen quickly and efficiently.*

Using two monitors

If your computer has the appropriate connections on its video output board and the necessary drivers, then you can use one monitor to display the image without being cluttered up by palettes, and the other monitor to show you the options. In the case of video editing, it is often useful to have two monitors to set up a "before and after" display. This saves you having to have two movies open on the same screen or flicking between one sequence and the other, which makes accurate comparison impossible.

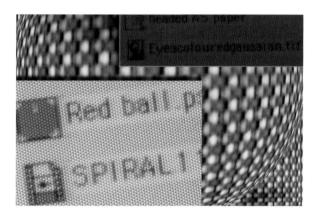
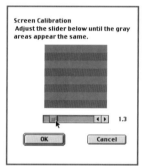

Above *Multimedia monitors feature built-in speakers that make them ideal for editing movies as well as image manipulation.*

Right *The blue casing and hood on this LaCie monitor ensure consistent lighting throughout the day. A hardware color calibrator is also available.*

scanners

We have looked at the various parameters of scanning from film (see chapter 5), from A/D conversion, bit depth, transfer method, resolution, and interpolation (see pages 14 to 20).

But what about the actual scanners themselves? Like cameras, scanners have an optical system that focuses the light from an object onto a sensor. Like digital cameras, the color and intensity of the light in a scanner are vital in determining the end quality of the image. But just as important are the physical rigidity of the scanner and the susceptibility of its electronic components to electronic interference or "noise." You are unlikely to see any mention of either of these elements on the presentation box that your scanner comes in, but you may well see their effects in the images that you create using the scanner.

As a general rule, it is a good idea not to position your scanner too near your monitor, or for that matter, near any transformer. This way you will cut down on the interference. Remember, your scan is initially just a series of voltages, and these can be affected by excessive electromagnetic radiation.

choosing a scanner for your needs

If you are going to be scanning exclusively from 35mm film images, your best option is to buy a dedicated film scanner. These vary greatly. The higher the dynamic range (see pages 124 to 125), the better the scanner.

If you need to scan from medium-format transparencies (these are 2.5 inches wide) you need a scanner that is capable of accepting images of this width. The larger the film format, the more expensive the scanner. With film scanners, the film is moved across a narrow gap between a light source and a sensing head. It is normally

Scanners

From slimline to specialist, scanners come in all flavors and have price tags to suit all pockets.

COMPACT
Though flatbed scanners necessarily have a large "footprint," modern models are particularly thin.

FLEXIBLE
Flatbed scanners are also available with larger scanning surfaces and can sometimes handle medium- or large-format transparencies.

SPECIALIST
For ultimate quality (particularly for smaller-format transparencies), dedicated film scanners are essential.

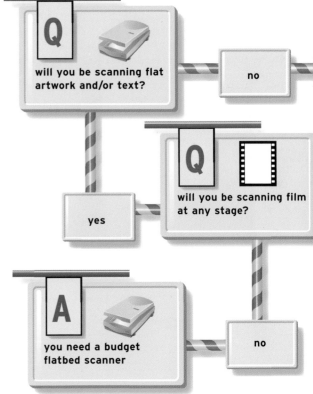

Q will you be scanning flat artwork and/or text?

no

yes

Q will you be scanning film at any stage?

no

A you need a budget flatbed scanner

gripped in a film strip holder, and the ability of these pieces of plastic to hold the film flat can make a considerable difference to the final quality of the image.

A typical budget scanner will have 24-bit color depth, which is adequate for most purposes. Professional models and film scanners may go up to 30, 36, or even 40 bits.

scanning large formats

If you are only working with prints or flat artwork you will need a flatbed scanner. These scanners use a system whereby a light tube is fixed to a line of scanning CCD (charged coupled device) elements (known as an array or raster) with a lightproof barrier between them. This moves across the image to be scanned in preset steps (whose size depends on the resolution selected). The light travels up through the glass and reflects from the scanned object down onto the sensor, which captures a horizontal line of information. Errors in the stepping of

the array's movement will show as horizontal strips, and any failings in individual cells of the CCD will show as vertical lines. General, or uncorrelated, noise will show as blobs. Good-quality scanners should be sturdy and sufficiently well built to avoid these problems.

If you are scanning flat artwork and transparencies, you will need a flatbed scanner with a transparency hood. For transparency (film) scans, turn off the light next to the scanning array and use the light in a hood above. The precision required for this is higher since the originals will be smaller and their dynamic range requirements much higher. Scanners that are specifically designed for reflective scans, but that are also supplied with a transparency hood, tend to have lower optical— e.g., uninterpolated—resolutions and less impressive dynamic ranges than professional film scanners. The latter machines may feature larger scanning area, better dynamic range and optics, and, unfortunately, a larger price tag.

Below *There's immense variation between scanner types and prices. Follow the flowchart to help you find your ideal type.*

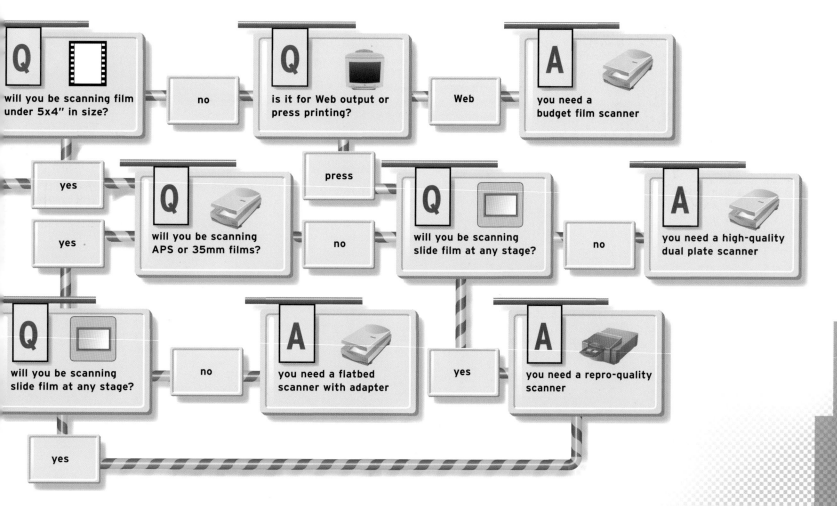

Q — will you be scanning film under 5x4" in size? → no → Q — is it for Web output or press printing? → Web → A — you need a budget film scanner

yes / yes → Q — will you be scanning APS or 35mm films? → no → press

Q — will you be scanning slide film at any stage? → no → A — you need a high-quality dual plate scanner

Q — will you be scanning slide film at any stage? → no → A — you need a flatbed scanner with adapter → yes → A — you need a repro-quality scanner

yes

cameras and camcorders

Capturing images digitally with a camera or camcorder is a quick and easy way to bring images into a computer. Like all other aspects of digital imaging, you get what you pay for. In the realm of digital cameras, that means that the higher uninterpolated resolution cameras are more expensive. So far, so obvious. But beyond a certain point (probably it is reasonable to use the three-million-pixel mark as a yardstick), other issues come into play. Optical systems (the lenses) and physical limitations (the size of the pixel) mean that there is a leap in price that comes with better cameras.

Compact models, where everything is built-in and predominantly automatic, may be acceptable up to a point, but in order to get the most possible out of the resolution, interchangeable lenses offer much more light-gathering ability, larger CCD or CMOS (complementary metal oxide silicon) sensors so that each pixel has more light falling on it, and, because of the higher signal-to-noise ratio, a "cleaner" image. The advantage of interchangeable lenses means you can get greater magnification at the moment of capture if you have a telephoto lens, and that will mean less need for digital

enlargement at a later stage. You can also use wide-angle lenses so you can fit more into an initial shot without having to resort to panoramic stitching. Again, the more detail you get at the moment of capture, and the less fiddling around you have to do with it, the higher quality your images will be. The interchangeable lens cameras are also often SLR (single lens reflex) models. These show you exactly what a picture will look like with more accuracy than a compact or an LCD (liquid crystal display) screen can offer. This raises the quality of the image, and therefor pushes up the price of the camera.

Right *The colorful rectangle inside the camera's lens throat is the high-resolution multimegapixeled CCD chip.*

CAMERA TYPE	Webcam	digital still 1024 x 768	3-megapixel still camera	3-megapixel still camera with video	SLR multi-megapixel still camera
FEATURES REQUIRED					
movie facility	YES	NO	NO	YES	NO
stills facility	YES	YES	YES	YES	YES
can be used away from pc	NO	YES	YES	YES	YES
video quality	LOW	N/A	N/A	LOW	N/A
stills quality	LOW	MEDIUM	HIGH	HIGH	VERY HIGH
interchangeable lenses	NO	NO	NO	NO	YES
controllable aperture	NO	NO	NO	YES	YES

Digital camcorders have a whole raft of digital features, including titling and special effects. You are better off ignoring these and aiming for the highest-quality output. Remember that for screen or Web work, a single frame from a digital camcorder is as acceptable as a shot from a still digital camera.

Interchangeable lenses, for the same reasons, are a key feature on professional models, which distinguish them from consumer models of digital camcorder. Other factors that help to explain the sometimes considerable difference between DV camcorders are the chips inside them. The broadcast-quality models may contain three CCD chips (one each for red, green, and blue capture) and this will make a significant difference to color fidelity, and your bank balance. Finally, one absolutely essential feature for your digital camcorder is that it must have the IEEE1394 (FireWire) connection (preferably for both input and output). This will enable you to take advantage of the "zero loss" aspect of digital video over analog. In short, if you use analog connections to your computer, you are throwing away one of the biggest assets of DV in that a copy made on DV is identical to the original. Digital output from the camcorder just makes for much simpler transport-action and copying of any movie you may make.

Digital cameras

This is a sophisticated multimegapixel still camera for resolutions of up to 2,048 x 1,536 pixels.

This camera uses three CCDs to capture an exceptionally sharp image.

A 10 x 300 lens means you do not have to make sectional enlargements.

This stylish component design is ideal for Web use or small printouts.

Several high-end cameras, such as the Nikon D1x, FujiFilm S1 Pro, and Canon EOS, use the same lens as a professional 35mm film camera system and are ideal for professionals turning to digital imaging.

scanning studio camera back	digital camcorder	video broadcast-quality digital video
NO	YES	YES
YES	YES	NO
NO	YES	YES
N/A	HIGH	BROADCAST
SUPERB	LOW	N/A
YES	NO	YES
YES	SOME MODELS	YES

printers

It is a truth universally acknowledged that despite the introduction of clear desk policies, endless talk of paperless offices, and the alleged imminent demise of physical reading matter like books and magazines, printing is an essential part of life. What the digital artist looks for from a printer is accuracy, fidelity, speed, flexibility, and the lowest possible cost per print.

Current market leaders in the desktop printing world are inkjet machines. They are cheap to buy, simple to use, and virtually everyone has one. As well as the inkjet there are two other types of printer that, if you are lucky, you may have access to: color laser and thermal printers. Note that thermal is a coverall term for any printer that uses heat to form an image, and encompasses the dye sublimation printer and the thermal autochrome printer. The latter is a proprietary technology and uses special papers with heat-sensitive chemicals to form an image in three layers (cyan, magenta, and yellow). Between each pass of the printing head, the image is fixed by exposure to an ultraviolet (UV) light source. The benefit of using this system is that UV light, which is one of the main problem factors for the fading of other types of color print, is actually used as a fixative.

Thermal dye sublimation works on a similar principle to children's wax crayons. Four different colors (cyan, magenta, yellow, and black) crayons are sublimated onto the receiving paper, using variable-sized dots in much the same method as traditional CMYK printing (see chapter 2). By building up tiny dots of these four colors, continuous-tone or graphic images of many thousands of different hues can be obtained.

Right *Different printer types can be used for outputting digital images but quality and prices vary considerably.*

Selecting the best printer

TYPE: THERMAL DYE
Speed: Slow. Requires several passes of the print head to achieve color print (two minutes per print is typical).
Quality: Very high print quality (despite comparatively low dpi) but limited in size.
Cost: Printer prices on a par with photo-quality inkjet printers, but media costs (for special paper and dyes) are high, leading to high cost per print.

TYPE: BUDGET INKJET
Speed: Dependent on print size and quality selected (two minutes for an 8 x 11-inch full-color print typical).
Quality: With the right type of paper, near-photographic-quality prints are possible.
Cost: Ink and paper costs are high (though cheaper papers can be used for "proof" work) but the printers themselves are modestly priced.

Color laser printers use electrostatic forces to bond four colors (including black) to paper. They are significantly quicker than any of the other types of printer, and their price is a more than fair reflection of that fact. Their longlasting toner cartridges carry a three-figure price tag, but for speed they cannot be beaten.

Inkjet printers come in three different flavors: desktop, DTP with RIP (Raster Image Processor), and iris inkjet. The last of these is a six-foot-wide machine that is used to make beautifully rendered inkjet prints. While the resolution of these printers is often lower than a desktop variety, given that the output size is two or three orders of magnitude above that of the desktop inkjet, the resolution of the image will break down before that of the printer. A 300ppi, 6 x 5-inch image would have to have about 200,000,000 pixels before any printer-introduced artifacts became evident.

rip it off

Although it sounds like a recommendation to bootleg someone else's designs, this refers to a piece of software called a Raster Image Processor (RIP), which performs the function of turning vector graphics and gradients into printable versions of the smooth, colorful images you see on your screen. For example, text in a given font is turned into a pattern of dots of the correct size, shape, and smoothness by an RIP. More sophisticated software RIPs can also provide the missing link in color management between printer and image manipulation software. Be warned, though, RIPs are specially designed for specific printers. Check whether your chosen printer is supported by an RIP before buying it if you feel that this is something you will need. Bear in mind, though, if you apply text in Photoshop, it will be bitmapped, so you will not need a RIP attached to your printer.

TYPE: SPECIALIST PHOTO INKJET

Speed: Similar to (or slower than) the budget inkjet, but speed depends on the quality selected.

Quality: Very good, particularly when specified paper and inks are used; many feature five- or six-color inks to deliver the best quality in (particularly) skin tones.

Cost: Printers (including increasing numbers of large document models) are moderately priced.

TYPE: COLOR LASER

Speed: Fast (up to several copies per minute, depending on the particular model).

Quality: Very good, though some models lack the fine control possible with more modest inkjet printers.

Cost: Very high purchase price and consumables. However, running costs are low since "ordinary" paper can be used for most printing tasks.

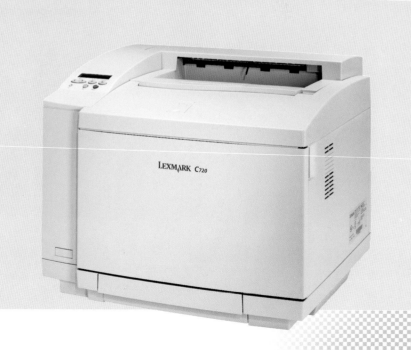

accessories

Twenty years ago, a mouse was a small rodent that lived under your floorboards. Now the computer mouse is ubiquitous, but that does not mean it is always the best tool for the job (*see pages 138 to 139*). If you are going to use a mouse, for maximum precision, try to get hold of an optical mouse. An optical mouse uses light to plot its position rather than wheels, rollers, and a rubber ball, whose sole aim appears to be to coat itself in gray debris and cause your cursor to jump. If you have an optical mouse, however, you cannot buy interesting mousemats with images that shift depending on where you view them from. The raised ridges of the mousemat (effectively vertical lenticular strips that focus the various images) will play havoc with the optical mouse's measurements. You can also get cordless mice, mice especially for the Internet (these have a wheel to allow you to scroll up and down without moving the mouse), and even tiny mice for computing on the move.

For most graphics applications, however, the graphics tablet is a very helpful alternative to the mouse. Its design is based on a simple enough idea. The tip of a stylus or pen held in your hand pushes on a slightly padded surface under which there is a sensing grid that tells the computer where the pen point is pressed, and so where the cursor should appear on screen. The screen size is defined by the edges of the tablet, and so the larger the tablet, the more accurately any movement appears on screen, and the easier it is to be precise. More advanced versions of the graphics tablet not only inform the computer of the position of the pen tip, but also detect how hard (in 1,024 increments) you are pressing down on the pen and then relay this information to the computer. The tablets themselves are smarter, too, and have their own menu sections together with extra features that allow you to concentrate on being creative, and worry less about the mechanics of the operation.

For digital video, you will find it helpful to have a separate mouse that features jog/shuttle controls for frame by frame advancing of video. The mouse should also offer about a dozen or so programmable buttons for executing quick edits, titling, and other special effects that enhance your creation.

Below *USB hubs permit several USB devices to be connected to a single USB port simultaneously.*

Connecting accessories

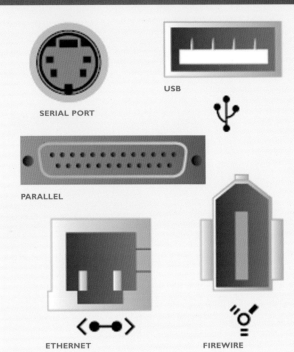

SERIAL PORT

USB

PARALLEL

ETHERNET

FIREWIRE

Parallel (sometimes called Centronics) connectors are used extensively for connecting PCs to printers and some other peripherals (such as scanners). Though found on some contemporary machines, the parallel interface is increasingly giving way to USB for such connections. Ethernet provides a simple and robust connection to networks, enabling computers (Macs and PCs) to share data, applications, and peripherals. An ethernet printer can be written to by a directly connected computer or any individual computer when connected on a network. USB is now found on most computers. It has the benefit of supporting multiple devices simultaneously (using a hub, as above), and most USB devices can be connected and disconnected without restarting.

FireWire (called IEEE 1394 on PCs, iLink on Sony peripherals) was developed by Apple and others as a high-speed link. Typically, digital video (DV) cameras, fast CD writers, and external hard drives use FireWire. Serial ports—a slower method—were used prior to USB for connection of keyboards, mice, and other peripherals not requiring substantial data transfers.

Right *The mouse is not ideal for graphics, so different kinds of stylus have been designed to give more of a "pen" or "brush" feel.*

Left *Color calibration of a monitor is essential if the image on screen is to match that printed. Calibration devices such as this make the process simple yet precise.*

Getting video in and out

If you are not getting a feed directly from a digital video camera, you will need a hardware accessory to help you get analog video into your computer. The latest digitizers allow you to take feeds directly from a television aerial (copyright issues aside) and plug them straight into a DV presentation. You can also get audio from radio input, and of course, take analog video and have it converted, in real time, into a DV-friendly format. The same box of tricks will also allow you to output in Web streaming or Web broadcast modes.

Alternatively, you can get an expansion card for your computer that allows you to take digital video input and convert it in real time to DVD-acceptable format for writing DVD videos in significantly less time than it would usually take to do this. The hardware also allows you to preview the image on a video monitor (as opposed to your computer monitor) so that you can check that all color, lighting, and audio levels are as they should be before you commit to burning the DVD, which is a great advantage (see pages 162 to 163).

Left *There is one simple truth about graphics tablets. The bigger they are, the more expensive they are.*

storage

The idea of storing all your information in a single place is less than ideal for two reasons. First, from a safety point of view, it is always worth having a backup on a different hard drive. Second, it is incredibly easy to fill up even the most seemingly capacious hard drive in a short period of time. Before starting this book, my new computer boasted an empty 30Gb hard drive, yet it is now nearly half full.

When you load a new piece of software onto your computer, it comes with a whole array of useful additions. You may find that many bits of software reinstall elements that you already have on your computer. The files you work on take up space. The programs you use like to "own" a protected portion of your hard drive in order to store their temporary files. Should your computer crash these temporary files, they might or might not find their way into the trash can. All the various bits (video clips, soundtracks, effects, transitions, and so on) of a movie file that may eventually end up being less than a megabyte, may need five hundred times that amount of storage in their original forms. While you cannot have too much data storage space, it pays to be organized about how you store things and allocate data space. Let us now have a look at the different types of storage on offer, and what you will most likely need.

hard drives

These can be built-in or external. Built-in is where your programs, fonts, and projects in progress live. As usual, you want the biggest, fastest drive you can afford. When buying a hard drive, the speed of the input/output bus your computer uses is one factor in a drive's speed. The speed of rotation of the drive is another. Avoid anything that is less than 5,400 rpm (revolutions per minute). A speed of 7,200 rpm is better, and you can get drives with up to 15,000 rpm. If a disk read head is traveling twice as fast, it can pick up more information than a slower one.

IDE (Integrated Drive Electronics) drives are cheaper than SCSI (Small Computer System Interface) drives, and, for most purposes, they are just as fast. External hard drives are where you back up to, and in the case of the new generation of portable hot-swappable drives, they are useful ways of transporting huge volumes of data. (Hot-swappable drives do not to be need to be turned on before the computer, and can be plugged in and unplugged without your computer crashing.)

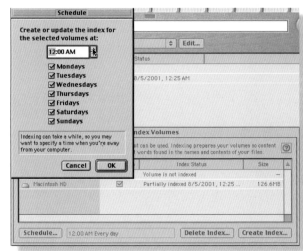

REGULAR INDEXING

Name	Date Modified	Size	Kind
doghinted.MOV	Sat, Apr 28, 2001, 9:07 AM	388.8 MB	MoviePlayer movie
RMOVO001.DV	Sun, Mar 18, 2001, 9:44 PM	188.6 MB	MoviePlayer document
RMOVO001.AVI	Sun, Mar 18, 2001, 9:19 PM	7.6 MB	MoviePlayer document
Mutto's sadness.mov	Thu, Apr 19, 2001, 10:30 AM	540 K	MoviePlayer movie
Joël Lacey's greatest Movie	Sun, Mar 18, 2001, 10:27 PM	4 K	iMovie document
Media	Sun, Mar 18, 2001, 10:23 PM	—	folder
RMOVO001.DV 01	Sun, Mar 18, 2001, 9:48 PM	188.6 MB	iMovie document
Flying Letters 01	Sun, Mar 18, 2001, 9:58 PM	21.7 MB	iMovie document
Drifting 01	Sun, Mar 18, 2001, 10:24 PM	14.4 MB	iMovie document

DIRECTORY LISTING

backup media

In addition to the writable media (see *pages 162 to 163*) there are dedicated recording devices that perform backups of your computer's work. These are not as useful as hard drives for day-to-day work, but they are quick, safe, and, most importantly, kept in a different place from the main computer in case of disaster.

partitioning

This is where you are effectively turning a single disk into more than one disk by allocating a fixed size to a partition. The benefits include forcing you to manage storage more effectively and making addressing more efficient. There are drawbacks in that you lose space and you may not be able to extend partitions after they have been made without reformatting (erasing) a drive. This is not wise unless you have backups of everything you have on that disk (see *pages 162 to 163*).

Storage solutions take many forms: a complete backup of your data, a short-term store for very large files, or the mobile yet capacious recordable media. CD-Rs are currently universal, as floppy disks were for a long time. Alternatives to compact discs are magneto-optical and removeable magnetic media, such as Zips.

Backup devices

When it comes to backup devices, speed of file transfer is more important than speed of access to an individual point on the medium. Special software keeps a record of what state the hard drive was in when it was last backed up and what was where. Restoring it is, depending on how much data there is to transfer, a relatively painless affair, certainly compared with the heartbreak of losing everything.

Remember, the data on your computer may well be more valuable than the hardware itself. Here are some backup options.

Below *Tape-based backup solutions allow the backing-up of extensive hard drives and, with appropriate software, make retrieval of specific files relatively easy.*

Left *Specialized software makes backing-up easy but rigorous. Restoration, where required, is equally simple.*

Below *Optical disk drives can store 1Gb or more of data and are useful for storing critical files and directories rather than complete hard drives.*

Below *Backup tapes can store many gigabytes of data, and even more if data compression is permitted.*

best practice in data storage

Whether you are backing up valuable data or burning (writing the data to an optical disk with a laser) a CD-ROM or DVD as a final product, there are certain things you should take into account to ensure that nothing goes wrong and that you have everything in the right location.

As far as backup goes, the important factor is how often you do it. You can use a tape system that automatically makes a backup of your hard drive every night (or at least makes a note of the changes since the previous full backup) or simply makes dual saves of everything you do as you go along. This second method is not only tedious, but you may not always remember to do it, and instead start working on a less-than-current version of your files.

writable media

Given the sheer amount of data that is involved these days, CD-ROMs are not the panacea that they once were. A 650Mb image is still quite large, but it pales in comparison with a complex video project. FireWire hard drives are a useful multipurpose backup and portable project helper, but specialist backup systems are the failsafe standard. Newly emerging 9.4Gb DVD-Ram disks are useful alternatives, and for smaller files, 1Gb or 2Gb Jaz disks are quick but relatively expensive in a memory per dollar equation when compared with CD-ROM or CD-RW (rewritable) disks. It is worth remembering, though, that the writing times for DVD and CD are significantly longer than those for magnetic media.

The choice of port—FireWire, USB, or SCSI—is again of prime importance when trying to determine which type of backup storage to use. It is all very well to have 20Gb of recoverable data, but if it takes literally hours to put it back onto your computer, then you might find that it is quicker, albeit slightly less safe, to try to recover the missing data on the original failed hard drive.

networking

If you have more than one computer on which you work, then while it is possible to use writable media to transfer data between one computer and the other, it is infinitely preferable to network the two together. Using a server-based system, which also has a hard drive for frequently

---

Image data memory cards

As well as CD, DVD, Jaz, and Zip drives, image data can also be stored on the same memory cards as used in digital cameras. Through a process that is partly historical and partly commercial, several "standards" have emerged in memory cards.

PCMCIA CARD

Oldest, in computer terms, is the PCMCIA card, now often known as the PC card. This is compatible with the card slots in many laptop computers and permits large amounts of memory storage. However, these cards are somewhat old now and their size precludes their use in contemporary compact digital cameras.

COMPACTFLASH CARD

CompactFlash cards are small, postage stamp-sized units that connect to the interface via a series of pins along one edge. They tend to be durable and are available in a range of capacities. Cards can be read and images copied to or from the card using a card reader or via a PC card adapter.

SMARTMEDIA CARD

SmartMedia are smaller and thinner than CompactFlash but offer capacities similar to those of the conventional CompactFlash card. Again, dedicated readers are available as are adapters for use in a PC card slot.

IBM MICRODRIVE

The Microdrive, introduced by IBM, offers a tiny hard disk in a case virtually identical to the CompactFlash. Microdrive capacities currently include those of 1Gb.

shared files, is the gold standard solution. A quicker and cheaper fix is to use inverted pair Ethernet cables. By using only four of the cable's wires, and reversing one of the pairs, each computer can be convinced that it is talking to a network rather than another computer. File transfer rates are more than adequate, but ensure that you only try to connect between the two when both computers are on, and that file sharing is switched on before attempting to connect. (File sharing lets one computer "see" the other.)

Networking is also by far the best way to connect one generation of Mac to another, as Ethernet ports have been included on Macs of all kinds for a number of years. You can also connect two older Macs by serial port. For example, a new minitower can be connected to a two-year-old iMac or a four-year-old laptop, which in turn can be connected to a ten-year-old laptop. This backward compatibility would allow a Webcam to be used on the oldest model and the results could then be transferred to the more powerful minitower for processing, without the need for any extra new hardware or software. This compatibility is one of the advantages of sticking to Macs.

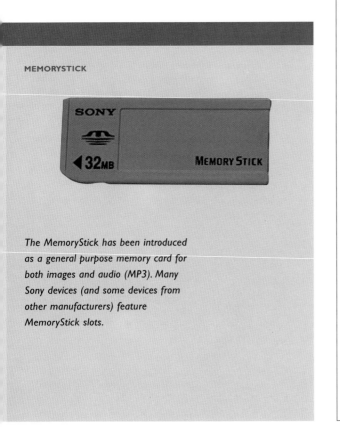

MEMORYSTICK

The MemoryStick has been introduced as a general purpose memory card for both images and audio (MP3). Many Sony devices (and some devices from other manufacturers) feature MemoryStick slots.

Storage devices

Left *Zip drives can record on 250Mb or 100Mb Zip disks (according to model), but in general, the 100Mb disks are more widely used.*

Right *With disk capacities of up to 2Gb, Jaz drives are excellent for archiving and backing up data, but the format is not as common as either CD-ROM or Zip disks.*

Left *CD-R recorders offer the ability to record up to 700Mb of data in under six minutes (for the fastest FireWire drives).*

Right *DVD writers also offer the ability to record CDs, but with the added benefit of recording on DVD media (but note that different DVD recording standards exist).*

7 software

There is usually something not quite complete about any piece of software you buy. You just know that in six months to a year, there will be a version 3.0 to replace your 2.0 or a 4.1.1 to iron out the bugs that version 4.0.5 was supposed to clear up. However, software is like a sibling. It changes, matures, and becomes more easy to understand as it gets older and learns a few more graces. Eventually, you and it will reach an accommodation where you know what you can and can't do with it. But which software do you really need?

basic software

Computers are like hothouse-educated children. They are very quick to do things that they can already do, but they have no ability to learn for themselves. If they want to take on new tasks, they need very specific instructions in a step-by-step fashion. In short, they need software. The range of software available is bewildering and the language with which it is described is impenetrable to all except those who already know how to use it. The producers of computer software mainly do not take the view that the computer is there to help you, but rather that it is up to you to bend to the computer's will and perform whatever tasks it decides in the way it prescribes: otherwise you will not get any joy from it. Such is life, so live with it. Software is not, by and large, user-friendly. For the most part, you will acquire software expertise with time, but only after you have endured hours of experimentation, heartache, failure, and crashes. Operating systems aside, there are four programs that you should learn to use: image manipulation, page layout, illustration, and Web authoring. These programs will not open doors for you, but not knowing them may leave a few swinging in your face if you are looking for a career in digital imaging and design.

the operating system

This is the bed on which all other software rests until it is required; the operating system performs an essential, if tedious, job within the computer. It keeps track of where everything is, calls applications to open in a given amount of memory, allows you to connect, with the appropriate software, to the outside world, and also acts as the

Right *Though the look is evolutionary rather than revolutionary, Mac OS X has some new desktop features, including the Dock (along the bottom of the screen), which shows all available resources, documents, and applications.*

Opposite *The latest Windows operating system, Windows XP, features an interface with larger icons and a customizable Start menu. Other new features include Home Networking, Internet Connection Sharing, and the Internet Connection Firewall—a basic personal firewall for broadband users.*

Opposite above *Despite the fact that Linux is a command-line operating system, it is most often packaged with a graphical interface, such as GNOME or KDE, to make it more accessible. It is the preferred OS for many technically proficient users.*

interface between all your hardware bits and software bits. These days, operating system software comes in three different flavors in the digital imaging world:

- Wintel (Windows 2000, NT, 98, 95, and XP), running on Intel- or IBM/AMD-chipped machines;
- Mac OS, running on Macs;
- Unix/Linux, running on pretty much everything (the new Mac OS X is a Unix-based system).

They all do pretty much the same things, but they have different ways of arranging them. While it is true there are probably half a million software titles for PC, and 50,000 for Mac, ultimately it makes little difference. All the packages you are actually ever going to want to use (about fifty in all) are made for PC and Mac (and Linux is catching up fast).

LINUX

WINDOWS XP

Copyright

You may already have received an email stating, "I can get you a copy of Adobe Photoshop 6 if you want." The sentence should really not have finished there. It should have said "...if you want to be liable to pay unlimited fines, and never be able to call anyone for support." The laws protecting software are among the most draconian in effect. Many employers consider copying software grounds for dismissal, and with good economic reason. The "I was just giving it a try" argument may well fall flat as a defense if your free trial of a program has been going on for more than a few weeks.

Meanwhile, your employer, who has otherwise been trying very hard to keep on the right side of the law, may decide it is simpler to summarily fire you rather than face the unlimited fine applicable. If you want some software, buy it; indeed, better still, if you possess the necessary skills, get someone to buy it for you. The possible alternatives are not worth thinking about.

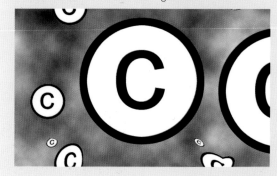

adobe photoshop

Why do digital imaging books always focus so heavily on Adobe Photoshop when there are so many other packages available? Because whether or not Photoshop is the best, it is the package that comes closest to being a universal standard in digital imaging. But why is it such a "must have" application?

First, life is simply too short to have to spend time learning yet another program once you have mastered Photoshop. And if you do decide to start working with a new package, you will invariably find yourself asking, "Why doesn't this behave like Photoshop?"

setting the standard

Second, at the risk of sounding pathetically like a child explaining that he decided to play truant from school because everyone else was going to do it, there is the fact that everyone else uses Photoshop. Every sector of digital imaging has its own champion piece of software. In digital still imaging, Photoshop is number one. Many of the software houses have come up with clever bolt-ons (known as plug-ins, *see pages 178 to 179*) that develop and extend Photoshop's existing flexibility.

Other software developers in fields associated with digital imaging make their programs so that images can be seamlessly introduced from, or into, Photoshop. PDFs, or portable document format documents, which have

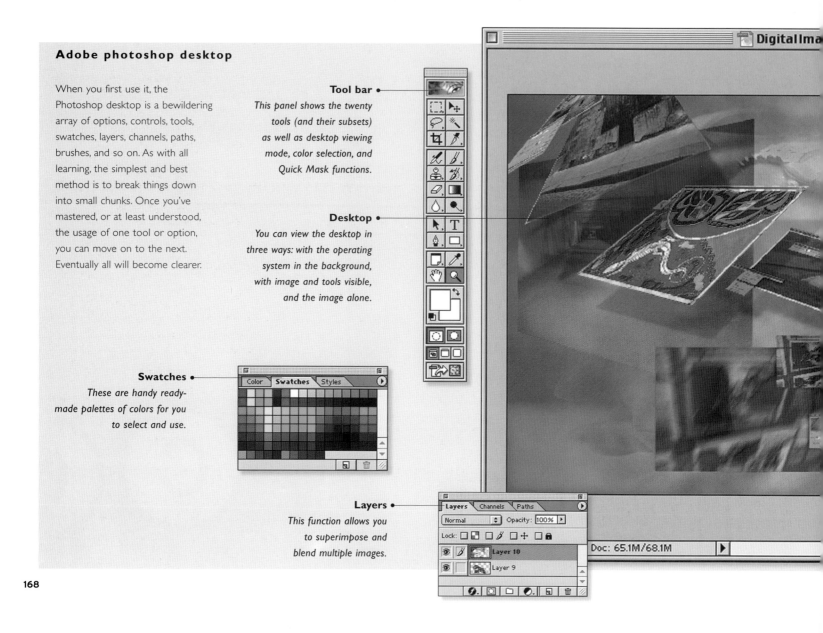

Adobe photoshop desktop

When you first use it, the Photoshop desktop is a bewildering array of options, controls, tools, swatches, layers, channels, paths, brushes, and so on. As with all learning, the simplest and best method is to break things down into small chunks. Once you've mastered, or at least understood, the usage of one tool or option, you can move on to the next. Eventually all will become clearer.

Tool bar •
This panel shows the twenty tools (and their subsets) as well as desktop viewing mode, color selection, and Quick Mask functions.

Desktop •
You can view the desktop in three ways: with the operating system in the background, with image and tools visible, and the image alone.

Swatches •
These are handy ready-made palettes of colors for you to select and use.

Layers •
This function allows you to superimpose and blend multiple images.

now established themselves as a Web standard, can be created from Photoshop. As far as any single product is concerned, Adobe Photoshop is quite simply the best thing since the inception of digital imaging. If you consider that to be a sweeping statement, ask yourself why everyone else uses it. The answer is because it can do everything you want it to do. That certainly cannot be said of every software package available on the market.

actions

One of the best features in Photoshop, although by no means unique, is that of Actions. These are macros (a series of program instructions activated at the press of a button) that you can use individually or in sets. If you are preparing a whole series of pictures that you want to have all the same style, look, resolution, and color space, you can simply open an image and apply an appropriate action. If you are outputting to print (*see pages 34 to 35*), you might want to have all your images with a 300ppi resolution, in CMYK format with a specific profile, and to be sharpened by a specific amount, so they all look the same when printed. All you have to do is to set action to Record, perform as many different changes as you want, then stop and save the action. By using the Automate: Batch function you merely point Photoshop to the folder where all the images are kept, choose your action, select OK, and then let Photoshop do the work for you.

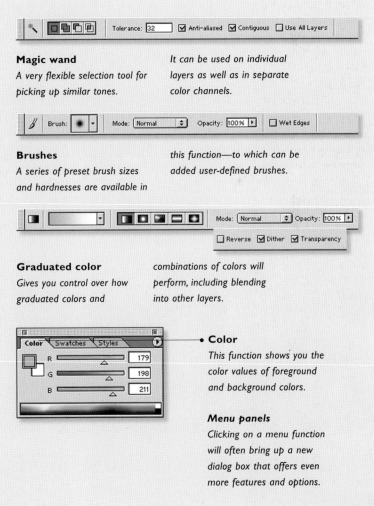

Magic wand
A very flexible selection tool for picking up similar tones. It can be used on individual layers as well as in separate color channels.

Brushes
A series of preset brush sizes and hardnesses are available in this function—to which can be added user-defined brushes.

Graduated color
Gives you control over how graduated colors and combinations of colors will perform, including blending into other layers.

Color
This function shows you the color values of foreground and background colors.

Menu panels
Clicking on a menu function will often bring up a new dialog box that offers even more features and options.

other digital still packages

After a long battle, Adobe has effectively seen off all major opposition at the high end of the still-image manipulation market. There remain competitors to Photoshop, and also some very useful complements to it.

There are programs like JASC's Paint Shop Pro (PC only) and Corel's PhotoPaint, although it must be said that despite the enthusiasm of their devotees, these programs are aimed at a slightly less sophisticated market than Photoshop. In this section of the market, even Adobe is attacking Photoshop with Elements, which is a less sophisticated version of Photoshop but costs only a fraction of the price.

Resolution-independent packages (where you could paste one digital image onto another without the same pixel ratios), such as Live Picture and xRes, are now virtually defunct. At the low end of the market, packages aimed at digital camera users include MGI Photosuite (which also incorporates some Live Picture technology).

The really interesting side of software in the digital imaging arena is the complements to Photoshop. For example, Corel (formerly Ultimatte) Knockout is a fantastic program adapting Hollywood technology to give absolutely sparklingly clean cut-outs of the most fussy of subjects. Extensis Mask Pro is a Photoshop plug-in that performs a similar job but lacks the same sophistication.

choosing software

For picture library and archive creation, there is Fotostation, and a whole host of add-ons in the form of plug-ins from Bryce such as Kai's Power Tools (KPT). The key to choosing software other than Photoshop is to establish which functions you don't already have with Photoshop and then find programs that complement it. There is no point in spending hundreds of dollars to get something that emulates most of Photoshop's functions. Better to find shareware (downloadable programs costing less than $150) that adds the specific functions you want. In this way you can gradually build an extensive storeroom of useful tools to access as you need them.

Below *I shot these five vertical panoramic shots with the aim of producing a digital panorama later using PanoramaMaker. The result is shown above right.*

COMPONENT I

COMPONENT 2

COMPONENT 3

COMPONENT 4

COMPONENT 5

Below *Panoramic applications allow you to make a single image from many components.*

Left *The final result shows the five separate images blended smoothly together.*

Making panoramas and fantasy pictures

Photoshop Elements includes an automatic panorama-generating feature, and panoramas can be "stitched" manually using the full version, but there are few software packages available that are dedicated to creating panoramic pictures from a series of shots taken consecutively. It is worth bearing in mind that if you try to glue together shots that were not taken at the same time, you are likely to end up with what some program errors euphemistically entitle "unexpected results," i.e., complete and utter garbage.

Depending on the package, you may have the option to specify which lens focal length you use for the pictures and what shape you want the final picture to be (letterbox for straight panoramic prints, or Apple QuickTimeVR). Some packages can zoom in on specific detail and move images up and down. Apple QuickTimeVR format makes for what are known as "immersive images," where the image looks as if it was projected on a barrel as seen from inside the barrel.

Both straight panoramas and VR images are storage-space-intensive, assuming you want your images to have any detail. This is to be expected. If you scan in ten 6 x 4-inch pictures at 300ppi, and only 2.5% overlaps with the next, you are going to have 20,520,000 pixels in your final image, which is nearly a 60Mb file. If your computer lacks plenty of memory, you may find the program hanging (i.e., refusing to do anything and causing the computer to freeze) halfway though an operation (see pages 148 to 149). ArcSoft PhotoMontage is something of a one-trick pony, but there has been a vogue for creating a single image from hundreds or even thousands of others. The key here is the size of the originals. Too small and the montage looks pixellated, too big and it takes forever to render.

FULL IMAGE

CLOSEUP

quarkxpress

If Photoshop is the main choice for still-image digital imaging, then QuarkXPress is the same for the desktop publishing (DTP) environment. While this package has historically been for "print" as opposed to the Internet, the manufacturers of Quark have been working hard to try to keep pace with their design audience as they move from paper to screen. Many designers believe page layout and Web design are completely different animals, and therefore Web designers will already have their own established loyalties in terms of preferred software. As far as page designers working with ink and paper are concerned, Quark has fostered an intense loyalty. There is

also the fact that, as with Photoshop, it has become the standard. If you are preparing images for an advertisement, a poster, a book, a magazine, or even a newspaper, then with few exceptions, it will be put together in Quark.

key features

Quark is considered quite a logical program. While page design was once thought to be the realm of the mouse, Quark, like Photoshop, uses keyboard shortcuts to speed work up dramatically. Just a word of warning, though: if you are using a keyboard and mouse together for long periods of time, you really should be aware of the possibility of RSI (repetitive strain injury) flaring up.

The QuarkXPress layout interface is based on organizing content within various "boxes." These can

QuarkXPress desktop

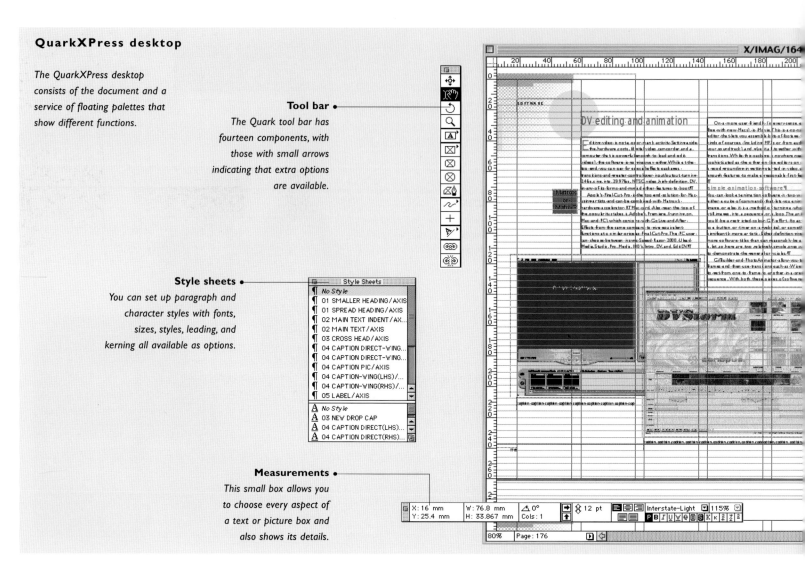

The QuarkXPress desktop consists of the document and a service of floating palettes that show different functions.

Tool bar •
The Quark tool bar has fourteen components, with those with small arrows indicating that extra options are available.

Style sheets •
You can set up paragraph and character styles with fonts, sizes, styles, leading, and kerning all available as options.

Measurements •
This small box allows you to choose every aspect of a text or picture box and also shows its details.

contain text, images, color, gradients, or combinations of these. A recent improvement has been the addition of basic Bézier drawing tools, which enable the boxes to be drawn to any shape. When importing images into boxes, QuarkXPress will allow a wide variety of file formats of virtually any printable bit depth and resolution, but only 8-bit images can be made negative or have their contrast adjusted within Quark itself.

When it comes to digital images, Quark has some advantages and disadvantages compared with Photoshop. If you need to preview images on paper (see *pages 34 to 35*), Quark is not ideal unless your printer has a RIP (Raster Image Processor). Quark shows images on screen at their screen resolutions (72ppi). If you print an image at that screen resolution (as Quark without a RIP will),

the quality will be poor: Quark is unable to rasterize (compute) the high-resolution images in certain formats.

Where Quark scores points is in the reduction of the size of screengrabs (see *pages 132 to 133*). If a file is saved in the correct format (EPS by choice), Quark will make a better job of resizing the image crisply. For enlarging screengrabs, you will find using Photoshop is a better bet.

While Photoshop has made great strides in its use of text, Quark is still the easier program for creative textual usage, especially once you are dealing with paragraphs.

Are there drawbacks? Well, the main deterrent is price. You can buy a sackful of other (non-DTP) packages for the price of a single copy of Quark. Also, Adobe's DTP newcomer InDesign is gaining an increasing user base and integrates well with other Adobe applications.

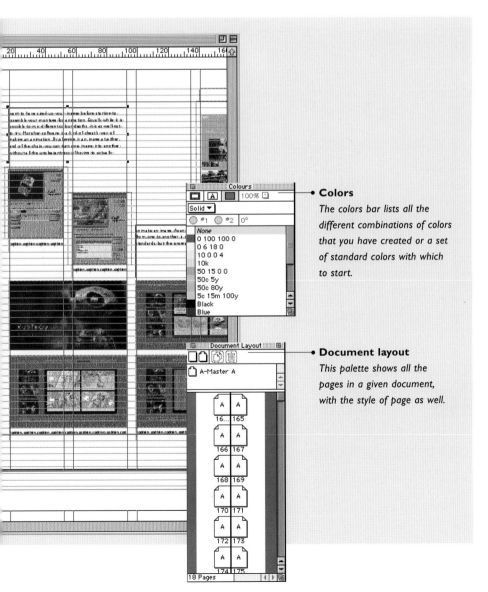

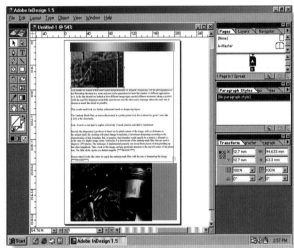

Colors
The colors bar lists all the different combinations of colors that you have created or a set of standard colors with which to start.

Document layout
This palette shows all the pages in a given document, with the style of page as well.

Above *Adobe's InDesign brings the Adobe interface and look to desktop publishing. The commonality of layout (with other Adobe applications) and powerful creative tools has won many converts.*

drawing applications

If you are creating an image from scratch, you are faced with a variety of drawing applications. The two most commonly used packages (out of a wide selection of others, including Corel Painter) are Adobe Illustrator and Macromedia FreeHand. Both these programs offer a huge array of tools that allow your imagination to run riot across your virtual canvas. Layers, multiple pages, and untold methods of transferring patterns, colors, lines, and curves mean that both of these packages offer an exciting toybox for the budding designer. Drawing applications, unlike image editing ones (which work with pixel-based graphics) produce scalable vector graphics.

The notable common feature is that the companies that make them have also developed significantly useful packages that focus on the animation, Web design, and development markets. For users of FreeHand and Illustrator, the benefit is that, assuming they have all the relevant programs, they have the ability to transform a graphic into a piece of animation or into a Web button, and so on.

opt for integration

If you are in the market for providing "high impact, low bandwidth," you are advised to opt for one of these integrated packages rather than a stand-alone application.

You can, of course move images from one type of package to another, but that requires producing everything in a linear fashion, i.e., pictures first, layout later. While this is undoubtedly an ideal way of carrying out the task, it is easier to have all the tools you need open at once on your screen, and to be able to backtrack and recreate a graphic, and then simply move it over to the other application.

Below *A sister product of Photoshop, Adobe's Illustrator has the same "look and feel" to its tool set as Photoshop, although it is a drawing application rather than an image editing application*

Adobe Illustrator desktop

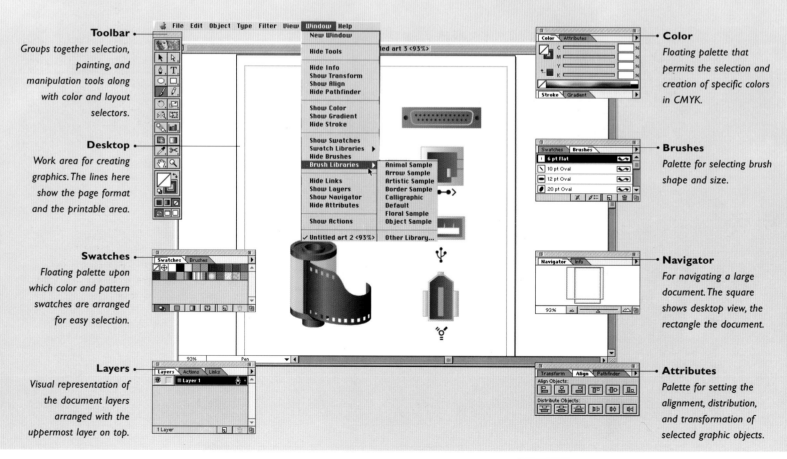

Toolbar •
Groups together selection, painting, and manipulation tools along with color and layout selectors.

Desktop •
Work area for creating graphics. The lines here show the page format and the printable area.

Swatches •
Floating palette upon which color and pattern swatches are arranged for easy selection.

Layers •
Visual representation of the document layers arranged with the uppermost layer on top.

• **Color**
Floating palette that permits the selection and creation of specific colors in CMYK.

• **Brushes**
Palette for selecting brush shape and size.

• **Navigator**
For navigating a large document. The square shows desktop view, the rectangle the document.

• **Attributes**
Palette for setting the alignment, distribution, and transformation of selected graphic objects.

FreeHand desktop

TOOL BAR •

DRAWING • CANVAS

MIXER • PALETTE

The standard standard

The portable document format (PDF) is the closest thing to a standard in the world of computers other than, perhaps, plain text. It has the advantage of being able to incorporate text, illustrations, and even photographic images in a frame that looks and behaves like a piece of paper. You can print from it even if you don't own the fonts used in the document, you can even search it and, if the author has allowed it, make changes to it and pass it on. The way to create a PDF is either to have an application like Photoshop, which can generate PDFs itself, or to use a "distiller," which is a program that changes whatever format the document is in currently to a PDF. You can get extensions to some programs, such as QuarkXPress, that allow

you to do this, or else you can use the full version of Adobe Acrobat that will write the files. All you need in order to read a PDF is Adobe Acrobat Reader. This program is given away free and is included on most application installation disks. You can be fairly confident that anyone who is connected to the Web either has Acrobat, or can install it easily. PDFs are completely cross-platform (Macs and PCs are able to run Acrobat Reader) and sophisticated design and typography do not necessarily mean huge files and prolonged downloads either. You can even save Web sites as PDFs. Adobe has sought to position PDFs as a standard for prepress work with some success, and it has been included as part of Apple's Mac OS X.

dv editing and animation

Editing video is not a poor man's activity. Setting aside the hardware costs (digital video camcorder and a computer that is powerful enough to load and edit videos), the software is no giveaway either. In fact, at the top end, you can pay for special effects packages, transitions and greater control over input/output, turning 24fps cine into 29.97fps, NTSC video, high-definition DV in any of its forms, and myriad other features to boot.

Apple's Final Cut Pro is the top-end solution for Mac-using artists, and can be combined with Matrox's hardware accelerator RTMac card. Also near the top of the popularity stakes is Adobe's Premiere (running on Mac and PC), which joins with GoLive and After Effects from the same company to give equivalent functions at a similar price as Final Cut Pro. The PC user can choose between in:sync Speed Razor 2000, Ulead Media Studio Pro, Media 100's Intro DV, and EditDV.

A more user-friendly version is iMovie (issued with new Macs). This is a no-nonsense editor that lets you assemble bits of footage from all kinds of sources (including MP3s or from audio CDs for your soundtrack) and glue it all together with titling and transitions. While this package is nowhere near as sophisticated as the other on-line editors available, it gives a good grounding in getting started in video, and still has enough features to make a reasonable first feature.

simple animation software

You can look at animation software in two ways. It is either a suite of commands that lets you animate a still image, or else it is a method of turning a whole series of still images into a sequence or a loop. The animation could be a restricted color GIF effort (to act perhaps

Left The simplest way to edit video on the Mac is Apple's own iMovie package, which comes free with new Macs.

iMOVIE

Right There are a number of good value video editing applications available, including EditStudio, Movie X One, and DVStorm, shown here.

DVSTORM

as a button or timer on a Web site), or something significantly more creative. Either definition gives access to more software titles than can reasonably be arranged in a list, so here are two relatively simple ones with which to demonstrate the general principles.

GifBuilder and PhotoAnimator allow you to add frames and then use transitions such as Wipe and Fade to get from one frame to another in a predetermined sequence. With both these pieces of software, you really should have sized up your images before starting to assemble your montage for animation. Equally, while it is possible to mix color depths, it is as well not to try. Morpher software is a kind of cheat's way of making an animation. By plugging in an image at either end of the chain, you can turn one image into another without having to animate it. As animations go, a smooth transition from one to another is not up to professional standards, but the program makes it quick and easy.

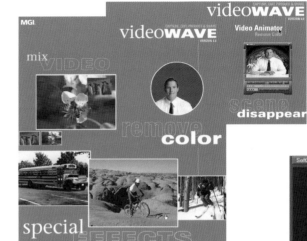

Left *Videowave has a number of transition components for use in PC video editing.*

Right *SX filters allow for special effects to be introduced and applied to video clips. Applications such as After Effects offer nothing else.*

Above, right, and below *Video editing software permits a range of special effects and compositions.*

plug-ins and xtensions

To unlock the power of an image editing program of whatever kind, it sometimes takes the talents of more than one software company. Whether Photoshop would have been as popular as it is without contributions from Kai Krause (from Kai's Power Tools or KPT plug-ins) is a moot point. The plug-ins available for use with Photoshop and Xtensions for Quark make life an awful lot more interesting and range from sophisticated masking programs and space-efficient color reduction programs, to graphically useful plug-ins, like lens flare effects, to the downright frivolous. They all offer, in that most hated of computer jargon, increased functionality.

saving time and hassle

The plug-in writers started off by writing extra bits of Photoshop and Quark that the main program writers should have included originally. But praise must go to the original application writers who allowed the architecture to be sufficiently open for this to be carried out at a later stage. Some of the additions fill gaps that, while not making the program unusable, certainly impede the worker in pursuit of a hassle-free life. The Group Resizing Xtension (allowing a group of items in a Quark document to be scaled all at the same time) has probably saved hundreds of thousands of working hours since its launch. It was so successful that it has been integrated into the latest version of the package. For Photoshop users, some of the filters (which add realistic ripples or sophisticated photograph emulation devices) make possible things that were not possible before.

On a more prosaic level, plug-ins can also take the form of specific import or export formats so you can port images between all kinds of weird and wonderful programs and still end up doing the bulk of any work in the familiar homeland of Photoshop. However, you have to exercise a little self-restraint, or else the effect completely overwhelms the image.

As far as filters in Photoshop are concerned, the approach is very similar to the use of filters in photography. Some will improve an image, but, as you can see from the selection shown below and right, some just make the image weird and not always wonderful. This is an area in which nothing can replace practice and experimentation. Eventually you will develop an instinct for what you can do to an image without making it silly.

Below and opposite
Photoshop includes many filters that transform the prosaic, not always for the better. Similarly, third party plug-ins (such as Holodozo and Frosty, shown here) can provide more extreme and sometimes more bizarre effects.

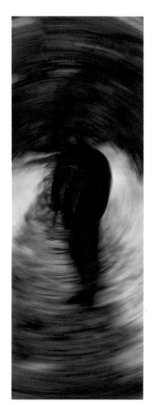

ORIGINAL SPHERIZE RADIAL BLUR GLASS EXTRUDE

MOSAIC

EMBOSS

HOLODOZO

LENS FLARE

COLORED PENCIL

SOLARIZE

DUST AND SCRATCHES

FROSTY

TRANSFORM

TILES

other applications

Surfing the Internet in search of useful bolt-ons, whether plug-ins or stand-alone applications, can prove to be a fruitful activity. Many of these products can add real power to your machine for a small fraction of the cost of a larger application.

Apple QuickTime Pro is probably one of the most underrated programs around. Apple successfully managed to port its QuickTime movie standard across to other platforms, and for many people the QuickTime player is excellent, spoiled only by the continual prompts to upgrade to QuickTime Pro. However, it is worth getting this update if only for its ability to import obscure movie formats and export them as files that the nonlinear editors can deal with in either PAL (UK and European) or NTSC (US) frame rate formats.

graphic converter

You may not have heard of Graphic Converter, but you should have. This wonderful translation package is effectively a lookup table that converts virtually any graphics format into any other and allows multiple "batch" processing. It will enable you to open documents and save them in a format that no other program will match.

You can even use Graphic Converter for nothing with a trial version from Lemke Software. It makes sense to buy a full version because, as with QuickTime, you soon get tired of waiting for the message asking you to upgrade to the full licensed version to scroll down the screen.

scion image

This is an analytical program for those who are truly interested in the structure of images, seeing behind the Fourrier transforms that digital cameras and other firmware/software functions produce. Once you get to

Left *Graphic Converter is a very flexible program that allows you to open and access all kinds of file formats.*

Below *Image browsers let you see what pictures you have on your hard drive.*

GRAPHIC CONVERTER

IMAGE BROWSER

know what you are doing, Scion image will also let you extract the maximum quality image from an unimpressively poor original. The program is not very user-friendly, so novices are recommended to buy a dedicated textbook, in addition to the accompanying manual.

photo tools

BoxTop Software's suite of preparation and compression programs (most of which sit within Photoshop) will save time for you as well as for anyone using a Web site for which you have created images. By squeezing the maximum out of JPEGs and GIFs, the suite of programs gives you absolute control over the size of the file and the number of colors within it. By using extremely accurate live previews (i.e., by letting you see what happens before you are committed to doing it), the BoxTop programs give sizeable reductions in file size, with little perceptible quality difference.

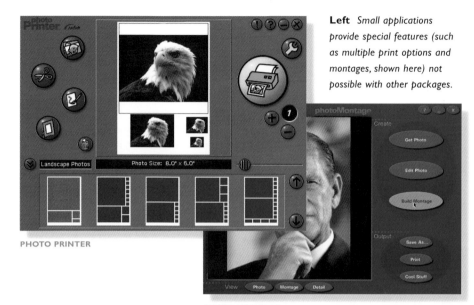

Left *Small applications provide special features (such as multiple print options and montages, shown here) not possible with other packages.*

PHOTO PRINTER

PHOTO MONTAGE

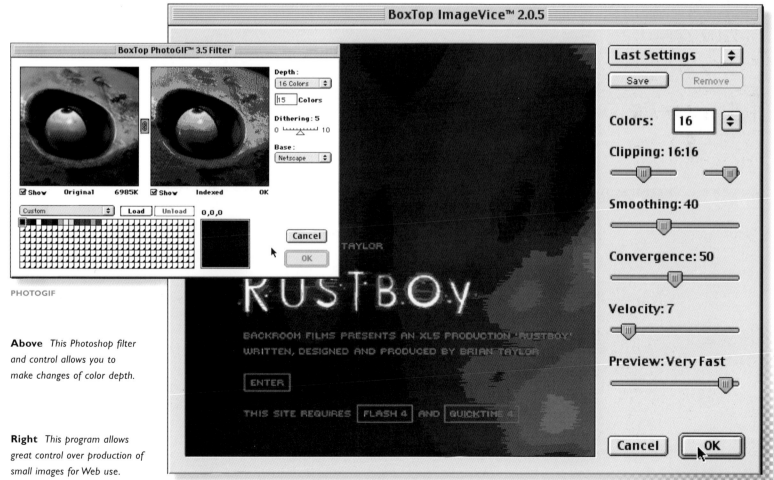

PHOTOGIF

Above *This Photoshop filter and control allows you to make changes of color depth.*

Right *This program allows great control over production of small images for Web use.*

IMAGEVICE

8 moving digital images

Once you have completed your digital image, the chances are that someone else will need to see it. So how do you get your image from where you are to where the client, for want of a better word, will be? Deciding which way to transfer the images depends on how you prioritize the speed, security, accessibility, compatibility, and delivery. As usual in the imaging chain, you need to consider what is easiest and quickest for the end user because that is likely to be quicker and easier for you in the long run. If the person to whom you are sending an image cannot open it, or even worse, cannot access it, it will be up to you to sort the problem out. Getting it right the first time is always the quickest way of doing something.

image transfer options / physical

The simplest method of image file transfer is what jargonauts term "sneakernet." It means that the print, slide, or disk is passed on in person. Make sure to write the digital image onto a recordable medium (disk) that you know the end user can read. Remember, the best solution is often the lowest technology. Put the image or disk in an appropriately sized and protected case with a small printout of the image on it, and physically take it to the person. In the case of a disk, ask them to open the image while you are there to make sure that it is suitable. If they have problems opening the images, don't just show them how to open them, teach them how as well.

Below *As with other aspects of digital imaging, a logical process makes the transfer process simple and safer.*

by mail/courier

Until broadband access is cheap and readily available, mailing will continue to be an important means of file transfer. You can track the delivery of a package by

Internet with many couriers now. It may seem strange to send something by mail when it is urgent, but in my experience, a telephone call to say that an item has been sent at five o'clock in the afternoon and is guaranteed to arrive before ten o'clock in the morning or midday is fast enough for 99% of cases. Even if this is not the primary method of delivery (i.e., if you use it as backup for a worst-case scenario), it will still be the one that people will prefer to use.

The great thing about either of these methods is that you can send the image at its maximum desirable resolution (which is not always the case with other means of transportation). But even with these two vintage methods of delivery, there are some technological questions that need to be asked.

What kind of computer will a digital image be opened on? Is the format that you have saved it in appropriate for its intended uses? Is your end point with the image the start point for someone else? Can they read your disks? Although you may be the proud possessor of the latest word in technology, that does not mean that the person receiving the image has the same setup. CD-ROM drives are ubiquitous on modern

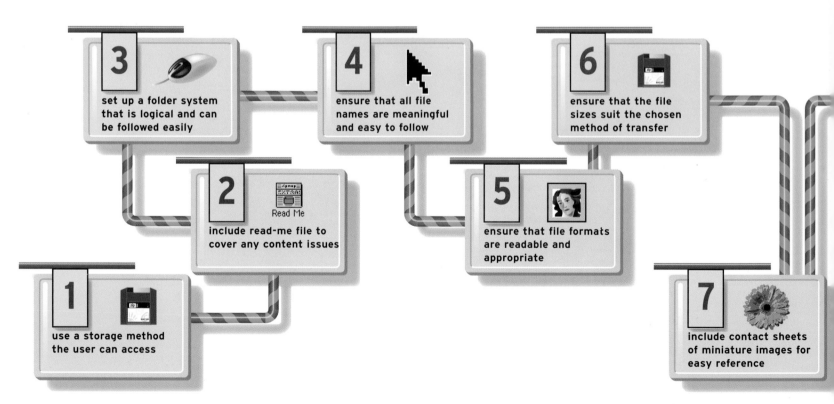

3 set up a folder system that is logical and can be followed easily

4 ensure that all file names are meaningful and easy to follow

6 ensure that the file sizes suit the chosen method of transfer

2 include read-me file to cover any content issues

Read Me

5 ensure that file formats are readable and appropriate

1 use a storage method the user can access

7 include contact sheets of miniature images for easy reference computers, but they are not all equal. You might be able to burn a large collection of images to a DVD-R disk, but it would be useless to a person without a DVD-R-compatible drive.

compatibility

Your client may say that a Zip disk is fine, but if you have a 250Mb disk and they have only a 100Mb drive, it is of no use to them. If you are sending to a Mac-equipped office, you can send it in a PC format and there's normally no problem. Send a Mac format to a PC office and there will be difficulties.

Which version of the software are you running? Is it significantly newer than the one at the reception end? If so, some of the formats may not be able to be read by the receiver. Working through this kind of checklist may be tedious, but it is better to be frustrated at the beginning and successful at the end than vice versa.

Finally, always be sure that any files have the correct three-letter suffix for the file type being used (e.g., PSD for Photoshop, TIF for TIFFs, and JPG for JPEGs).

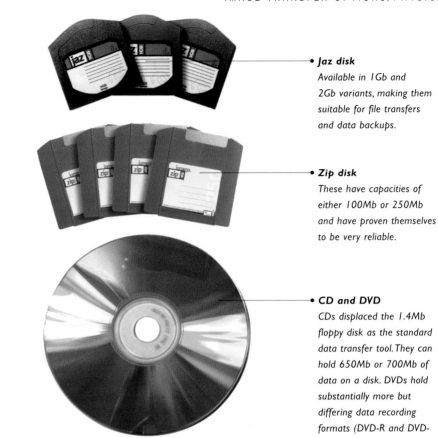

Jaz disk
Available in 1Gb and 2Gb variants, making them suitable for file transfers and data backups.

Zip disk
These have capacities of either 100Mb or 250Mb and have proven themselves to be very reliable.

CD and DVD
CDs displaced the 1.4Mb floppy disk as the standard data transfer tool. They can hold 650Mb or 700Mb of data on a disk. DVDs hold substantially more but differing data recording formats (DVD-R and DVD-RAM) can lead to compatibility problems.

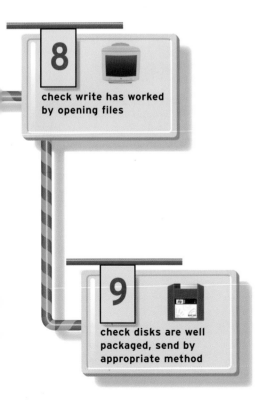

8
check write has worked by opening files

9
check disks are well packaged, send by appropriate method

What opens what

Sharing images—or files generally—can be fraught with problems. In general, users of Macintosh computers are well placed. Macs, by virtue of their smaller market share, have had to understand "foreign" file formats. Thus a disk created on a PC can usually be read by a Mac. Most file types can be opened (including many of those normally "native" to a PC) but, in general, programs and applications designed for the PC will not run on a Mac. Conversely, files created on a Mac will not run automatically on a PC. Hybrid CDs can be recognized by either platform, but again, applications may be specific to one platform. File conversion utilities, such as Conversions Plus and Debabilizer, enable specialized file formats to be opened on "foreign" computers and saved back in a format that will be understood by the originator. Mac users can also run emulators like SoftWindows that create the Windows environment on their computer. Such emulation software permits Windows software and applications to be run as if on a Windows PC. There is some crude software that permits the MacOS to be run on a PC, though not reliably.

image transfer options / direct electronic

Below and right

Communication routes can be direct to the intended recipient or indirect via an Internet service provider (ISP). Connections can be via modem, ISDN, or DSL.

If you are in an office where you share the same network as the people to whom you are sending the image(s), then either you or they can set up a section of their hard drive that can be accessed directly by anyone on that network (*see page 187*). To do this, you simply choose the recipient's hard drive with AppleShare in your Chooser (Mac), or by logging on as if it were a network (PC), and then you just drop the images into the hard drive of their computers. With two Ethernet equipped computers and a switchover cable (an Ethernet lead swaps two of the wires over inside) you can transfer images directly between computers without having to go through a network. ISDN (Integrated Service Digital

Network) was the holy grail when it first arrived. Seemingly huge files could be transferred in an instant, with absolute confidence. That was, of course, against the background of lower-resolution images and slow modems. A few years later, as file transfer traffic increased in popularity and size, the system quickly clogged up, making the perfect future offered by ISDN seem nothing more than a cruel joke.

home connections

For the smaller home office, ISDN, DSL (digital subscriber line), or cable offer many benefits, the most significant of which is increased speed. ISDN has a maximum download speed of 64 Kbps (and dual ISDN doubles this to 128 Kbps). DSL usually has a maximum speed of about 512 Kbps, while cable is usually around 500 Kbps. In practice, however, the Internet user will rarely achieve transfer rates that high. You can also

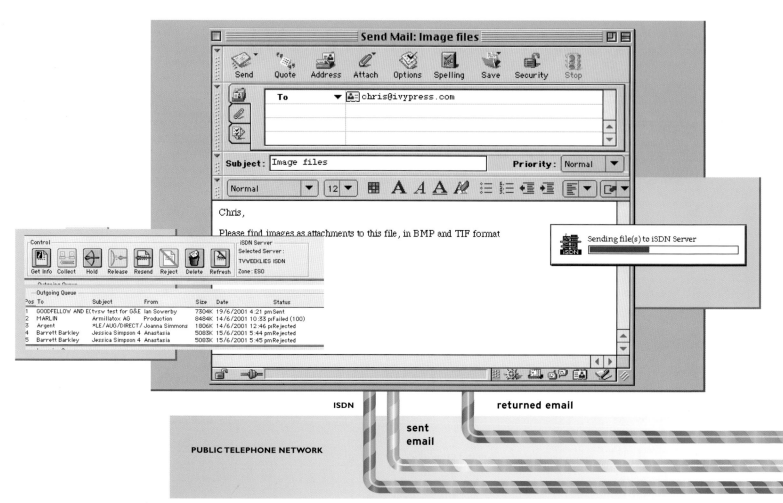

obtain verbal confirmation from the other end of the line that the file is readable. With these relatively broadband (i.e., high data throughput capacity) systems, images can still just about be transferred uncompressed. However, if you are trying to send a movie rather than an image, you might find that you could have used sneakernet by the time the file transfer is complete. This is especially true for POTS (Plain Old Telephone System), the basic analog crackly telephone line attached to your computer. Bear in mind also that your connection is only as quick as the slowest part of the chain. A slow server will inevitably mean a similarly slow connection.

email

It is important to remember that email is not a direct connection between computers, and work can even sometimes go "missing" for several days before it finally reaches the recipient (see pages 188 to 189).

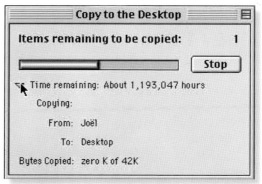

LONG TRANSFER TIME

Left *Sometimes software time predictions are wildly pessimistic. Luckily this operation did not actually take this long!*

Below *The firewall of a recipient computer doesn't just limit the type of content that can be received, it can also restrict file size.*

Right and below *The Internet abounds with sites offering free resources such as file storage and data transfer routines.*

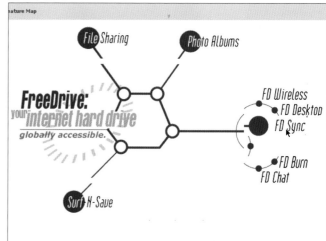

FREE FILE STORAGE

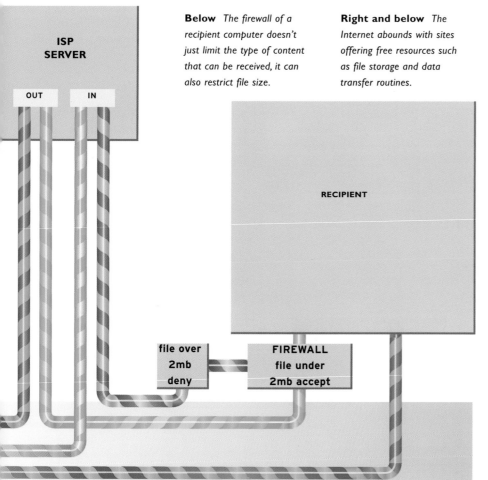

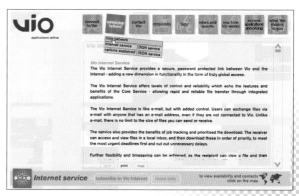

INTERNET DATA TRANSFER

image transfer
options / remote server

Sending digital images by email can be a quick and easy solution, or it can be a nightmare. Which of these two outcomes occurs depends on the email software and the savvy of the user on the receiving end of the pictures. If they are on their toes and have a relatively modern email package, they should be fine.

If the user is part of a larger organization with the usual draconian corporate security measures, it can be difficult to pass images through the receiver's company's firewall (software that makes a snap decision whether to let an email or a remote connector through). Sometimes the receiver may not even be notified that someone has

tried to send them an email. Depending on how many gateways you have to jump before your email arrives at its destination, you may or may not get an email notification of its arrival. Anything larger than 2.5 to 3.5Mb will experience problems getting through some Web mail servers. Many of the firewalls that are set up on email systems in large companies still stop mail with attachments that are even smaller than 2.5Mb.

In case the receiver's software cannot identify the file type you are sending, it is always worthwhile putting a three letter file-type indicator at the end of the file name (e.g., picture.jpg for a JPEG, or layeredimage.psd for a Photoshop Document). This will prevent the file from being turned into a very long text document. It is also worth checking that the recipient's email software has the File Type Helpers activated, and that the correct Helper application is being used to launch the image you send.

Using a network

Right *With a Mac, you select an AppleTalk zone and then a file server within that zone.*

Below *On a PC you will usually connect to the main network via the "Network Neighborhood" window.*

Below *You will need to have a legitimate user name and password to get in.*

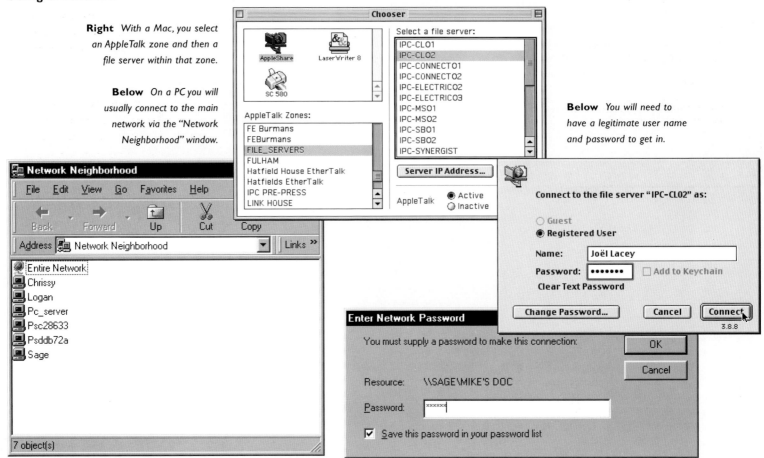

network servers

Office networks have become a lot more robust over the last five years, but they are not always to be trusted. Any server that is communicating with both Macs and PCs has the tendency to corrupt image files, and you may only realize it too late. For this reason, always keep a copy of images on your hard drive, and preferably make a copy on some removable media, too.

To make the transfer, you simply drop the image into a shared folder on the network, tell your colleagues where it is, and leave it to them to pick it up. Unless they acknowledge receipt of the image, you cannot know whether they have picked it up, let alone whether they can open it or like it. This is not the most secure approach, either; in lightly regulated office networks, many people have the right to delete files if they think the server is becoming too overloaded and slow.

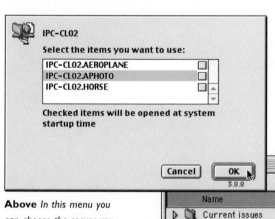

Above *In this menu you can choose the server you want to gain access to.*

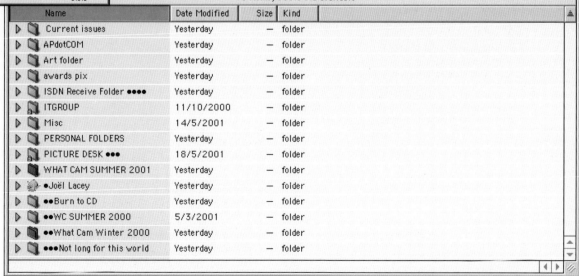

Left *File helpers and exchange programs can be engaged by adding the correct three-letter suffix to a file.*

Below *You now have access to the network and can obtain information stored here.*

internet file transfers and storage

Recently there has been an explosion in the amount of free Web space available. Mostly this has been space to allow people to set up their own Web pages. More recently, free space has been offered on shareable Web servers where hard-pressed computer users can store their files. Most of these have a limit on how much data you can store and how much you can transfer in a day without incurring charges, and do not in any case necessarily have the fastest transfer rates either. Again security, by virtue of it being a shared site, is unlikely to be stringent. Given that some of these Web servers are already turning away new clients, this may be a transient method of file storage, and as such is probably to be avoided.

FTP transfer

A File Transfer Protocol (FTP) site is an established means of storing computer files; also, FTP is the usual method for uploading files to a Web space on a server. The protocol itself uses cryptic command-line parameters, but many shareware or freeware applications utilize interfaces that make it easier to use. Also, most browsers now have FTP capacity built in, and although these usually do not allow you to upload files, they are adequate for downloading. These may include images you stored on your FTP server at work to download at home, or software drivers from hardware manufacturers' public FTP sites.

Shareware or freeware FTP applications—such as GlobalSCAPE's CuteFTP for Windows machines or Fetch by Fetch Softworks for Mac OS—usually list a variety of public FTP sites by default. These will generally be hosted by software developers and hardware manufacturers, and usually contain a variety of free files for various purposes.

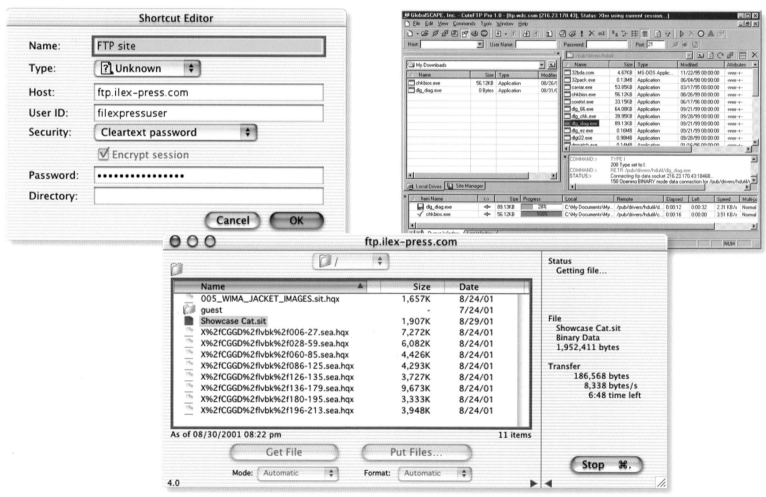

You can't use these to store your own files, however. Either contact your network administrator at work and ask to have an FTP site set up for you, or obtain access to an existing one.

Often, your Internet service provider will grant you a certain amount of password-protected file space on their servers, which is intended for Web files but can be used as FTP storage space. You should keep in mind that this is browser-accessible Web space, so if a person knows the URL and the filenames contained there, they may be able to download or view the files. So it is not a secure option, but it is an adequate short-term storage solution.

cross-platform multispeed servers

One of the newer solutions to appear in the virtual market is a combination of ISDN/leased line/telephone/ email whereby you send and receive to a hub or gateway service at the speed that your system can manage. The hub then sends the image(s) to the recipient at the fastest available rate for his or her setup. This has the advantage that you can connect to almost any type of direct connection system, but there are drawbacks too.

These systems charge for sending data on a per-Mb level for occasional users, or a fixed fee for higher-volume users. Furthermore, both sender and recipient need to have installed the appropriate software to get it to work. This might entail a change in Internet browser. It is, however, worth considering, since there are two other benefits. The first is relevant to security. The files are directed to a specific address and to that address alone. Second, you are notified when the job has been received, and also when the job has been looked at. Therefore there is no scope for plausible deniability, when the recipient later claims not to have seen or received the image.

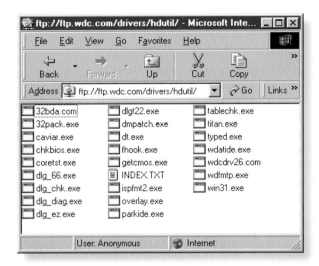

Left *Most Web browsers allow basic access to public FTP sites. For example, Western Digital hosts a public FTP site with drivers and other files to supplement their hardware. Microsoft Internet Explorer allows you to navigate through the site, view, and download files and folders.*

Left *Apple's iDisk (part of the iTools suite) offers extendable space hosted on Apple's own servers, albeit only for Macintosh OS users.*

Above *There's no shortage of vendors offering free Web space. Just be sure to read any small print that may limit space expansion or restrict visitor numbers.*

file sizes and compression

JPEG compression

JPEG is probably the most useful image compression format, but even within those four letters lies a multitude of variations. When you save your images from Photoshop, you are presented with three options for the format you wish to save in. These are Baseline Standard; Baseline Optimized; or Progressive.

As well as the actual format, you can choose a quality option. This ranges from 0 to 12 (0 to 10 in earlier versions). As you might expect, 0 does not give tremendous results, and 12 is virtually indistinguishable from the original file. But what kinds of saving in file size (and thus transmission time) does JPEG compression of whatever type afford?

The images on these pages show the same detail from a 7Mb Photoshop file compressed using different JPEG options. This is not a huge file (it could be printed at 7 × 4 inches at true photographic quality), but it is still likely to test your patience if you try sending it by a traditional telephone modem. You may notice that an unfamiliar format "ProJPEG" has been included. ProJPEG is a Photoshop plug-in from BoxTop software that squeezes a little more quality into, and a little more file size out of, compressed files. While this in itself is a recommendation, the real benefit is the on-screen preview, which shows you the differences between settings without having to save them and then open them up again. The plug-in costs $50 and, depending on how you charge your own time, it will earn its keep in time savings quite quickly.

The only thing that should happen to a JPEG file after it is compressed is that it is expanded. There should be no more file correction, absolutely no further sharpening, no color curve changing, and no major changes in contrast or orientation of the image.

GIF compression

Graphics Interchange Format (GIF) image files work best with graphics that have large, uniformly colored areas. These files employ the LZW (Lempel-Zif-Welch) compression technique. While this is not necessarily a "lossy" means of reducing file size, reducing the image color palette or removing stray pixels using software such as ImageReady or Fireworks can often reduce file sizes even further with very little noticeable reduction in file quality or appearance.

ZIP and Stuffit files

There are various lossless compression formats available for both Windows and Mac, but the most common are ZIP and Stuffit. These files can be created and decompressed using freeware or shareware programs, such as WinZip Computing's WinZip (Windows) and Aladdin Systems's Stuffit Dropstuff/Expander (Mac). The process used for all of these types of files is basically this: the software creates a small "dictionary" of repeating elements in the text or data file and allocates numbers to them. Each occurrence of the repeating element is then replaced with a number, thus reducing the overall size of the file. This process produces better results with large files than it does with small ones, and, because many image files already use similar compression methods, results can vary greatly. However, multiple files can be "Zipped" or "Stuffed" into a single archive. Also, the latter can be made into "self-extracting" archives containing the basic procedures required to rebuild the file. In this situation, the end viewer does not even need extra software to decompress them.

Modem compression

It should also be noted that most modems have a series of protocols built into their hardware for various purposes, such as error correction, and even file compression. These automatically allow easily compressed files (such as text documents) to be transferred more quickly. Downloading the HTML in a Web page, for example, generally takes less time than downloading the equivalent number of bytes in an already heavily compressed image file.

Right and opposite This series shows the differences in file sizes and download times for various types of JPEG images. Progressive JPEGs are used to provide the viewer with something to look at while the image downloads. While a normal JPEG image will slowly appear from top to bottom, a progressive JPEG will appear almost immediately at low quality, then with each successive "pass" or "scan," will increase in quality until the full image is displayed. The labels refer to: JPEG type, quality level, number of scans, and approximate file size and time to transfer at 28.8Kb/sec.

BASELINE, QUALITY LEVEL 0, 1 SCAN, 105KB

PROGRESSIVE, QUALITY LEVEL 0, 3 SCANS, 103KB, 29s

PROGRESSIVE, QUALITY LEVEL 0, 5 SCANS, 107KB, 31s

BASELINE, QUALITY LEVEL 100, 1 SCAN, 1.2MB, 350s

PROGRESSIVE, QUALITY LEVEL 100, 3 SCANS, 1.1MB, 306s

PROGRESSIVE, QUALITY LEVEL 100, 5 SCANS, 1.3MB, 380s

PROJPEG, QUALITY LEVEL 0, 38KB, 12s

PROJPEG, QUALITY LEVEL 60, 287KB, 83s

PROJPEG (SMOOTH), QUALITY LEVEL 100, 1.1MB, 317s

PROJPEG, QUALITY LEVEL 100, 1.2MB, 350s

9 real-time practice

This section of the book looks at getting you started quickly on the individual aspects of input, manipulation, and output. Each of the projects within this section leads you through a procedure no more than 20 minutes long, at the end of which you should be able to complete your task. If there is something you can't quite follow, simply refer back to the appropriate chapter.

20-MINUTE PROCEDURES

image capture 1

There are a number of ways of getting an image into a digital format and then into your computer. Scanners and digital cameras are the easiest methods, but alternatives include PhotoCD (or Picture CD) transfers of conventional film media and download via certain photoprocessing labs. Such labs will process your film and post a digital copy onto the Web for you to download or to order prints from. Here we take a look at using a flatbed scanner and a digital camera to capture digital images and get them onto your computer.

Scanners

Ensure scanner is properly connected and turned on.

Launch the scanner software. This may be as an independent application or as a plug-in from within a graphics or image editing application.

Place artwork on the scanner's glass plate, accurately aligned.

Choose the right scanning size based on your required output (*see chapter 2*).

| 00:01 | 00:02 | 00:03 | 00:04 | 00:05 |

| 00:01 | 00:02 | 00:03 | 00:04 | 00:05 |

Digital cameras

Ensure that camera is turned on, is in the correct mode, and that there is sufficient capacity in both the batteries and memory card. (It is wise to have at least one backup set of each.)

Select minimum compression, and check sharpening settings.

Check that the white balance setting of the camera is correct for the scene (this could be set to auto) particularly if you are using problematic light sources such as fluorescent or tungsten.

Check that the resolution settings are correct.

scanners

Scanners are an ideal tool for digitizing prints. Flatbed scanners are best for flat artwork, but most are less successful for scanning slides. Dedicated slide scanners work in much the same way as the flatbed.

digital cameras

Digital cameras vary in complexity, but they all operate in basically the same way. Though much of the picture-taking process is similar to that of conventional cameras, we pay particular attention to the digital-specific elements.

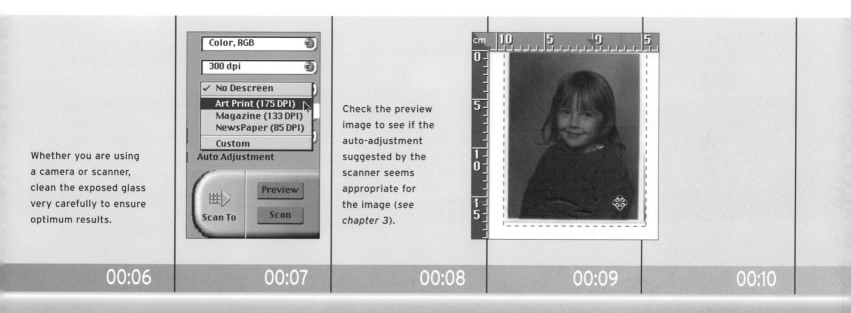

Whether you are using a camera or scanner, clean the exposed glass very carefully to ensure optimum results.

Check the preview image to see if the auto-adjustment suggested by the scanner seems appropriate for the image (*see chapter 3*).

00:06   00:07   00:08   00:09   00:10

00:06   00:07   00:08   00:09   00:10

Check sharpening and any other camera-set parameters (*see pages 120 to 121*).

Compose and take picture.

20-MINUTE PROCEDURES

image capture 2

With the image recorded, either using a scanner onto a computer or on the digital camera's memory card, we now need to optimize it in order that the image may be reproduced to the highest quality and with the highest level of authenticity.

scanned images

Scanned images may need more modification than those from a digital camera. Scanning can increase contrast levels and reduce tonal ranges. Dust and alignment problems are also common.

If you are happy with how the image preview looks, scan the picture in at your chosen resolution and color depth (see *page 125*).

If you are not happy with the image, use a more advanced manual level to get the image exactly as you want it (*see chapter 3*).

| 00:11 | 00:12 | 00:13 | 00:14 | 00:15 |

| 00:11 | 00:12 | 00:13 | 00:14 | 00:15 |

At this stage some cameras (or cameras set to certain picture modes) will store the image automatically. Others will permit the image to be previewed on the LCD panel to assess the quality of the image.

Check preview screen for focus and red eye; zoom in if necessary. If the image is not entirely as expected, retake the shot.

If all is okay, the image can be saved to the camera's memory card.

Transfer the image to your computer (*see pages 118 to 119, 155*).

A general rule for image capture: if memory space is not at a premium, use uncompressed file types in-camera.

THE END RESULT

digital camera images

When taking a digital photograph, you can use the preview screen to assess the image immediately after exposure. It is usually possible to zoom in on details (such as the branches of trees) to check for focus or other defects.

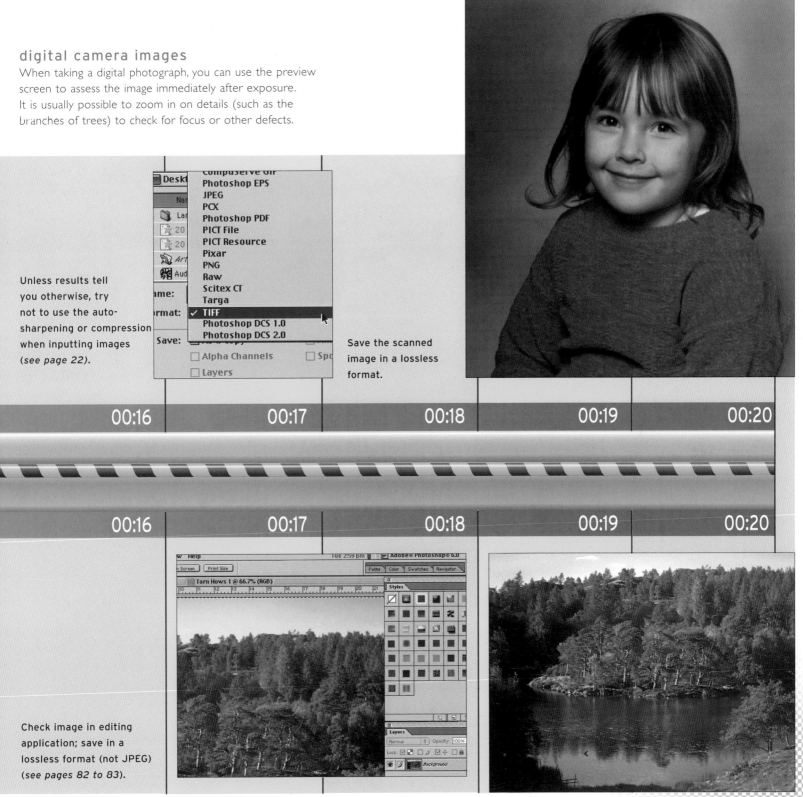

Unless results tell you otherwise, try not to use the auto-sharpening or compression when inputting images (*see page 22*).

Save the scanned image in a lossless format.

00:16   00:17   00:18   00:19   00:20

00:16   00:17   00:18   00:19   00:20

Check image in editing application; save in a lossless format (not JPEG) (*see pages 82 to 83*).

THE END RESULT

20-MINUTE PROCEDURES

image correction 1

The "raw" images delivered by a scanner or digital camera (such as those in the previous procedure) are just that—raw. This is still a long way from being a finished product. To convert them into true, high-quality images suitable for output, we will need to perform some

edits and manipulations. We are using Photoshop here, but you could equally use any other image editing application. All the tools and processes used here are common to most applications and the process itself remains the same.

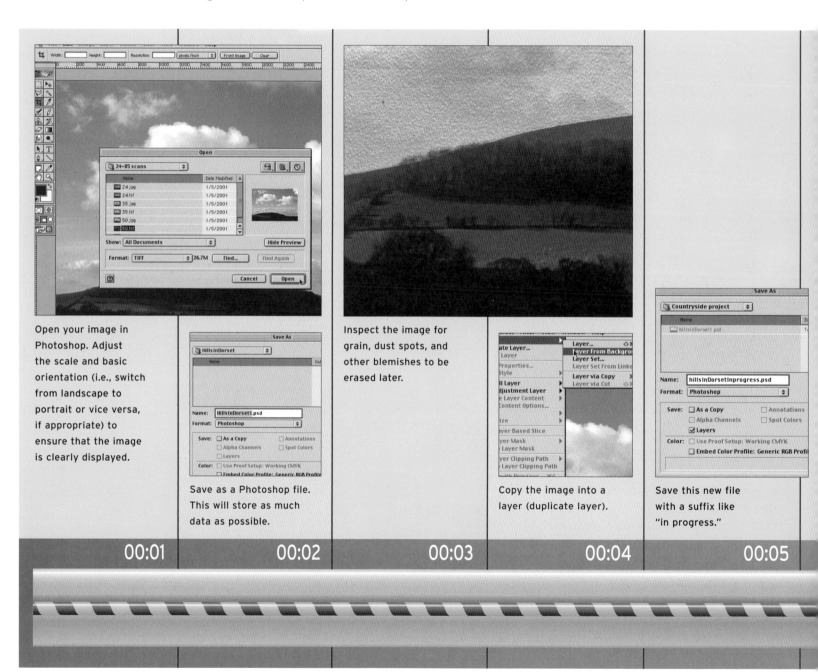

Open your image in Photoshop. Adjust the scale and basic orientation (i.e., switch from landscape to portrait or vice versa, if appropriate) to ensure that the image is clearly displayed.

Save as a Photoshop file. This will store as much data as possible.

Inspect the image for grain, dust spots, and other blemishes to be erased later.

Copy the image into a layer (duplicate layer).

Save this new file with a suffix like "in progress."

00:01   00:02   00:03   00:04   00:05

orientation

Digital camera images are correctly orientated (or need only a simple rotation through 90 degrees), but those from a scanner are often slightly skewed. Check for "true" verticals and horizontals (particularly horizons).

dust and scratches

Scanned images will inevitably display some marks due to dust and scratches. Some of these may have been on the original image but most will have occurred as part of the scanning process, no matter how clean your scanner is.

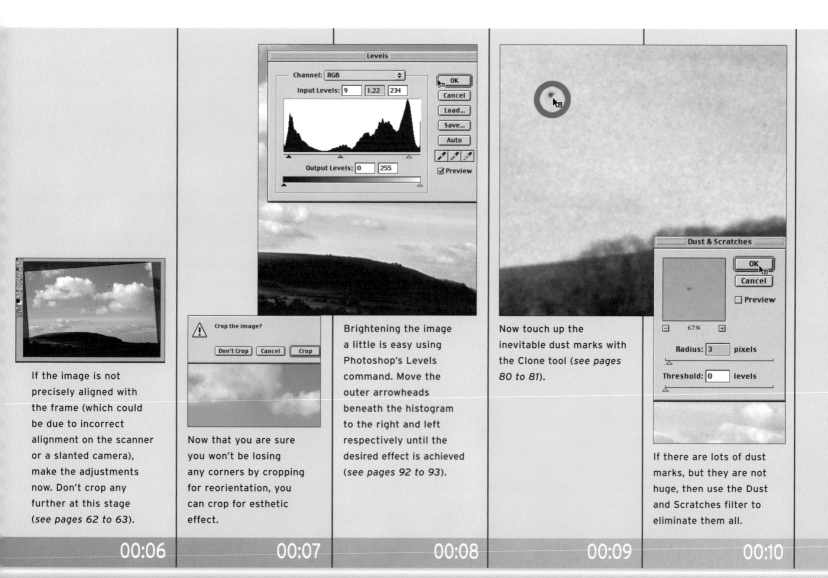

If the image is not precisely aligned with the frame (which could be due to incorrect alignment on the scanner or a slanted camera), make the adjustments now. Don't crop any further at this stage (*see pages 62 to 63*).

Now that you are sure you won't be losing any corners by cropping for reorientation, you can crop for esthetic effect.

Brightening the image a little is easy using Photoshop's Levels command. Move the outer arrowheads beneath the histogram to the right and left respectively until the desired effect is achieved (*see pages 92 to 93*).

Now touch up the inevitable dust marks with the Clone tool (*see pages 80 to 81*).

If there are lots of dust marks, but they are not huge, then use the Dust and Scratches filter to eliminate them all.

00:06   00:07   00:08   00:09   00:10

20-MINUTE PROCEDURES

image correction 2

Image editing and manipulation is seen by many as a black art. Often this perception arises because there are few hard and fast rules; each image creator has his or her own ways of going about the processes. This often leads to slightly different end results, as well as different problems and advantages. The examples shown here should really be regarded as starting points and inspiration rather than strict procedures to be followed. Here we look at improving the tonal range of our selected image and the presentation.

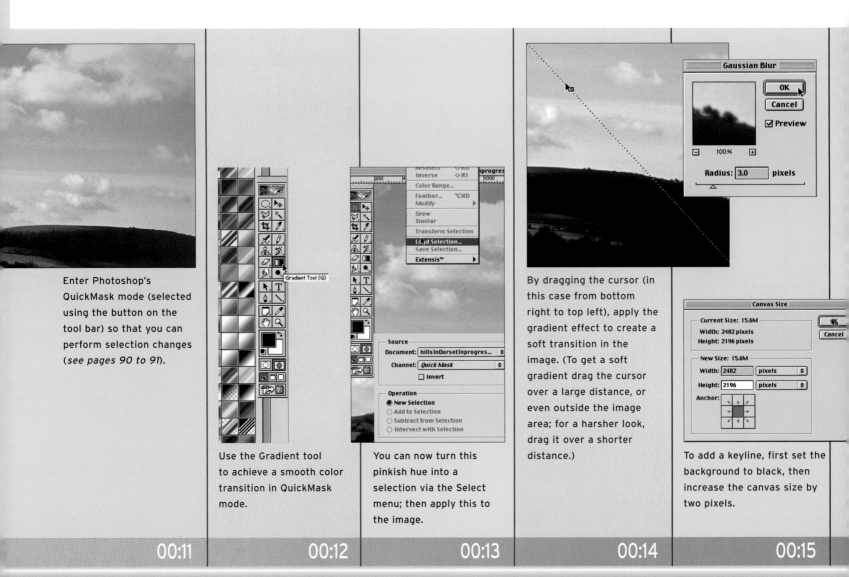

Enter Photoshop's QuickMask mode (selected using the button on the tool bar) so that you can perform selection changes (*see pages 90 to 91*).

Use the Gradient tool to achieve a smooth color transition in QuickMask mode.

You can now turn this pinkish hue into a selection via the Select menu; then apply this to the image.

By dragging the cursor (in this case from bottom right to top left), apply the gradient effect to create a soft transition in the image. (To get a soft gradient drag the cursor over a large distance, or even outside the image area; for a harsher look, drag it over a shorter distance.)

To add a keyline, first set the background to black, then increase the canvas size by two pixels.

| 00:11 | 00:12 | 00:13 | 00:14 | 00:15 |

QuickMask

The QuickMask feature shown here is one of those invaluable selection tools found in the full version of Photoshop; it enables conventional tools to be used to protect elements from subsequent manipulations.

Photoshop format

Saving an image using the Photoshop Format (and with the .psd file extension) ensures that any changes or enhancements—such as layers—are stored with the image and not lost.

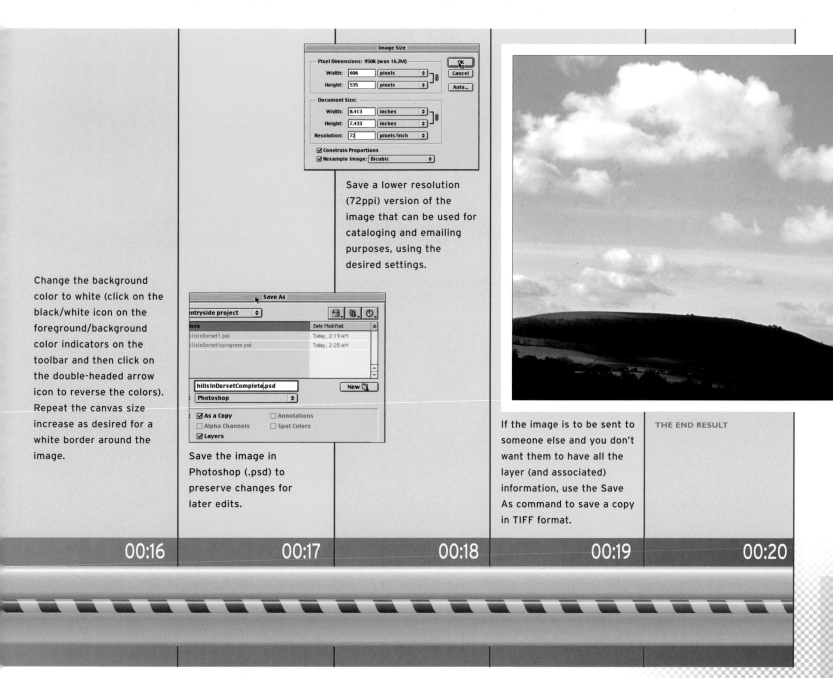

Save a lower resolution (72ppi) version of the image that can be used for cataloging and emailing purposes, using the desired settings.

Change the background color to white (click on the black/white icon on the foreground/background color indicators on the toolbar and then click on the double-headed arrow icon to reverse the colors). Repeat the canvas size increase as desired for a white border around the image.

Save the image in Photoshop (.psd) to preserve changes for later edits.

If the image is to be sent to someone else and you don't want them to have all the layer (and associated) information, use the Save As command to save a copy in TIFF format.

THE END RESULT

00:16   00:17   00:18   00:19   00:20

10-MINUTE PROCEDURES

preparing still images for the web

Preparing an image for use on the Web (for example, for emailing to friends or for use on a Web page) requires the use of a slightly different set of techniques than would be used to prepare the same image for use in print or on screen. Here we first look at Web use and second at how a series of still images can be combined into an effective Web animation. There are some concerns that vary between print and Web publishing, one of the most crucial being the ratio between file size and image quality.

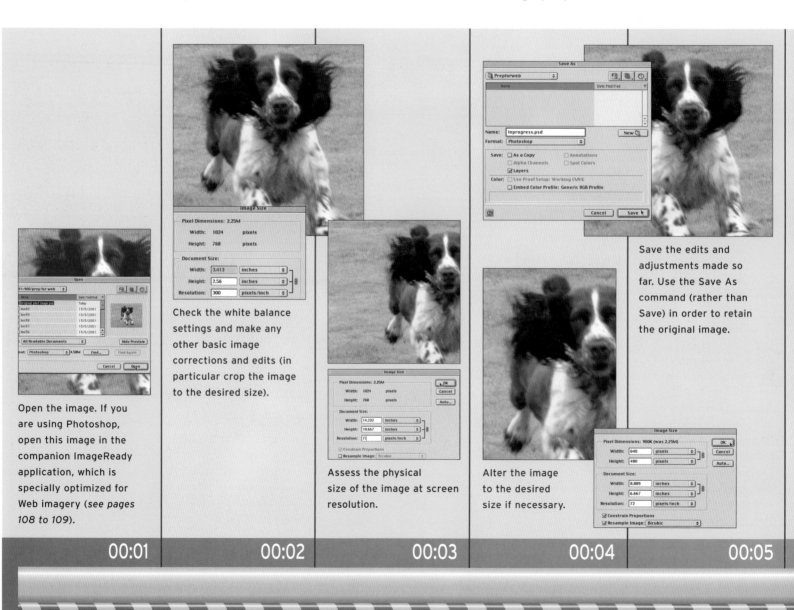

Open the image. If you are using Photoshop, open this image in the companion ImageReady application, which is specially optimized for Web imagery (*see pages 108 to 109*).

Check the white balance settings and make any other basic image corrections and edits (in particular crop the image to the desired size).

Assess the physical size of the image at screen resolution.

Alter the image to the desired size if necessary.

Save the edits and adjustments made so far. Use the Save As command (rather than Save) in order to retain the original image.

00:01   00:02   00:03   00:04   00:05

JPEG

The JPEG is considered by many to be ideal for Web images. Though it is lossy, it produces small file sizes that are perfect for the Internet. It is also almost universally accepted by graphics applications and Web browsers.

GIF and PNG

GIFs use 8-bit color. They suit graphics and simple images and support animations. Portable Network Graphics (PNG) gives 10 to 30% lossless compression and supports variable transparency through "alpha channels."

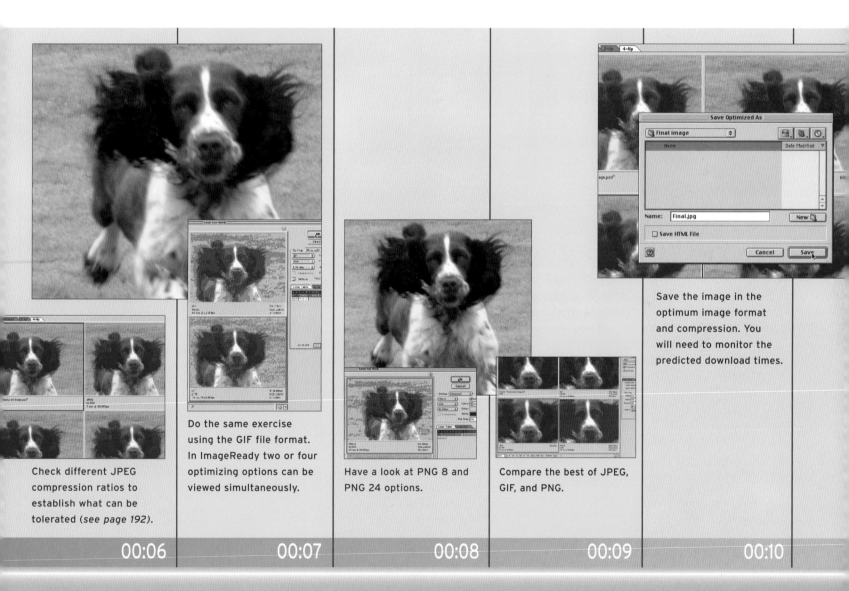

Check different JPEG compression ratios to establish what can be tolerated (*see page 192*).

Do the same exercise using the GIF file format. In ImageReady two or four optimizing options can be viewed simultaneously.

Have a look at PNG 8 and PNG 24 options.

Compare the best of JPEG, GIF, and PNG.

Save the image in the optimum image format and compression. You will need to monitor the predicted download times.

00:06   00:07   00:08   00:09   00:10

10-MINUTE PROCEDURES

preparing an animation for the web

If you have captured a sequence of images (time-lapse photos or some edited graphics, for example), they can be combined to create an animation sequence. These are quite simple to create using most image processing applications. Animations are the ideal way to enliven or enrich a Web site, providing the essential addition of movement to the page. To start with you will need to ensure that the images in your sequence are in an identical format or even converted into individual layers of a Photoshop format image.

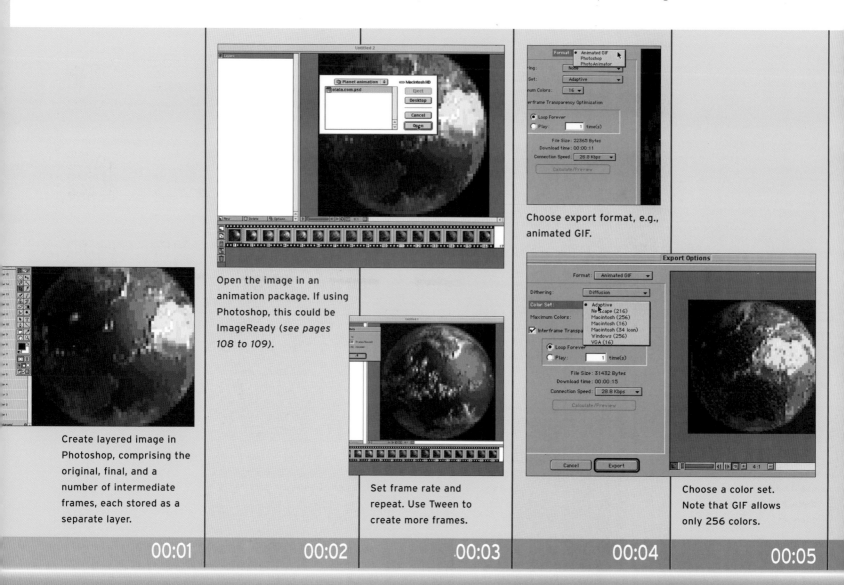

Create layered image in Photoshop, comprising the original, final, and a number of intermediate frames, each stored as a separate layer.

Open the image in an animation package. If using Photoshop, this could be ImageReady (*see pages 108 to 109*).

Set frame rate and repeat. Use Tween to create more frames.

Choose export format, e.g., animated GIF.

Choose a color set. Note that GIF allows only 256 colors.

00:01   00:02   .00:03   00:04   00:05

frame rate and repeat

Conventional TV has a twenty-five or thirty frames per second rate, depending on the format (*see page 50*). Web animations work successfully with lower rates. You'll also need to specify the repeat: once-only sequence or a loop.

tweening

The "Tween" command creates intermediate frames between existing frames to help "fill out" a sequence. The automated nature means that tweened frames may not always represent an accurate intermediate image.

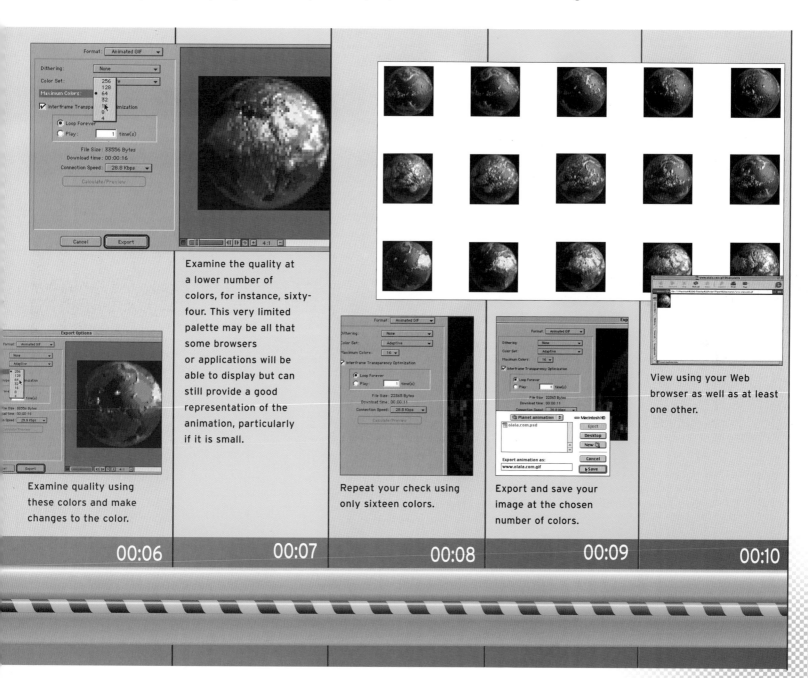

Examine quality using these colors and make changes to the color.

Examine the quality at a lower number of colors, for instance, sixty-four. This very limited palette may be all that some browsers or applications will be able to display but can still provide a good representation of the animation, particularly if it is small.

Repeat your check using only sixteen colors.

Export and save your image at the chosen number of colors.

View using your Web browser as well as at least one other.

00:06 00:07 00:08 00:09 00:10

20-MINUTE PROCEDURES

preparation for press 1

Normally when working with images we use the RGB color mode to ensure accurate reproduction on screen. However, when we send images—say, to a magazine—with the intention that they will be reproduced and published, they will need to be converted to CMYK in order that color separation plates can be produced, one for each of the inks used: cyan, magenta, yellow, and black. In this procedure we look at optimizing such a conversion and ensuring that the image created in RGB remains true in CMYK.

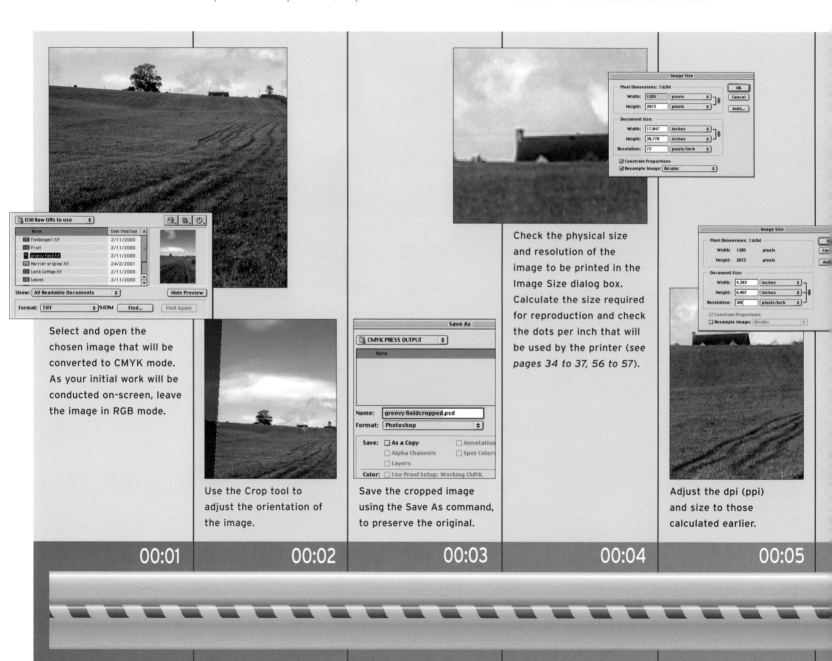

Select and open the chosen image that will be converted to CMYK mode. As your initial work will be conducted on-screen, leave the image in RGB mode.

Use the Crop tool to adjust the orientation of the image.

Save the cropped image using the Save As command, to preserve the original.

Check the physical size and resolution of the image to be printed in the Image Size dialog box. Calculate the size required for reproduction and check the dots per inch that will be used by the printer (*see pages 34 to 37, 56 to 57*).

Adjust the dpi (ppi) and size to those calculated earlier.

00:01   00:02   00:03   00:04   00:05

color spaces

The CMYK and RGB color spaces are somewhat different in that the range of colors that can be reproduced on a color monitor is different to the range that can be printed with the CMYK inks. There is a considerable overlap between the two color spaces but there are some that are unique in each case. It is rare that the unique colors are so crucial that an RGB image cannot be reproduced with a high degree of accuracy in CMYK (or vice versa) but differences can, and do, occur.

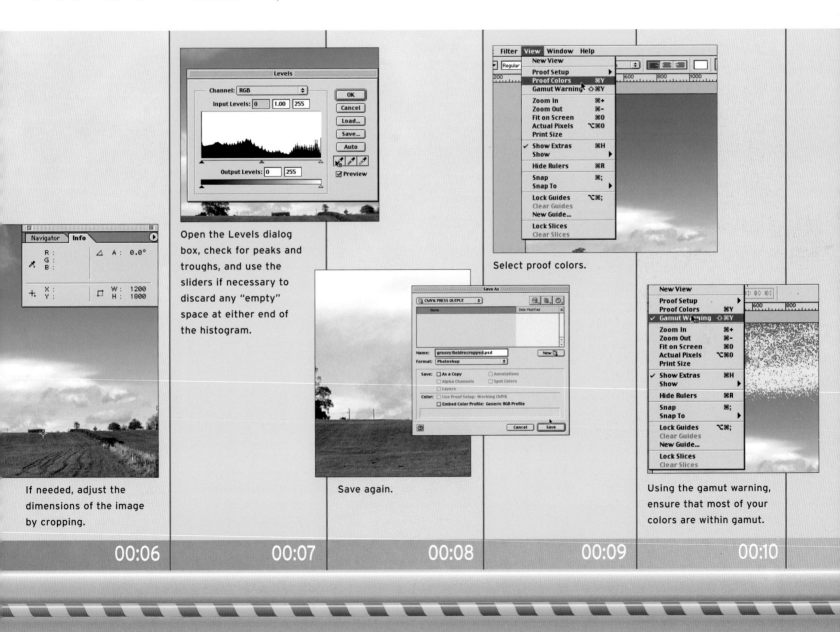

Open the Levels dialog box, check for peaks and troughs, and use the sliders if necessary to discard any "empty" space at either end of the histogram.

Select proof colors.

If needed, adjust the dimensions of the image by cropping.

Save again.

Using the gamut warning, ensure that most of your colors are within gamut.

00:06   00:07   00:08   00:09   00:10

20-MINUTE PROCEDURES

preparation for press 2

Based on predigital techniques of combining an image with a blurred negative to achieve subtle sharpening effects, the Unsharp Mask uses three control parameters: Amount, Radius, and Threshold. Amount determines the amount of contrast added to boundary (edge) pixels;

Radius describes the number of pixels adjacent to that boundary that are affected by the sharpening; and Threshold sets a minimum value for pixel contrast below which the filter will have no effect. It is a powerful filter, but it is easy to overdo its effects.

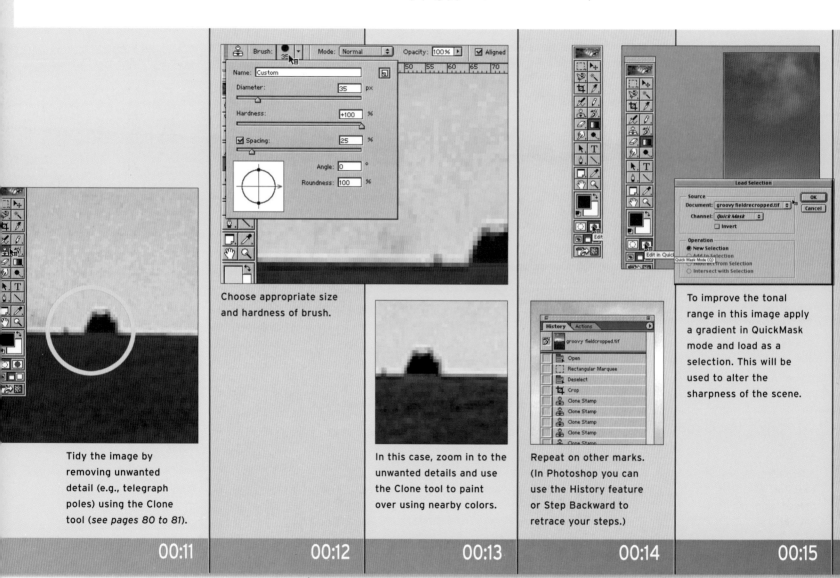

Choose appropriate size and hardness of brush.

Tidy the image by removing unwanted detail (e.g., telegraph poles) using the Clone tool (*see pages 80 to 81*).

In this case, zoom in to the unwanted details and use the Clone tool to paint over using nearby colors.

Repeat on other marks. (In Photoshop you can use the History feature or Step Backward to retrace your steps.)

To improve the tonal range in this image apply a gradient in QuickMask mode and load as a selection. This will be used to alter the sharpness of the scene.

00:11   00:12   00:13   00:14   00:15

gaussian blur

Gaussian Blur is a specialized blurring filter found in image editors. It applies a weighted average (based on the bell-shaped curve of the Gaussian distribution) when identifying and softening boundaries. It also introduces low-frequency detail and a mild "mistiness" to the image, ideal for blending out discrete image information, such as noise and artifacts. Unlike the Sharpen and Sharpen More filters, the Gaussian Blur permits a controllable amount of softening that yields more realistic end results.

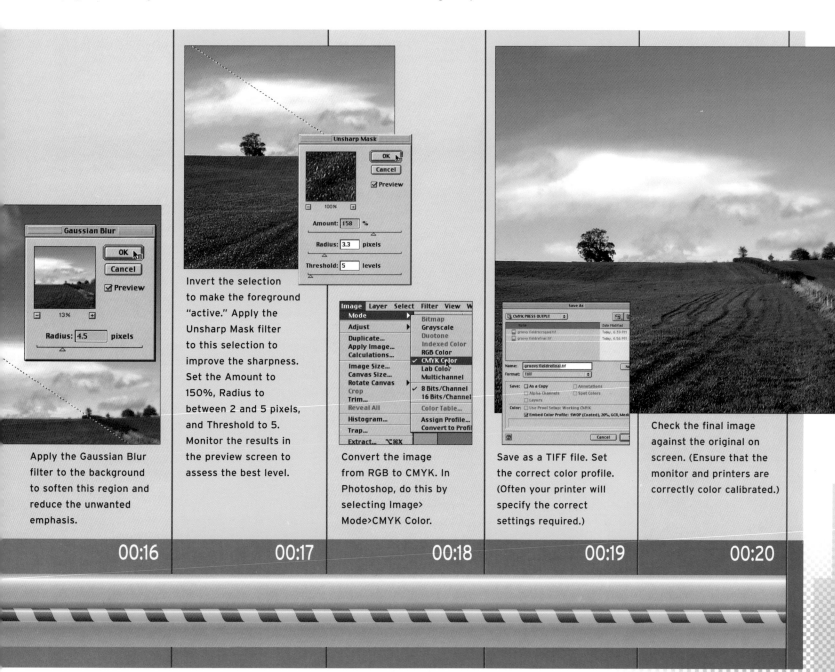

Apply the Gaussian Blur filter to the background to soften this region and reduce the unwanted emphasis.

Invert the selection to make the foreground "active." Apply the Unsharp Mask filter to this selection to improve the sharpness. Set the Amount to 150%, Radius to between 2 and 5 pixels, and Threshold to 5. Monitor the results in the preview screen to assess the best level.

Convert the image from RGB to CMYK. In Photoshop, do this by selecting Image> Mode>CMYK Color.

Save as a TIFF file. Set the correct color profile. (Often your printer will specify the correct settings required.)

Check the final image against the original on screen. (Ensure that the monitor and printers are correctly color calibrated.)

00:16   00:17   00:18   00:19   00:20

glossary

Acrobat Reader (Adobe)
A program that allows you to view PDFs on virtually any computer platform.

A/D conversion
Conversion of an analog voltage to a digital number (0s and 1s). The higher the number of bits used to describe the analog signal, the more accurate it will be.

additive colors *(see also subtractive colors)*
Describes the light-based primary colors of red (R), green (G), and blue (B) which, added together, create white. RGB is used to form every other color for display monitors and photographic reproduction.

Adobe
A major software developer, Adobe is responsible for products such as Acrobat, GoLive, Illustrator, ImageReady, InDesign, Photoshop, Premiere, and Type Manager.

aliased *(see also antialias)*
Jagged edges on images with a low resolution or that have been enlarged.

alpha channel *(see also masks)*
An additional channel to the RGB or CMYK channels. It contains masks that can be manipulated to create effects.

Amiga IFF
Color format used by programs including DeluxePaint. Allows you to save between computer platforms.

analog
A signal from an input device that needs to be converted to a digital form the computer can understand.

anchor *(see also paths)*
Adjustable points, such as curve or corner points, added when changes of direction are introduced into a path.

animation
A moving image created by moving quickly through a sequence of still images.

Animation
A lossless compression setting in QuickTime. The lack of compression makes it slow to write but relatively quick to load—from a local hard disk at least.

antialias
Removes the jagged edges of bitmapped images by blending the image with surrounding pixels. If antialiasing is not used, block effects known as aliasing occur.

Autochrome (Thermal)
A FujiFilm technology for the production of photo-realistic prints.

bicubic interpolation *(see also interpolation)*
Used for smooth, exact results, but tends to be slow. Compares the colors of all of the surrounding pixels when assigning color values to any new pixel in the image.

bilinear interpolation *(see also interpolation)*
Used for medium-quality results. It only compares the colors of the nearest four pixels when assigning color values to any new pixel in the image.

binary
A system that expresses values as 1 or 0.

bit depth
The number of bits per pixel (expressed as 8-bit, 16-bit, 24-bit, 32-bit, and so on).

bitmap
A bitmap is a "map" describing the location and binary state (on or off) of "bits" which defines a complete collection of pixels or dots that comprise an image.

black generation *(see also UCR and GCR)*
When printing, black is needed as the fourth color because 100% of CMY makes dark brown, not black, when added together. Black generation also describes the way that black ink can be used to replace CMY when these colors would combine to make a gray.

bleed
An area that goes outside the cropmarks of an image to allow it to print to the edge of the cut page.

BMP
A Windows bitmap file. Can be up to 24-bit.

BoxTop
Manufacturer of several programs designed to ease the production of Web images. Products include very useful plug-ins for Photoshop including ProJPEG and PhotoGif.

brightness
The strength of luminescence from light to dark (the amount of black or white present). Defined by Photoshop as a measured percentage from 0% (black) to 100% (white).

bump map
A bitmap image file, normally grayscale, frequently used when creating a lighting effect in some programs.

burn tool (see *dodge tool*)
Allows you to brush over areas of an image to gradually make that part darker.

calibration
The adjustment of a monitor or other device to conform to an established standard so that the image is displayed as accurately and consistently as possible.

cascade
Open file windows displayed one above another.

cast
When the color balance of a scan is wrong; for example, if the image appears too blue or red.

CCD (Charge-Coupled Device)
The array of light-sensitive square receptors used to pick up the image in a digital camera or scanner.

CD-ROM (Compact Disc Read-Only Memory)
Optical disk with a capacity of 650Mb or 700Mb.

channel (see also *alpha channels*)
A file in RGB has three channels. A file in CMYK has four channels. You can also make additional channels for creating effects or for masking.

cine (cinematographic)
Refers to moving film cameras, usually using 8mm or 16mm film.

Cinepak
A DV compression format.

clip art
Collections of ready-made pieces of artwork often available on a royalty-free basis on CD or via the Web. Clip art images are more often a very useful basis for a digital image than finished images in themselves.

clipboard
Temporarily stores the last item that you cut or copied.

clipping path
Most image files are saved and imported into layouts as rectangles. Using a path tool, a clipping path creates straight and curved lines around a shape. When exported as an EPS format, a file containing a clipping path can be imported into a layout in the shape that has been created.

CLUT (Color LookUp Table)
An existing table of 256 colors used by the operating system. Where a color used in an image is not available in the table, the application selects the nearest color to the one used. You can also save an exact set of colors (indexed colors) from an image. This is useful for animation packages. With indexed colors, the number and range of colors do not constantly change.

CMYK (see *subtractive colors*)

ColorSync
Apple's color management technology, meant to ensure color accuracy throughout the digital workflow.

color curve
Curves are used to adjust the overall tone of a picture. You can make an image darker or lighter at any point between white and black. You can also change the amount you do this at more than one point, producing effects such as solarization.

color gamut (see also *color model*)
The range of colors available on a device is described as its gamut or color space. Colors that a monitor cannot display are said to be "out of gamut." Similarly an RGB monitor can display more colors than a CMYK printer can print.

color mode
Some devices and computers have a very limited ability to display color; in order to work properly they need certain colors. When you change color mode, you select one that is more appropriate to the device.

color model (see also *HSB, indexed color, L*a*b*)
The method of defining color space. The two principal models are additive (Red, Green, Blue) where adding two colors creates a third, and subtractive (Cyan, Magenta, and Yellow) where subtracting a color creates another.

color separations
When an image is color-separated for the printing process, four films (one each of CMYK) are made to recreate a color image.

color space (see *color gamuts*)

color systems
PANTONE, FOCOLTONE, TRUMATCH, TOYO, DIC, and ANPA are all color systems used for specifying colors. Some are sets of colors based on CMYK; others are additional colors to the standard CMYK set. These colors are referenced using a color book or swatch to achieve an exact match.

color trapping
Slight overlapping between two colors to remove any unsightly gaps or mismatches in printing. Most of the comprehensive programs that incorporate graphics to be printed will also include color trapping rules.

CompuServe GIF (see *GIF*)

continuous tone
Any image with subtly graduated tones, such as a photograph or artwork.

corner point (see *paths*)

crop
To conceal or trim unwanted areas of an image.

CRT (Cathode Ray Tube)
Standard video display system for most TVs and monitors. It fires electrons at tricolor phosphors.

curves (see *paths*)

cut, copy, and paste
When you choose Cut, your selection is removed from its original position in your file and placed in RAM (temporary memory). Copy makes a duplicate of your selection and places it in RAM. Select Paste when you are ready to return the selection or duplicate to your current or any other file.

cutout (see *clipping path*)
An image in which the background has been removed. Shooting pictures with plain backgrounds specially for cutouts is recommended to avoid time-consuming masking.

DCS (Desktop Color Separation)
File format for saving color separations for output. DCS saves a low-resolution image for displaying on screen as well as the individual color channels.

desaturate
To reduce the purity of a color, thus making it grayer.

digital
Any information or signal described in binary digits.

digital camera
Rather than film, uses an array of light-sensitive cells to capture an image. The resolution depends on the size of the array, and the quality depends on how much information the chip can handle.

disk cache
A small amount of RAM set aside for temporary storage of information that is used frequently.

dithering
A method of introducing randomness to either printing patterns or screen colors by adding extra pixels to smooth the jagged effects of pixellation (blockiness).

dodge tool (see *burn tool*)
Allows you to brush over areas of an image to gradually make that part lighter.

dot gain
In the printing process, when the ink hits the paper, the ink spreads out. The amount varies, so you can change this in your Preferences to compensate for the printer, paper, or press being used.

DPI (Dots Per Inch) (see also *LPI*)
Represents the resolution of printing devices.

duotone
A monochromatic image combining two halftones with different tonal ranges made from the same original, so that when printed in different tones of the same color (usually black, thus sometimes described as a "double-black duotone"), a wider tonal range is reproduced than is possible with a single color.

DV (Digital Video)
Movie images created in, or converted to, the digital domain and thus editable on computer.

EPS (Encapsulated PostScript)
A standard file format that includes all the PostScript data necessary to display and reproduce images in a large number of graphics and layout programs.

export
Saves a version of your file into a format that can be read by another application.

feathering
Similar to antialiasing, this blurs the edge pixels of a selection to give a soft border.

filter
Creates different effects on an image or partial image using presets from the menus.

FireWire
An Apple-developed technology that allows high-speed communications between the computer and peripherals such as external hard drive and digital cameras.

Flashpix
A file format that has pixel-independent resolution. When you alter an image at screen resolution (72ppi), the software makes the same amendments to the master file, making for faster editing.

flatness (see RIP)
PostScript files can get very complicated and contain lots of curves, which can lead to PostScript printing errors. Changing the flatness can simplify the paths in a complex graphics file. Instead of printing every pixel on a curve, it will join, say, every three pixels to form a straight line. The term is also used to refer to an image where the contrast between the lightest and darkest tones is insufficient, resulting in a "flat" image.

frame grabber
Software that captures an image (usually quite a low-resolution one) by acting as a still video camera.

gamma
A measure of how much light, dark, and contrast is contained within an image. Gamma curves can be used in the software that may come with a scanner so that you can preset the amount of light and dark and contrast on input.

gamut (see color gamut)

Gaussian Blur
A method of giving an impression of defocus to an image. Also helps to hide blemishes.

GCR (Gray Component Replacement)
A method of color separation where black ink is used instead of CMY to create gray.

GIF (Graphic Interchange Format)
A "lossless" bitmapped graphics format particularly suited to line images and other graphics, such as text.

GifMation
An animation program based on the GIF graphics format.

graduation (also gradation)
The measure of smoothness of transformation from one color to another.

grayscale
The mode used for re-creating black-and-white photographic images and smooth black-and-white blends.

halftone
A series of monotone dots, set in a pattern or screen. These dots are smaller or larger, closer or further apart, to simulate each particular shade.

highlights
Brighter areas of an image.

Histogram
Shows in graphical terms (a horizontal array of vertical bar charts) the amount of each particular shade of gray across the range from white to black.

HSB
A color model based on the variables of Hue, Saturation, and Brightness.

HTML (HyperText Markup Language)
A text-based "page description language" (PDL) used to format documents published on the Web.

hue
A color as found in its pure state in the spectrum.

import
To bring a file created by a different program into your program.

indexed color (see also CLUT)
An RFB file that contains a maximum of 256 colors.

inkjet
Printing system that fires tiny inkdrops at a sheet of paper.

interpolation (see also bicubic and bilinear interpolation)
A computer process used to add or delete pixels when resizing an image.

JPEG (Joint Photographic Experts Group)
A "lossy" file format for compressing an image. Particularly suited to continuous-tone images, such as photographs.

Kodachrome
A color slide film system that discontinued in 2002.

L*a*b color (see also color mode)
A color model designed to achieve consistent color whatever the device. L*a*b color consists of a luminance component (L) and two chromatic components: a (green to red) and b (blue to yellow).

lasso
A tool for making an irregular (that is, not rectangular, circular, or ovoid) selection on an image.

layers
A method used in graphics programs to overlay different images or sections of the same image.

line art
Usually a black-and-white drawing. Can be pixel-based but is usually an EPS.

lossless / lossy
Refers to data-losing qualities of different compression methods: lossless means that no image information is lost; lossy means that some (or much) of the image data is lost in the compression process.

LPI (Lines Per Inch) (see also halftone)
The measurement used to define the dot frequency of a halftone.

LZW (Lempel-Ziv-Welch) (see also TIFF)
A lossless compression method for bitmapped images.

Mac
Abbreviation for Apple Macintosh.

masks
A photographic technique that allows you to show or hide areas of an image. You can work on areas that are inside or outside the mask that you "paint." Masks can also be used to make holes through layers and reveal what is underneath.

midtones
These are not the lightest or darkest areas of an image, but the middle of the range.

mode (see color mode)

montage
Image that includes a number of other images.

multichannel mode
When you convert an image to multichannel mode, you separate each color channel into multiple layers, each containing a maximum of 256 levels of gray. To make edits, you would have to edit each channel individually. This is only useful for very specialized tasks.

nearest neighbor
The most basic kind of interpolation, this should only be used for screengrabs where the image is pixellated anyway.

Nyquist Frequency
The factor by which the resolution of a subject to be scanned or photographed needs to be exceeded by the capture resolution in order for its detail to be properly recorded (see page 126).

opacity
Describes how nontransparent an item is. Something with an opacity of 0% is completely transparent, something with 100% opacity lets no other detail through.

out of gamut (see color gamut)

output
Any printed matter or screen image produced from a digital file.

parallel
PC port used by printers and scanners. Not to be confused with SCSI, which appears to have similar plugs and sockets. Connect a SCSI device to a parallel port or vice versa and you will damage your device.

paths (see also clipping path)
Using paths in programs that work with "vector graphics" you can create a series of lines, curves, and corners. Paths can be used for producing cutouts and for creating graphics that are "resolution-independent."

PDF (Portable Document Format)
A standard that can be read across all platforms with the appropriate "reader" installed. PDFs can also be used for high-resolution graphics.

PhotoAnimator
Animation program from Extensis.

Photoshop (see also Adobe)
A digital imaging program.

PICT
Pixel-based file format that can be used in most graphics and layout programs (Macintosh only).

pixel (picture element)
A single dot of color contained in an image. When scanning a picture you can specify the image resolution (the number of pixels you want to an inch (ppi)). The resolution of an image depends on what it is: line art is high-resolution and is often reproduced at more than 2000ppi; professional quality photographs would need a resolution of about 300ppi. Monitors typically display at 72ppi; this does not reflect the actual resolution of your scan, but an image with a resolution of 300ppi will appear much larger on the screen than it actually is.

pixellation
Where an image appears blocky and the pixels are visible.

PNG (Portable Network Graphics)
A file format for images used on the Web that provides 10 to 30% "lossless" compression.

PostScript (see also RIP)
A powerful programming language on which the DTP revolution is based. It is used to describe items such as fonts which, because they are independent of pixel resolution, can be printed at any size. PostScript also describes vector graphics and is able to talk to all RIP-enabled printer devices.

PPI (Pixels Per Inch) (see also pixels)
Measurement used for image pixel resolution.

preferences
Sets of values that can be stored so as to preset your copy of a software to always work in a particular way.

prepress
Any or all of the reproduction processes that may occur between design and printing. Often specifically used to describe color separation and planning.

Process colors (see spot colors)

PSD
Default Photoshop file format.

Q factor
The amount by which the dot screen of a printing device needs to be multiplied in order to get a resolution that will guarantee high-quality, moiré-free images.

quadtone (see duotone)

QuarkXPress
Widely used desktop publishing program.

QuickTime
Apple's now "standard" Web movie format. QuickTime provides editing features for moving images and automatic compression and decompression of both movie sequences and still image files.

RAM (Random Access Memory)
The memory "space" in which you work on your PC: generally speaking, the more, the better. Imaging software such as Photoshop needs up to five times the size of the files that you are working on to process images.

rasterized (see RIP)

Raw file format
A digital file format that saves image data for transferring between applications and computer platforms.

resample
Altering an image by modifying pixels to either increase or decrease its resolution.

resolution
Describes the number of pixels per inch in an image.

RGB (see additive colors)

RIP (Raster Image Processor)
A device that converts data generated by a page description language such as PostScript into a form that can be output by a high-resolution imagesetter for printing. If fonts and some graphics files are described in terms of lines and curves, then they will need to be converted to dots in order to be printed. This is what the RIP does.

saturation
A variation in color of the same total brightness from none (gray) through pastel shades (low saturation) to pure (fully saturated) color with no gray.

scanners (see also CCD)
These devices allow users to capture images from reflective (paper-based) and transparent (film-based) originals. Most scanners use CCD technology. There are two basic types of scanner: flatbed and film.

screen (see halftone)

SCSI (Small Computer System Interface)
Using a SCSI connection system, you can attach a string of devices such as hard drive, removable drives, and scanners to your computer. SCSI is faster than USB.

smoothing
Method of reducing the visibility of unwanted artifacts in highly compressed images.

Sorenson
Video encoding format that treads a fine line between small file size and speed of loading. It is particularly suited to showing video over the Internet or local area network.

spot colors
Printing colors that are not composed of CMYK. In other words, you only need to output two films if your image comprises just black and green. If your printer has the exact green ink required, then you can define that color as a spot color. The alternative is to combine cyan and yellow and possibly a little magenta and black in various percentages in order to make up the color you want.

sRGB
Standardised Red, Green and Blue colour space. A colour system based on the characteristics of an 'average' PC monitor. It has a somewhat restricted gamut.

subtractive colors (see also additive colors)
Color model describing the primary colors of reflective light: cyan (C), magenta (M), and yellow (Y). Together with black (K), they are used in most forms of printing. The letter K is used rather than B to avoid confusion with blue. High-resolution pictures should be saved in this format to be printed.

threshold
A determining value for a pixel. Setting a threshold level for a particular function causes those pixels either above or below that level to be affected by the result of the function.

thumbnail
A small fixed-size representation of a larger picture or contents of a picture file for reference.

TIFF (Tagged Image File Format)
TIFFs are picture files that can be used in a large number of programs. They are one of the preferred file formats for including in layouts that are going to be printed. TIFFs can also be compressed using the lossless LZW compression.

transparency
A photographic slide.

trapping (see color trapping)

TWAIN
Software protocol for connecting scanners and computers. TWAIN often comes with programs so that if you are not using original software supplied with the scanner, it will still work.

UCR (Undercolor Removal)
Used in the printing process for high-resolution images. When the values (across a given range) for CMY combine to make a neutral gray or black, then those three color inks will be replaced with black ink. GCR works in a similar way but across a wider tonal range. UCR tends to confine ink replacement to the darker tones.

unsharp mask
There is a lack of clarity in scanned images due to the deficiencies of the scanner. Unsharp masking is a way of making the edges within an image sharper again, thereby restoring an image more nearly to its original.

USB (Universal Serial Bus)
A connection standard that may eventually replace serial and parallel ports on PCs and ADB serial and SCSI ports on Macs.

vector graphics
A graphics file that uses mathematical descriptions of lines, curves, corners, and angles. When using vector graphics; it does not matter how large or small you print the file, it will still reproduce perfectly because there are no bitmapped pixels.

VGA (Video Graphic Array)
Standard definition of 640 x 480-pixel resolution.

watermark
A product from Digimarc that embeds information about the ownership of a picture into the digital file itself.

Websafe
Color that will not be changed when an image is optimized for the Web.

zoom
Makes pixels look bigger or smaller on the monitor. If this feature is taken to its logical conclusion (1,600% is the maximum zoom in Photoshop), you will eventually be looking at just a few colored squares on your screen. Can be used to creative effect where pixellation is desirable.

1-bit
The lowest level of color definition in digital imaging. A 1-bit pixel can only be black or white.

1000s of colors
A 4-bit per channel color depth used as a memory-saving level when using monitors that aren't supported by a good video memory.

16-bit
16-bits per channel gives a huge variety of different shades of color (approximately 281,475,000,000,000 different shades of color); the square of 8-bit color.

16.7 million colors
The maximum number of different shades of color an 8-bits per channel system can record.

16:9 format
A widescreen format often available as a recording format in digital camcorders. Its longer aspect ratio is still taller than true anamorphic panoramic film formats.

24-bit
8-bit per channel color depth producing 16.7 million color possibilities.

25 fps
The frame rate used by PAL system television and video sets. The frame rate was set by EMI in the 1930s and is based on the 50Hz British electric power frequency.

256 colors
The maximum number of colors normally used in any image created for the Web. If the image contains any more than this (and the image is a continuous-tone one, i.e., 24-bit), then it is likely to take much longer for the viewer's computer/modem to download from a Web site, and is therefore impractical.

29.97 fps
The NTSC frame frequency. Based on half the frequency of the electric power supply (59.94Hz) in the United States.

4:3 format
The current standard aspect ratio for television pictures. It is being superseded by 16:9—especially for the viewing of professionally produced movies.

8-bit
The de facto standard for "natural color"; 8-bits per channel (24-bit color) gives sufficient hues for the output to be practically indistinguishable from colors in nature. When 8-bit refers to a grayscale image, it delivers a sufficiently smooth image such that even a monochrome image appears to be continuous tone.

bibliography and web site addresses

BOOKS

Digital imaging and photography

Ang, Tom, *Dictionary of Photography and Digital Imaging*, Argentum London, 2001

Ang, Tom, *Silver Pixels*, Watson-Guptill, New York, 2000

Davies, Adrian, *The Digital Imaging A to Z*, Butterworth-Heinemann, Woburn, MA, 1997

Davies, Adrian, & Fennessy, Phil, *Digital Imaging for Photographers*, Focal Press, Oxford, UK, 2000

Davies, Adrian, & Fennessy, Phil, *Electronic Imaging for Photographers*, Butterworth-Heinemann, Woburn, MA, 1996

Daye, David, *Digital Photography Handbook*, Argentum, London, 1999 (reprinted 2000)

Galer, Mark, & Horvath, Lester, *Digital Imaging*, Butterworth-Heinemann, Woburn, MA, 2001

Graham, Ron, *Digital Imaging*, DIANE Publishing, Collingdale, PA, 1999

Johnson, Simon, *The Digital Photography Handbook*, Metro Books, London, 2000

Schwaderer, W. David, *Digital Imaging and the World Wide Web*, Wordware Publishing, Inc, New York, 1998

Application-Specific Titles

Adobe Creative Team, *Adobe Photoshop 6 and Illustrator 9.0: Advanced Classroom in a Book*, Adobe Press, San Jose, CA, 2001

Bain, Steve, *CorelDRAW 10: The Official Guide*, Osborne/McGraw-Hill, Berkeley, CA, 2000

Baumgardt, Michael, & Baer, Marjorie, *Adobe Photoshop 6.0 Web Design*, Peachpit Press, Berkeley, CA, 2001

Binder, Kate, *Easy Adobe Photoshop 6*, Que, Indianapolis, IN, 2001

Copestake, Stephen, *Paintshop Pro 7 in Easy Steps*, Computer Step, Southampton, UK, 2001

Evening, Martin, *Adobe Photoshop 6.0 for Photographers*, Butterworth-Heinemann, Woburn, MA, 2000

Evening, Martin, *Adobe Photoshop 6.0 for Photographers*, Butterworth-Heinemann, Woburn, MA, 2000

Huss, Dave, *Corel Photopaint 10*, Osborne/McGraw-Hill, Berkeley, CA, 2000

Illustrator 9: Advanced Digital Illustration, Prentice Hall, Paramus, NJ, 2000

Kantaris, N., *Paintshop Pro 7 Explained*, Bernard Babani (Publishing) Ltd, London, 2001

Lee, Lisa, *Adobe Photoshop 6 Digital Darkroom*, Prima Publishing, Rosewood, CA, 2001

WEB SITES

Note: Web site addresses change, and sites can appear and disappear almost daily. Use your search engine to help find new arrivals or check addresses.

Absolute Cross Tutorials (including plug-ins)
www.absolutecross.com

Adobe Software (Photoshop, Illustrator, ImageReady)
www.adobe.com

Canvas Software
www.deneba.com

Corel Software (Draw, Photo-Paint, Painter, Dabbler, Knockout)
www.corel.com

Creativepro.com (e-magazine)
www.creativepro.com

Designing Tutorials
www.designing.com/photoshop/tutorials/

Digital Photography
www.digital-photography.org

Digital Photography Review (digital cameras)
www.dpreview.com

Everything Photographic
www.ephotozine.com

Paintshop Pro
www.jasc.com

Laurie McCanna's Photoshop Tips
www.mccannas.com/pshop/photosh0.htm

Planet Photoshop (portal for all things Photoshop)
www.planetphotoshop.com

ShortCourses (digital photography: theory and practice)
www.shortcourses.com

index